A Scholium

to S. L. Jaki's

SCIENCE AND CREATION

Παντα μετρω και αριθμω και σταθμω διεταξας.
Omnia mensura et numero et pondere disposuisti.
"Thou hast ordered all things in measure, and number, and weight."
Wisdom 11:21

The machinery of the world has been built for us by the Best and Most Orderly Workman of all.

– Copernicus

One of the severest tests of a scientific mind is to discern the limits of the legitimate application of scientific methods.

– James Clerk Maxwell

Those who devote themselves to the purpose of proving that there is no purpose constitute an interesting subject for study.

– A. N. Whitehead

Much is spoken today about the power of science and rightly. It is awesome. But little is said about the inherent limitations of science and both sides of the coin need equal scrutiny.

– Vannevar Bush

It is not the uranium but the heart of man that should be purified.

– Albert Einstein

There is but one thought greater than that of the universe, and that is the thought of its Maker.

– J. H. Newman

The rebuilding of this bridge between science and human nature is one of the greatest needs of mankind.

– G. K. Chesterton

Religion without prayer is as defective as physics is without mathematics.

– S. L. Jaki

* * *

About the quote on the preceding page:

"Every reader of medieval Latin texts knows that few Bible verses are so often quoted and alluded to as the phrase from the Wisdom of Solomon, 11:21, '*omnia in mensura, numero et pondere disposuisti*'," as pointedly noted by E. R. Curtius in his magisterial monograph, *European Literature and the Latin Middle Ages*, translated from the German by W. R. Trask (London: Routledge and Kegan Paul, 1953), p. 504.

Jaki, *The Origin of Science and the Science of Its Origin*, 85 note 61

* * *

For more information, visit

http://TheDuhemSociety.blogspot.com

http://www.sljaki.com

* * *

A Scholium
to S. L. Jaki's
SCIENCE AND CREATION

Peter J. Floriani

Preface by Stacy A. Trasancos, Ph.D.

Foreword by Antonio Colombo

Dedication

Ad Majorem Dei Gloriam

and to the memory of

STANLEY L. JAKI, O.S.B.
PIERRE DUHEM
JOHN HENRY CARDINAL NEWMAN
FRANCES AND GILBERT CHESTERTON

and my parents and my teachers

With special thanks to
Rita M. Floriani
Nancy Carpentier Brown
James M. Waclawik
Wayne Stahre
Dennis Musk
Antonio Colombo
Stacy Trasancos
Magdalen Ross

About the cover photograph:
On the left: a few of the books of S. L. Jaki.
On the right: a few of the books he references in his work.
In the background is the Septuagint in parallel Greek and Latin
open to Wisdom 11:21, near the bottom of the right-hand page.

For more information about the works of Stanley L. Jaki, visit
http://www.realviewbooks.com

ISBN-13 978-1536867718
ISBN-10 1536867713

Table of Contents

Preface

A "scholium" is an explanatory note that precedes an important work. This compilation is more than that; it is an introduction to Fr. Stanley L. Jaki and his major historical review of the birth of science, *Science and Creation*, and it is a guide to the fabric of his life's work in general. One may well wonder why a book, which ought to be self-contained, needs external introductions and guides. The answer is that Fr. Jaki integrated theology, physics, philosophy, and history, not as the telling of a story, but as a unique perspective of the landscape in which the story unfolds. It is difficult to pick up a single book by Fr. Jaki and grasp its full color unless you understand this context.

For example, when Fr. Jaki uses the word "science," he means "exact science," a concept that crystallized in his mind over time. Exact science refers to the quantification of motion of physical objects, a much narrower definition than newcomers may realize, yet a definition that aims at the heart of modern science nonetheless, so taken for granted as to be missed by many a modern mind. Fr. Jaki used this phrase like a razor's edge to cut to the storyline of the history of science.

Peter Floriani has provided a collection of insight into a chapter-by-chapter guide to *Science and Creation*, useful terms and foreign terms, major characters and prominent original sources, and the personal goals of Fr. Jaki's efforts, as if Dr. Floriani is giving a tour. This present work is a companion for the one who wants to read Fr. Jaki. Use it as a reference book, as hindsight now that scholars turn to mining and analyzing the depths of Fr. Jaki's thought.

Stacy A. Trasancos, Ph.D.
August 2016

Dr. Trasancos is the author of *Science Was Born of Christianity* and *Particles of Faith*.

Foreword

There are several arguments which are taken for granted, and never really dealt with by the general population. Information about them is taken from the mass media, and never really discussed. One such argument is the relationship between science and religion. One of the stereotypes on the subject is "the Catholic Church is an enemy of science," usually accompanied by a mention of the Galileo case.

Peter Floriani, who, as a Chesterton enthusiast, soon discovered that GKC fiercely opposed Scientism, which was and still is now one of the main secularist trends, met in 2004, at a Chesterton Conference, Father Stanley Ladislas Jaki, who devoted his whole life to the study of the history and philosophy of science. Father Jaki carried on the work started at the beginning of XX Century by the French physicist and historian Pierre Duhem. Both Jaki and Duhem found out the close relationship between the birth of science and the Catholic Middle Ages (known to the general public as "Dark Ages"). In other words, far from being an enemy of science, the Catholic Church made possible the birth of exact science.

As sometimes happen, meeting Father Jaki was for Peter a life-changing encounter. Being an informatician, he was able to help him, and got to know very well his works.

Of the several books Father Jaki devoted to the matter, the one examined in this *Scholium* (*Science and Creation*) is one of the most meaningful. It shows in ample details how science failed to became a self-sustaining enterprise in all ancient civilizations. And it also shows how science happened to become what we call "exact science" only in Christian Europe, starting not from the XVII Century (the Century of Galileo and Newton), but from the XIV Century Sorbonne University in Paris.

That's why Peter decided to write this *Scholium*. It is a good introduction to the matters of the *Science and Creation* book, and to the works of Father Jaki. The reader can find in it a lot of reasons to overcome the stereotypes on the matter of science and religion, with indications on how to get a better grasp on the whole matter. This *Scholium* follows a long overdue reprint[*] of the said book by Father Jaki, a reprint made possible also by the tireless work of Peter Floriani.

Antonio Colombo
August 2016

Antonio Colombo has translated several of Fr. Jaki's works into Italian. He is the Secretary of the Stanley Jaki Foundation.

---

[*] This new edition was recently released in both paperback and electronic forms.

A Preliminary Note

This year, 2016, was an important year for the history of science: it marked the 100th anniversary of the death of the great scholar Pierre Duhem, and the 50th anniversary of Father Stanley L. Jaki's first book, *The Relevance of Physics*. It is fitting, therefore, that this book follow the 2017 re-publication of Jaki's great work, *Science and Creation: From Eternal Cycles to an Oscillating Universe*.

Science and Creation is one of the most important of Jaki's books, a study of six ancient civilizations which failed to give rise to sustained science, and an examination of the antecedents of the singular viable birth which occurred during the Christian Middle Ages and enabled the work of Galileo, Newton, and their more recent followers. It is not an easy book to read, and it has even been found controversial, but its scholarly qualities, its usefulness, and its fascination are inarguable. It may be that some readers will find it rough going, even challenging; however, some readers may want to know where to go for further reading.

I have named this book a "scholium" after the famous *Scholium* added to the second (1713) edition of Newton's *Philosophiae naturalis principia mathematica*.[1] The dictionary defines a "scholium" as a "remark or observation subjoined, but not essential, to a demonstration or reasoning." The contents of this volume are subjoined to Jaki's work, and are certainly not essential – yet they may be helpful.

As we read and study these works, studies of Science and the history of Science, let us often turn in thanksgiving to the One Who made Heaven and Earth, for, as Father Jaki reminded us so many times, God "ordered all things in measure, and number, and weight."[2]

Paradoxically yours,
Peter J. Floriani, Ph.D.

---

[1] Jaki, *Science and Creation*, 297. Note, all page references in this work cite the 1986 edition, which differs from the new edition by no more than a page or two.
[2] Wisdom 11:21. See below (pp. 74-5) for more on this important verse.

I. An Introduction to S. L. Jaki

Stanley L. Jaki, O.S.B.
Born: August 17, 1924, Győr, Hungary
Died: April 7, 2009, Madrid, Spain
Joined the Benedictine Order (O.S.B.) in 1942.
Ordained a Roman Catholic Priest in 1948.

S.T.D. (Theology) Pontificio Ateneo S. Anselmo, Roma, 1950
Dissertation: *Les tendances nouvelles de l'ecclésiologie.*
Ph.D. (Physics) Fordham U., New York, June 1957.
Dissertation: *A study of the Distribution of Radon, Thoron, and their Decay Products above and below the Ground.*

Gifford Lecturer, 1974-5 and 1975-6.
Recipient of the Templeton Prize, May 1987.
In 1990 Pope John Paul II appointed him an honorary member of the Pontifical Academy of Sciences.
Author of over 50 major books,
dozens of booklets, pamphlets, and numerous journal articles.[3]

Outside of the above sort of data which may be found in typical reference works, the best source of information about Jaki the man is to be found in his published works. From the huge number of his carefully researched scholarly works, one quickly obtains a picture of a great intellectual, a multi-lingual polymath, a writer who takes extreme care with details, resorting whenever possible to original sources. There are several recordings of his addresses, such as those given at the Conference of the American Chesterton Society in 2004, 2005, and 2006. The best additional source is his *A Mind's Matter* (2002), his "intellectual autobiography."

– PJF

* * *

A historian never starts from absolute scratch. Still, apart from offering a fairly long monograph in which meticulous attention was paid to the original publications, there was something original in my focusing on the motivations that compel the scientist to prefer one particular explanation, or one specific type of explanation. *A Mind's Matter* 40

At this point I should make it very clear that I did not become a scientist as if I had become disappointed in theology. True, my first intellectual experience, which may be indicative of my mind's eventual coming of age, had a distinctly scientific touch to it. The event takes me back to the fall of

---

[3] A list of Jaki's books is given in Appendix I. For his publications to 2002 see his *A Mind's Matter*. A more recent list is available on-line at
http://www.sljaki.com/publications.html

1937. I was then just turning twelve, attending the third form of the Gymnasium run by Benedictines in my native town, Győr, Hungary. One of them taught me mathematics in all eight forms, that is, from 1934 till 1942. He also gave occasional public lectures on the latest advances in science, one of which had the cosmic rays for its subject. I attended and, though only twelve, I felt I understood everything. If this was true, the credit should go to the invariably clear presentation of that Benedictine priest. Little did I suspect then that I would eventually do my doctoral research in 1956-57 in physics under the direction of Dr. Victor F. Hess, who, in 1936, received the Nobel Prize for his discovery of cosmic rays. *A Mind's Matter* 17

I could but antagonize others in the lab by asking them questions that related to historical details of instrumentation and to broader aspects of the history of physics. They simply did not like being confronted with their indifference to such matters. To most practicing physicists it does not matter whether Euler preceded Lagrange or vice versa, or whether Maxwell came first and Boltzmann afterwards.

Professors were not to be troubled with such inquiries. I still remember the embarrassment of an excellent teacher of quantum mechanics, whom I asked in class as to why certain very useful polynomials are called Hermite polynomials. He answered that probably because of their mysterious character they were found to resemble those elusive figures, called hermits. Perhaps he was joking. But that was the last time I raised such questions in class. As I came to see later on, only one out of ten textbooks of quantum mechanics would reveal that Hermite was a 19th-century French mathematician. None of those textbooks contained a single word on a historically far more intriguing, and epistemologically far more revealing, fact of modern physics. Both in relativity theory and in quantum mechanics crucial role was played by mathematical functions that had been worked out for decades, at times a century earlier before physicists found them useful, indeed, indispensable. *A Mind's Matter* 25

Experimental verification, a work at times exceedingly tedious, demands more than ordinary determination and patience. Lab work was tedious and at times odious for me, especially after I was almost electrocuted by putting my fingers in the wrong place. I can still almost feel the shock that went through my right arm. Decades later I have found myself to be no more at ease, even with connecting laptops with scanners. Jazz drives and other jazzy computer paraphernalia can easily drive me to despair. *A Mind's Matter* 24-5

A few years ago, Cardinal Ratzinger [who became Pope Benedict XVI] told me in a chance encounter that he has for *Les tendances* [Jaki's theology dissertation] "a place of honor" in his library. *A Mind's Matter* 17

When one's energy is largely spent on writing books (now over forty [Jaki is writing in 2002]), the first major among them may represent the mind's coming of age. I was forty-two when, in late 1966, the University of Chicago Press brought out my book, *The Relevance of Physics*, a volume of over six hundred pages. By then I had earned two doctorates, one in theology, another in physics. The mind is greatly enlarged by absorbing the material comprised in a doctorate, let alone in two, especially when these relate to very disparate fields. But the mind really matures or takes a measure of its powers – and here anyone who has written a serious book would agree – through the effort to produce something new from the material it has absorbed. *A Mind's Matter* 1

About those books of mine that deal with the history of science I should say above all that they were invariably a delight to write. This should be of no surprise if one's basic bent of mind is to home in on the history of whatever one wants to understand. Apart from this, historical research implies the reading of original sources which in turn are an inexhaustible source of novelty. Satisfying as it does an inveterate sense of curiosity, the flow of ever new details into one's ken can but delight one's mind. There is further the excitement of finding data that have been ignored beforehand, at times a long chain of documents and data that generations of scientists (and historians of science) failed to notice, or if they did, they passed them up. *A Mind's Matter* 31

My method [in preparing the Gifford Lectures] consisted of portraying the natural theology of a particular thinker and then relating it to what he said on, or did in, science. In some cases the field had already been well researched, but the re-reading of the original texts disclosed not a few novel aspects and details. *A Mind's Matter* 94

Personally I am very satisfied with having published the [Gifford] lectures in almost exactly the same form as they were delivered. Usually I look up my published books only for a reference or two. To re-read one's books is not usually a rewarding experience. It is equivalent to looking at one's old photographs. Every phrase one writes is the product of one's mind at a particular time. Whatever the power of one's mind to help one re-live past moments, the mind stubbornly lives in the present tense. But now that I had to re-read *The Origin of Science and the Science of its Origin* in connection with writing this chapter, I found it a very rewarding experience. *A Mind's Matter* 60

* * *

About his languages:

Latin, French: I could not have delved into the study of medieval science, had Latin not become a second language for me from early on. But equally important was my early training in French. It enabled me not only to write my doctoral dissertation in theology in French, but also gave me an easy access to the riches in the writings of Duhem. It certainly opened for me the door to those very few who had known him and were still alive sixty years after his untimely death in 1916. *A Mind's Matter* 68

Italian, German: I could safely concentrate on the history of early Copernicanism and on the late-16th-century Neapolitan dialect in which Bruno wrote *La Cena*. Luckily, Firestone Library had on its shelves a huge dictionary of the Italian language based on historical principles. But this was only part of the problem, and the easier one. The other was common to all translators. None of them can entirely escape the truth of the Italian saying: *traduttore, traditore*. [Roughly, "to translate (is) to betray."] For one thing, no two languages are isomorphic, a point of which more in another chapter. For another, and this is the crux of the matter, a translator has to decide whether fidelity or beauty is to be honored more. What is true, according to an Italian dictum, of women, is also true of translations: if beautiful not faithful, if faithful not beautiful.

Instead of stylistic beauty, I chose fidelity to the original as my chief guideline. This is true of my two other translations as well. The fact that both were written in mid-18th-century German made the task somewhat easier. And certainly so with respect to Johann Heinrich Lambert's *Cosmologische Briefe über die Einrichtung des Weltbaues*, first published in 1761. He hardly wrote a phrase longer than five lines, a great contrast with the syntax in Immanuel Kant's *Allgemeine Naturgeschichte und Theorie des Himmels*. There one encounters on occasion phrases that are twenty-five or even thirty lines long. Sentences half as long are typical in it. This can only make for obscurity of expression even when the thought is clear. Lambert's was certainly a clear mind as befitted a first-rate mathematician and logician. About Kant, let me recall here a remark of E. Rommel, the son of the "Desert Fox," who, as Mayor of Stuttgart, once complained to a scholarly gathering there about the fact that Kant had made obscure diction *de rigueur* for German academics. Herr Rommel would have hit his target better had he pointed out that Kant set a standard for academic excellence by promoting obscure thought through convoluted phraseology. *A Mind's Matter* 44

* * *

A personal note: obviously Jaki first learned Hungarian, more accurately called Magyar; his vast publications demonstrate his powerful command of English. During one of my visits, he told me he knew "four or five" languages fluently, another "four or five" less well, and was familiar with yet another "four or five." From the evidence he was fluent in at least six.

– PJF

II: A Brief Guide to SCIENCE AND CREATION

0. Some Initial Observations

Jaki's *Science and Creation: from Eternal Cycles to an Oscillating Universe* is of major importance to the history of science and one of his major works, along with *The Relevance of Physics* (1966) and his Gifford Lectures (1975-6) published under the title *The Road of Science and the Ways to God* (1978). It is, as Jaki declares, "my first sustained study of the history of science during the Middle Ages and the Renaissance."[4]

It is the fifth of his more than 50 major volumes, preceded by his *The Relevance of Physics* (1966), *Brain, Mind and Computers* (1969), *The Paradox of Olbers' Paradox* (1969), and *The Milky Way: an Elusive Road for Science* (1972). Its size – slightly over 200,000 words on 400 pages arranged in 14 chapters, each with an average of almost 100 footnotes – may daunt some readers, and the style is definitely academic and often discursive. However, the arrangement of the material is very clear and simple, being merely a carefully researched defence of the claim that Science (writ large, as Jaki was fond of saying) – that is, Science in the modern high-tech sense, Science in general, and most particularly Physics – came, in *every* ancient culture, to a "stillbirth" due to the ubiquitous Pagan infatuation with the idea of the "Great Year" – the idea that *all* events of history, natural and human, had occurred before countless times, and will repeat forever without change.

Furthermore, Jaki argues that Science came to life only in the Christian Middle Ages, a life which has continued since that time, despite the opposition of some who worked – and some who are still working – to return to that Pagan view.

Other works by Jaki present further details about the rise of Science in two major aspects: the pioneering research into medieval science carried on just over a century ago by the great French scholar Pierre Duhem,[5] and the connection[6] of Science to the

---

[4] Jaki, *A Mind's Matter*, 56.

[5] Sree Jaki's books: *Uneasy Genius: The Life and Work of Pierre Duhem*; *Scientist and Catholic: an Essay on Pierre Duhem*; *The Physicist As Artist: The Landscapes of Pierre Duhem*; *Reluctant Heroine: The Life and Work of Hélène Duhem*; and essays: "Christian Culture and Duhem's Work" in *Chance or Reality*, "Pierre Duhem: Uneasy Genius" in *A Late Awakening*, and "Science and Censorship: Hélène Duhem and the Publication of the *Système du monde*" in *The Absolute Beneath the Relative*.

[6] See Jaki's books: *The Savior of Science*; *The Virgin Birth and the Birth of Science*; and essays: "The Hymn of the Universe" and "The Universe in the Bible

intellect-freeing and culture-changing belief in Jesus Christ (*not* the "universe") as the Only-Begotten[7] Son of God.

Jaki's *Science and Creation* is primarily an argument against the "Great Year," though it reveals the essential underpinnings of Science in three incomparable chapters: Chapter 7, "The Beacon of the Covenant," examines the role of the ancient Israelites and their unique distinction among the ancient peoples of the Near East. Chapter 8, "The Leaven of Confidence," presents the view of great scholars of the early Church, and finally chapter 10, "The Sighting of New Horizons," reveals the great discoveries of Pierre Duhem: the work of Buridan and Oresme, scholars at the Sorbonne in the 1300s, who pioneered the work credited to Galileo and especially to Newton.[8]

In the midst of these is chapter 9, "Delay in Detour," which Jaki himself found generating controversy:

> I have to take it in stride when a public lecture of mine is interrupted by Muslim demonstrators, waving in their hands a copy of *Science and Creation*, which, in its chapter, "Delay in Detour," contains a number

---

and in Modern Science" in *The Only Chaos*, "Faith, Reason and Science" in *The Gist of Catholicism*, and "Christ and the History of Science" in *A Late Awakening*.

[7] Greek: μονογενης (*monogenês*). Latin: *unigenitus*. For the most well-known use of this technical term, see the Nicene Creed: *Credo... in unum Dominum Jesum Christum, Filium Dei unigenitum...* = "I believe ... in one Lord Jesus Christ, the *Only-Begotten* Son of God..." This form of the Creed is recited weekly at Catholic Mass, and claims adherents in very many Christian denominations.

[8] The chain of evidence is revealed elsewhere (see e.g. "Pierre Duhem: Uneasy Genius" in *A Late Awakening* and "Science and Censorship: Hélène Duhem and the Publication of the *Système du monde*" in *The Absolute Beneath the Relative*) but the point may be put succinctly:

> He [Newton] did not care because he was a very proud man unwilling to give credit to others, as was all too often the case with other seventeenth-century scientists and authors. Galileo and Descartes are two chief examples of this intellectual stinginess. Had Newton cared to say something about the origin of those three laws, and had he been utterly candid, he might have proceeded something like this: The credit for the third law (force equals mass times acceleration) belongs to me though not in the sense that I had formulated the notion of uniform acceleration. Credit for the latter should go to Galileo. As to the second and first laws, Newton should have made a special effort to be candid. The reason for this was that both those laws could be found in the books of Descartes, of whose reputation Newton was terribly jealous. He did not want anyone to suspect that he owed anything to Descartes. In his later years, Newton spent much precious time on erasing from his manuscripts and notebooks the name of Descartes, lest posterity learn a thing or two. [Jaki, "God and Man's Science: A View of Creation" in *The Absolute Beneath the Relative*, 62]

As yet I have not been able to find Jaki's source for this claim about Newton's erasures, which he declares (but contrary to his usual style does *not* attribute) in several places, starting with *The Road of Science and the Ways to God*, 85.

of quotations from the Koran that reveal its world view to be markedly voluntaristic and therefore antiscientific.[9]

That chapter examines the role of certain medieval writers, including the great commentators on Aristotle: Ibn-Rushd and Ibn-Sina, better known as Averroës and Avicenna.

However, the four concluding chapters contain another sort of controversy. As Jaki examines the work of the last four centuries – the Renaissance, Galileo and Newton, the philosopher-scientists of the 17th, 18th, and 19th centuries and recent times – we find a distinct warning. In his 1986 Postscript he saw that even modern workers in Science were recurring to the Pagan view of infinite recurrence, though now framed in technical quips about an oscillating universe.

Jaki did not live to write a promised second Postscript,[10] but he left a pungent hint of his views:

> During the 20th century the idea of an oscillating universe was seized upon by materialists who greeted it as something germane to the Great Year. Very recently the same perception propels the praises of the idea of an inflationary universe and, what it logically leads to, the idea of many universes, and the replacement of the idea of the Universe with that of a Multiverse. There, to anticipate a point to be discussed later, even the word "cosmology" is no longer applicable. In its place inflationary theorists should introduce the term "cosmetology," or the art of sprucing up mere cosmic fiction with the semblance of science. All this further illustrates that the basic choices in cosmology are only two: cyclic or linear, or rather, chaos or order.[11]

Nevertheless, this book contains a sufficiency of both warning and inspiration. We are warned against recurring into the endless cycles of the Pagan "Great Year" while we are inspired with delight, with curiosity, with zeal to study and to search ever more for the truth about this singular and unrepeatable cosmos, this real and created universe. As Newman observed, "There is but one thought greater than that of the universe, and that is the thought of its Maker."[12]

---

[9] Jaki, *A Mind's Matter*, 56.

[10] Personal communication, March 9, 2006, when I had finished a fresh typesetting into electronic form of *Science and Creation*. He intended this new postscript to cover the 20 years since the first (1986) postscript.

[11] Jaki, *A Mind's Matter*, 56-7.

[12] Newman, *The Idea of a University*. VIII. Christianity and Scientific Investigation, §3, quoted in Jaki, *Science and Creation* 402.

1. The Treadmill of Yugas

Locale: ancient India
Belief-system: Pagan – Hinduism, Buddhism, Brahmanism, Jainism

This chapter begins with seven paragraphs which form an excellent introductory summary of Jaki's thesis. Its very first sentence is almost Chestertonian in wit: "In the genesis of scientific ideas, as Duhem once noted, there is no well-defined starting point." In the middle of his introduction Jaki introduces the ancient view of the Hindu classics, tying its cycle of 4.3 billion years to very modern speculations on hypothesized cosmological cycles of the expansion and contraction of the universe.

Having set the stage, Jaki goes into the ancient Hindu speculations on these cycles, which gets into computations of very large numbers. For example, the term "yuga" in the chapter title is 12,000 divine years divided by 4, or 3,000 divine years, and since 1 divine year = 360 years, hence we have 1 yuga = 1,080,000 years.

Just to keep from confusing any attentive reader, a factor was dropped in the computation of how long a "twinkling of the eye" is. See the quote beginning "Oh best of sages..." (SC 3) which defines the following time-intervals:

15 "twinklings of the eye"	= 1 Kashtha
30 Kashtha	= 1 Kala
30 Kala	= 1 Muhurtta
30 Muhurtta	= 1 "day and night of mortals"

Hence one "day and night of mortals" = $30 \cdot 30 \cdot 30 \cdot 15 = 405000$ "twinklings of the eye." Since one (mean solar) day = $60 \cdot 60 \cdot 24 = 86400$ seconds, thus one "twinkling of the eye" = 0.2133 seconds.

Jaki goes on to show more of these astronomically large computations from ancient India, but also shows how these were all tied to the perception of the cosmos as a living being, going through the cycles of life – all of which leads inexorably to pessimism and defeatism, the futility of human action, and even the irrelevance of making a distinction between good and evil.

> As the teacher in the *Vishnu Purana* tells his disciple, the most fundamental dissolutions occur at the end of periods which in terms of years correspond to a number that "occurs in the eighteenth place of figures enumerated according to the rule of decimal notation." The occurrence of the expression "decimal notation" in a jungle of morbid world view is of no small relevance. It evokes one of the most portentous questions that can be raised about intellectual history – the question of why science was born in the West and not in the East. (SC 13)

This question Jaki will answer in chapter 10.

2. The Lull of Yin and Yang

Locale: ancient China
Belief-system: Pagan – Mohist, Confucius, Taoist

The ancient Chinese also take an animistic view of the cosmos with cycles of life: the "custom" of Confucius, the dualism of the Yin and Yang, and the undescribable Tao, whose "paradoxical tenets do not issue in practical implementation." (SC 29)

As usual in the first six chapters Jaki mentions some of the stunning advances of the culture being studied. He then adds:

> ...for all their gunpowder, magnets, and printing skill the Chinese remained hopelessly removed from the stage of sustained, systematic scientific research. They had rockets for centuries, but failed to investigate their trajectories, or to probe into the regularities of free fall. Unlike in the West, bookprinting did not lead in China to a major intellectual ferment. Although magnets were installed on Chinese ships, which formed the best navy in the world during the fourteenth and fifteenth centuries, their captains never had the urge of a Vasco de Gama, Columbus, and others to circumnavigate the globe. SC 32

Jaki goes on to examine the impact of Western knowledge of mathematics and science when it arrived in the person of Father Matteo Ricci in 1583, but "Traditional Chinese mentality posed a major barrier to a genuine assimilation of the data and method of science." (SC 39) The point was made even more explicit by

> [Joseph] Needham, the leading Western historian of Chinese science, and an avowed Marxist. According to him, it is the a-theological orientation of traditional Chinese thought that should ultimately be singled out as the decisive factor which blocked the emergence of a confident attitude toward systematic scientific investigations. All this stood in sharp contrast with the situation prevailing in Western Europe. There, according to Needham's admission, all the early cultivators of science drew courage for their pioneering efforts from their belief in a personal and rational Creator. ... He also recognized somewhat ruefully that it was the reluctance of the Chinese to accept the idea of a personal, supreme lawgiver (God) that ultimately blocked their vision toward scientifically formulated laws of nature. ... For Needham, a Marxist interpreter of science, it must have been a frustrating pill to acknowledge the crucial role played by faith in a personal Creator in the rise of modern science. (SC 40, 42)

Either a supreme lawgiver, or a lawless dualism:

> The categories of the Yin and Yang came to dominate the theory of magnets as well as the rituals of divinations. ... The properties of the sun, moon, and stars could only receive poetical descriptions within a conceptual framework in which the Yin and Yang ruled supreme. Speculations about the seasonal and cyclic variations of this famed pair of opposites put the crowning touch of irony on the efforts of the Chinese to understand nature, man, and cosmos. It turned out to be a patently self-defeating enterprise. SC 45

3. The Wheels of Defeat

Locale: pre-Columbian Mexico, Yucatán, Peru
Belief-system: Pagan – Aztec, Inca, Maya

This chapter considers the three great pre-Columbian cultures of the western hemisphere, each of which had a handful of amazing accomplishments. And yet,

> The Maya, as was the case with all pre-Columbian Americans, had no wheeled vehicles. They also lacked familiarity with any practical use of the wheel whether as a pulley, a potter's wheel or a water wheel. SC 58

Though without wheels they were trapped in the cycles of an animistic view of the cosmos, and in each case, this fatalistic view was an important factor in their demise. The Aztec belief that

> ...within the relatively short span of some 2500 years the world was destroyed and re-created four times could hardly generate a feeling of stability. Continuity could not be safely claimed in a world resembling a wheel, the four spikes of which, symbolizing the four main directions, served not so much as guideposts for orientation but rather as dim warnings about inevitably occurring cosmic destructions. SC 52

For Aztecs, the end always came in a "1-Reed" year. The year 1519 was such a year, the year of Cortés' march on Tenochtitlán:

> Moctezuma's powerful army proved no match, despite its great numerical superiority, for a small band of adventurers. It is, however, to be remembered that these, in addition to some strange weapons, were also armed with an outlook on nature, life, and history, which could not have been more different from that of Moctezuma and his people. Cortés triumphed over an enemy already defeated, if not in body, certainly in mind and spirit. SC 54

It was similar with the Incas whose superlative roads and suspension bridges spanned a huge empire:

> Equally incapable were the Incas to break out from the cycles of nature, though it should seem that the concept of a perennial, immutable Inca Empire would have encouraged an interpretation of the cosmos and history free of cycles. What is actually known is that the lunar months formed the basis of their ceremonial calendar while the solar year regulated their agricultural system. SC 56

And the Maya found nothing better to do with their stunning invention of a "zero" than to tick over like an odometer their *tun*s and *baktun*s in an unending series of dates chiseled into hundreds of monuments, monuments to the tyranny of cycles. And so, in 1698,

> ...the validity of Maya prophecies concerning the impending abandonment of their ancient faith was not questioned. ... The sound of a hundred or so firearms signalled not only the routing of the Itza canoe flotilla. It also triggered the pent-up defeatism of some 5000 Itza soldiers lined up on the shore. Without joining the battle, all took to flight, leaving behind their families, homes, and everything they had built for centuries. SC 63-4

4. The Shadow of Pyramids

Locale: ancient Egypt
Belief-system: Pagan – Egyptian

The Egyptians made stunning advances such as making 6-layer plywood and making paper from the papyrus plant. In some things they were amazingly practical but in others backwardly committed to their traditions. Behind all of which was their animistic pantheon of gods and goddesses:

> For the ancient Egyptian the understanding of existence, individual and cosmic, meant an immediate, general overview, which in the end prevented him from achieving an objective analysis of the parts of nature. A case in point is the failure of ancient Egyptians to achieve at least a rudimentary form of a systematic study of the animal world with which they were wholly obsessed. Theirs was an almost endless line of mawkish gods and goddesses having the head of a bull, an ass, a hawk, a cat, a ram, a cobra, a goose, a scorpion, or a vulture. In ancient Egypt there were not only sacred trees but also sacred fishes and sacred insects. For the ibis, the sacred bird of Thoth, a huge sanctuary was kept at about 25 miles north of Hermopolis, but for purposes other than the satisfaction of natural human curiosity about their ways of life. Obsession with animals resulted in representations that boldly fused the bodies of different animals. SC 72

This was carried to extremes in their cosmogonies:

> The process of the self-unfolding of the "god-of-all" is recounted in heavily biological terms... Needless to say, the legend's account of the "creation" of humans goes along the same physiological lines... ...In such an animistic concept of the world, cyclic notions played a basic role. SC 76

And yet even this *cyclic* view had odd gaps:

> ...the real technological mystery of the pyramids lies in their enormous proportions. ... In general, the engineering technique employed in the construction of pyramids represents a strange mixture of ingenuity and backwardness. The lack of familiarity of ancient Egyptian engineers with the pulley provides a striking illustration of this. Even with pulleys, the intricate placing of hundreds of thousands of huge blocks of stone, at considerable heights, is an enormous feat. Without pulleys, such a task should appear well-nigh insuperable. Again, the builders of pyramids could not rely on wheeled vehicles for the transportation of heavy stone blocks. This had to be done on wooden sleds. SC 79

But their views did not only impair their engineering:

> Caught up in an animistic, cyclic outlook, the Egyptians had grown insensitive both to scientific reflections and to historical ones as well. ... Science and historiography are but different types of a causal and rationally confident probing into the space-time matrix in which external events, physical or human, run their irrevocable courses. To achieve science one has to recognize that these courses are not returning on themselves in a blind circularity in close analogy to the workings of perpetual motion machines. SC 80

5. The Omen of Ziggurats

Locale: ancient Sumer, Mesopotamia, Assyria, Babylon
Belief-system: Pagan

Jaki begins with an interesting comparison of Egypt with the region called Mesopotamia, Greek for "between-the-rivers" of the Tigris and Euphrates. Both had "high pointed structures": pyramids and ziggurats. However, the latter land had no stone and its people were forced to build using sun-dried bricks – but

> weather conditions have always been very erratic in the Tigris and Euphrates valley with frequently disastrous consequences. Unexpected torrential rains, followed by savage floods, could destroy in a matter of hours all buildings and irrigation works over large areas and reduce life to a mere subsistence level. ... Most of those ziggurats that are entirely or in part excavated show only the remnants of the first or ground tier from their usually three-tiered construction. The same holds true of the temple complexes at the centre of which stood the ziggurat. SC 85

And the deities of these temples were as animistic as the Egyptians:

> Sumerians, Babylonians, and Assyrians were convinced that every part of nature had a will of its own, often capricious and standing in continual conflict with one another. ... All this was in line with the picture of the world as a huge animal with apparently no beginning and end, subject to the various periodic changes evident in the life of the animal kingdom. Changes in human life, in society, and in the immediate physical surroundings of man were naturally pictured as the effects of the periodic clashes of large-scale forces and phenomena in nature. Most of these... were readily connected with the heavens. The observation of the heavens seemed, therefore, to be the logical clue for learning something about the course of events on earth. SC 94-5

But instead of astronomy they had astrology.

> The non-scientific character of Babylonian astronomy is strikingly evident from the fact that it has never developed even tentatively a geometrical, or a mechanical model of the system of the planets. ... Babylonian astronomy was not interested in the facts of heaven as scientific data. Its interest lay exclusively in providing a fairly correct lunar calendar, completely subordinated to the service of religious rites. These in turn were expressions of an animistic and cyclic world view that provided no fertile soil for the development of the scientific enterprise. SC 89, 90

And so, the peoples of Mesopotamia

> remained trapped in the disabling sterility of a world view in which not reason ruled but hostile wilfulness, the crushing blows of which threatened with repeated regularity. Believing as they did that they were part of a huge, animistic, cosmic struggle between chaos and order, the final outcome appeared to them unpredictable and basically dubious. All they could see was the endless alternation between the two. SC 99

6. The Labyrinths of the Lonely Logos

Locale: ancient Greece
Belief-system: Pagan

Some of the greatest intellectual advances of all time occurred in ancient Greece, the work of men like Socrates, Plato, Aristotle, Pythagoras, Euclid, Eratosthenes, Aristarchus, Thales, Archimedes, Sosigenes, Erasistratus, Hippocrates, Galen, and many others. And yet,

> ancient Greek scientific thought fell prey to the lure of sweeping generalizations that sidetracked the cultivation of physics for two thousand years. In short, the mistake consisted in the reduction of physics to biology... The extraordinary feats of Aristotle in biology were in a sense responsible for his failure in physics. The cultivation of the study of many aspects of the living organism invited a methodology which took its start from the purposiveness of biological systems. The emphasis on goals and purposes served biology only too well throughout its long history... ...in the days of Aristotle the espousal of final causes was far more than a methodological expedience. The realm of final causes stood then for the bedrock of intelligibility. The result was that investigation of any realm, living or not, was not considered satisfactory without attributing, rightly or wrongly, purposes to processes and phenomena of every kind, ranging from the fall of stones to the motion of stars. SC 103, 104

The cyclic character of the cosmos followed from this animistic view:

> ...the daily rotation of the sphere of the fixed stars was in Aristotle's eyes a perfect image of the innermost activity of the Prime Mover. As all other motions were derivatives of the primary physical movement, the daily revolution of the fixed stars, it followed that throughout the cosmos this cyclic pattern of changes had to evidence itself. SC 110

And this view had its effect on religion:

> It is not only the impotency and disarming confusion of a certain religious or theological outlook which is revealed in passages like these [of Epicurus ascribing control of the heavenly bodies to the gods]. They should also convey with an almost brute force the inhibitory influence of the belief in eternal returns. It was under such influence that scientific enterprise could appear to Epicurus as a road leading to an enslavement by "the destiny of natural philosophers." SC 119

Hence for the Greeks there was nowhere to turn, not even to their "Logos," that is, to reason, or logic:

> Aristotle's seemingly innocuous dictum that "time itself is regarded as a circle" had indeed been pregnant with momentous implications for the ultimate fortunes of the Greek Logos. For all its brilliance, for all its spectacular initiatives, it remained trapped within a spacious labyrinth where every move and enterprise led in the final analysis back to the same starting point. SC 130

7. The Beacon of the Covenant

Locale: ancient Israel
Belief-system: the monotheism of Israel now known as Judaism

We quote here without apology Jaki's superlative rhetoric of the opening paragraph of this most amazing chapter:

> In a history of science, which is mainly a meticulous listing of particular discoveries (and most histories of science are still of this type), there can be no room for a discussion of the culture of the Old Testament. After all, the scientific attainments of the Hebrews are practically non-existent when set beside the achievements of the Greeks, and are insignificant even compared to the much less developed science of ancient Babylon and Egypt. The historian of science, who notes the nomadic character of the ancient Hebrews and their heavy dependence on the culture of their more powerful neighbours, may feel justified in limiting his remarks on the people of the Bible to a few pages. If, in addition, he recalls the religious genius of the Hebrews, he implicitly offers a convenient excuse for their inferiority in matters scientific. The widely shared conviction about the fundamental opposition between religious and scientific orientation then readily cloaks such a procedure in the aura of objectivity. SC 138

And yet:

> For an analysis of the history of science which dares to extend its search beyond the glitter of easy listings of facts and data, the foregoing procedure is doubly inadequate. This holds true particularly of an inquiry into such tantalizing questions of the history of science as to why science failed to develop in half a dozen great cultures, why it came to a standstill in Greece after a splendid start, and why it finally emerged more than a thousand years later in clearly identifiable circumstances. Such a probing into the history of science cannot easily brush aside factors however extraneous they may appear to the mentality in which science is today cultivated. *Ibid.*

The rest of that stunning chapter is Jaki's probing, rich with quotes from Scripture and especially the Psalms and the Prophets, with the remarkable contrast it shows between the creation story of Genesis and that of Israel's pagan neighbors. But then, "The God of the Bible is the God of Abraham, Isaac, and Jacob; that is, the God of the Covenant, or a God who freely binds Himself to the welfare of mankind through the mediation of Abraham's progeny." SC 139

* * *

For further reading, see Jaki's books: *Bible and Science, Genesis One Through the Ages, Praying the Psalms,* and essays "The Universe in the Bible and in Modern Science" in *The Only Chaos and Other Essays,* and "The Biblical Basis of Western Science" in *The Limits of a Limitless Science.*

8. The Leaven of Confidence

Locale: Europe (imperial Roman times)
Belief-system: Christianity (Roman Catholic)

If the previous chapter on Israel was stunning, this one is even more so, linking as it does the topic of science with the only spiritual system which (to many) is even more absurd than that of Israel. But then it was found necessary in Alexandria, which was

> the chief focus and haven of cultural activity and aspirations during late antiquity. It was there that history witnessed the emergence of the first school of Christian thought... a considerable part of their efforts [Clement and Origen] aimed at vindicating the Christian message by showing its decisive superiority over a culture steeped in paganism. ...their achievement consisted in giving full body to an already existing Christian intellectual tradition which showed a twofold aspect. On the one hand, it further articulated that part of the message of the Covenant which was primarily meant for those who already possessed the faith. On the other hand, the inevitable exposure to the pagan world necessitated reflections of more apologetical character with distinct bearing on cosmology. ... The cosmological content of such a conviction was too explicit to remain unexploited in the encounters with those outside the fold professing a basically different explanation of the ultimate origin of the universe. SC 163

Granted, Christianity opposed the surrounding paganisms:

> "let none of you worship the sun; rather let him yearn for the maker of the sun. Let no one deify the universe; rather let him seek after the creator of the universe." SC 168

And yet, at the same time, Christianity

> prompted a trust in the positive achievements of a pervasive though distinctly hostile culture, in its philosophy and science to be specific. ... Such a firm conviction could only rejoice at the presence of genuine fragments of truth in antique learning. ... What, then, was ultimately wrong with a culture that could rightly be proud of so many "rational insights" and remarkable "dialectical speculations"? Origen gave the answer in a straightforward manner as he distinguished between two types of return, that proposed by the philosophers and that which formed the backbone of his theological speculations. The former amounted to a blind treadmill, the latter was goal-directed, and animated by purpose because everything that happened did so under the guidance of a rational and benevolent Creator. SC 168, 174

Even more stunning is St. Augustine's *The City of God* and his commentary on Genesis (SC 182, to be highlighted later), as well as the work of John Philoponus, whose

> firm faith in the first tenet of the Christian creed made him thoroughly aware of the fundamental paganism of Aristotelian cosmology. The alleged divinity of celestial matter and the eternity of motion in a pantheistic world could not be accommodated in the Christian interpretation of the cosmos. SC 187

15

9. Delay in Detour

Locale: From the Middle East to Spain (ca. 600-1300)
Belief-system: Islam

While Christianity became legal and the Roman empire waned,

...within exactly 100 years after Muhammad's death much of the *oikumené* formed again a unity with incalculable possibilities for learning in general and science in particular. What made the new unity so special transcended the usual advantages coming with the political unification of a land area reaching into three continents. ... The Muslim conquest was primarily the spread and imposition of a new religious conviction codified in the Koran. For the first time in world history a giant and vigorous empire was steeped in a conviction that everything in life and in the cosmos depended on the sovereign will of a personal God, the Creator and Lord of all. SC 192

Yes, in fact:

In all three caliphates [Persia, Egypt, Spain] serious concern for the promotion of learning was in early evidence. .. In Cordova the caliph al-Hakim II (961-76) amassed more than 300,000 volumes for the library which almost immediately began to attract eager scholars from the Christian West. An impressive proof of Muslim interest in learning was the hospitality extended to foreign scholars. SC 193-4

And yet in the end, this led nowhere.

The cases of Averroës and Avicenna are principal illustrations of the symptom of which the whole history of Arab science is a classic paradigm. Muslim science made notable contributions to those parts of science which had, in the historical context at least, little or nothing to do with the laws of the physical world at large. ... The heavily voluntaristic and organismic world picture that dominated the cosmology of medieval Muslim scholars ... agreed with the world view of the Persians and the Hindus... Although several of its features stood in opposition to fundamental tenets of the Koran, Muslim scholars made that world picture their own. SC 195, 200

As noted in Maimonides' *Guide for the Perplexed*, "in which both reason and faith were given their due" (SC 214), the most the Mutakallimun (a branch of Muslims) were willing to admit

about lawfulness in the universe was that it resembled human habits, such as the customary riding of the king of a city through its streets. Still, a king could readily break his habits, and so could any or all parts of the universe shift to a different "habit." SC 214

* * *

For further reading, see Jaki's essays: "The Physics of Impetus and the Impetus of the Koran" in *The Absolute Beneath the Relative and Other Essays*, "Myopia about Islam, with an Eye on Chesterbelloc" and "Islam, Science, and Christianity as Seen by a Muslim Physicist" in *Numbers Decide and Other Essays*, and his booklet *Jesus, Islam, Science*.

10. The Sighting of New Horizons

Locale: Europe (the High Middle Ages, 1200s-1300s)
Belief-system: Christianity (Roman Catholic)
Philosophy: Scholasticism

This, the most surprising chapter of the book, begins in the 1100s with Adelard of Bath and Thierry of Chartres, and moves into the 1200s with Grosseteste, "a most influential figure of medieval scientific thought" who "could not have been more explicit about anchoring his methodology of science in the notion of God as a Creator ... a wholly rational, personal Planner, Builder, and Maintainer of the universe." (SC 221-2, 223) After William of Auvergne came Albert and Aquinas, and a Franciscan named Roger Bacon, leading up to the dramatic event which took place on March 7, 1277, when a list of 219 propositions was condemned by Étienne Tempier, bishop of Paris. (SC 229) And though it "stated nothing new" nor was "binding on the universal Church," it was important:

> The prominence of the University of Paris, the large number of points covered in the decree, and its timing, endowed it nevertheless with special significance. The decree is a classic manifestation of the firmness of medieval Christians already in possession of the Greek philosophical and scientific corpus. They made their stand in the conviction that their belief in the "Maker of Heaven and Earth" imposed on them radical departure from some basic assumptions of Greek learning and world view. One may, therefore, look with Duhem at the decree as the starting point of a new era in scientific thinking, provided it is kept in mind that the decree expressed rather than produced that climate of thought which Whitehead once rightly presented as the most crucial ingredient for the eventual creation of modern science. (SC 230)

(See *medievalism* below for Whitehead's quote.) Here we meet Buridan and Oresme... but one must read this entire chapter in order to see the "new and reliable horizons" (SC 243) they saw.

* * *

For further reading see Jaki's four books on Duhem, and his essays: "Science and Censorship: Hélène Duhem and the Publication of the *Système du monde*" in *The Absolute Beneath the Relative and Other Essays*, "Christian Culture and Duhem's Work" in *Chance or Reality and Other Essays*, "Pierre Duhem: Uneasy Genius" in *A Late Awakening and Other Essays*. Also "The Modernity of the Middle Ages" in *The Only Chaos and Other Essays*, and "Medieval Creativity in Science and Technology" in *Patterns or Principles and Other Essays*.

11. The Interlude of "Re-naissance"

Locale: Europe (1400s-1500s)
Belief-system: Christianity (Roman Catholic and Protestant)

Here we begin finding names who are not what most would classify as "scientists" but rather as "philosophers," while many of them indeed performed various studies of a scientific kind – and yet they are important because their writing was helping shape the thought of society and hence scientists: Petrarch, Boccaccio, Ficino, Pico della Mirandola, Diacceto; Nicolas of Cusa (Cusanus), Machiavelli, Thomas More... and Leonardo da Vinci, who "was strongly influenced by Cusanus" followed by "Tartaglia and Benedetti, the sole notable contributors to the science of motion during the sixteenth century." (SC 261)

At this time we also find Copernicus:

> Simplicity was an avowed ideal for ancient Greek astronomers, still they found it impossible to abandon for a higher measure of it the evidence of senses and geocentrism. In his *Almagest* Ptolemy called it ridiculous and absurd to remove the earth from the centre of the universe. Copernicus, as Galileo later pointed out, had to commit a rape of his senses in putting forward the heliocentric ordering of planets. Galileo could hardly contain himself in praising the faith of Copernicus in the simplicity of nature. Such a faith, as Galileo explained in another context, rested on the Christian faith in the Creator, whose nature demanded that His handiwork should reflect His own perfect simplicity. SC 260

He is followed by Galileo as the telescope brings amazing details of the lunar landscape, sunspots, and the four Galilean moons of Jupiter; at this time was Paracelsus and Kepler and Tycho Brahe, who "did not get wholly trapped in the morass of that [animistic] 'physics'... due to his commitment to observational and mathematical astronomy, in which he saw a most exquisite service to the Creator." However, "When such a faith was lacking, the safeguards of reason also vanished rapidly. The classic case is that of Giordano Bruno..." (SC 262) beneath whose "weird reasoning lurked the spectre of a treadmill." (SC 265) The chapter concludes with mention of Bodin, Descartes, Boyle, Hooke, and Huygens, some more on Kepler, and a hint of the advent of Newton.

* * *

For further reading, see Jaki's essay, "The Transformation of Cosmology in the Renaissance: Facts, Myths and Mythmaking" in *The Only Chaos and Other Essays*.

12. The Creator's Handiwork

Locale: Europe (1600s-1800s)
Belief-system: Christianity (Roman Catholic and Protestant)

We take a deeper look at Galileo and Descartes, who are the immediate intellectual predecessors of Newton. With Descartes comes Francis Bacon. We also meet Father Mersenne,

> ...possibly the most selfless servant the scientific community had ever had. ... the rare combination of theologian, scientist and, above all, of a virtuous Christian. It should not, therefore, be surprising that Mersenne wrote more extensively than others in his century about the relation of science and theology, and he did so with a consistently high level of judiciousness. In the clarity of the new mechanistic science he saw a powerful antidote to crude and refined forms of obscurantism alike. He fought with equal zeal the astrological tradition and the pantheistic animism... As Mersenne saw it correctly, the belief in the Creator was incompatible with both. SC 284

Pascal, Boyle, Hobbes are mentioned, and then Newton:

> Newton's warning against imagining God as a soul of nature reveals his awareness of the pantheistic world view, which dominated ancient thinking and which represented a natural option for those ready to part with Christianity. SC 288

And yet it was unnoticed that "the concept of a cyclic universe was slipping in through the back door when the young Kant published anonymously his *Universal Natural History and Theory of the Heavens.*" (SC 289) Kant was no astronomer, but his contemporary Lambert was. Then come Hume, Laplace, Lagrange, Condorcet, the Herschels, Humboldt, still suggesting

> ...the idea of a wheel-work universe operating as a clock. By then this notion had been the hallowed shibboleth of science for well over two hundred years. But the world of science soon had to learn that the cosmic clockwork was not likely to run forever. (SC 294)

This was the result of the thermodynamics of Carnot, Joule, Kelvin, Rankine, Boltzmann, Tyndall, Faraday, and Maxwell... but good science led to bad speculations on the part of writers such as Herbert Spencer, Wundt, Mach, Zöllner, Arrhenius, Zehnder, Riemann, and others:

> ...fascination with mathematical glitter and mistrust in traditional patterns of reasoning can trap a mind even as cautious as that of Boltzmann. The real thrust and preferences of his thinking came to the fore as he advised his reader about the difference between time as a straight, infinite line, or as a closed circle: "In any case, we would rather consider the unique directionality of time given to us by experience as a mere illusion arising from our specially restricted viewpoint." This choice he seemed to take seriously. SC 300

19

13. On Murky Backwaters

Locale: Europe (1800s)
Belief-system: Christianity (Roman Catholic and Protestant)

Jaki's introduction sets the tone: "Much about health is learned from the analysis of disease, and the outlines of the rules of rationality can be more sharply discerned against the dark background of obscurantist aspirations. ... Most modern forms of pseudoscience have their roots in the rise of Romanticism." (SC 306)

Then we meet Fichte, Shelling, and Hegel, the architects of *Naturphilosophie*, in which the

> flat rejection of the Christian idea of a Creator is even clearer in Fichte's crudely immanentist and subjectivist account of the reduction of the Creator to the awakening of the human mind to the level of complete self-consciousness... SC 307

These writers and ideas may seem terribly irrelevant, but

> ...scientific sanity became a principal victim of willfully posited principles. A classic and early illustration of this is the interpretation of the laws of physical science by F. Engels, a chief architect of Marxist dialectic. His admiration for Hegel was unbounded. ... [Engels] called Newton "an inductive ass"... SC 311, 312

Another writer of this time was Blanqui, "a dilettante in matters scientific" who "did not perceive the grave contradictions" in "the concept of an infinite space filled with an infinite number of stars." (SC 315. This, the famous "Olbers' Paradox," is discussed later.)

The entire second half of the chapter is on Nietzsche: "the idea of eternal recurrence kept Nietzsche's mind and moods in a permanent grip." (SC 319)

> The sadly mistaken discourses of Nietzsche on science have an eloquence of their own. The sickly lingering of science within the ambience of a Naturphilosophie inspired by the pantheism and dialectic of German Idealism is an open book only to the professional student of the history of science. The setbacks suffered by science in institutionalized Marxism constitute a less esoteric matter. But in both cases the harmful consequences of a more or less overt acceptance of eternal, cosmic returns can only be seen if one is willing to take an exacting look beyond the horizons of stereotyped accounts of the principal factors at work in the history of science. Readers of Nietzsche should be in a far easier position. From the pages of the tragic prophet of eternal returns there blares forth in shocking directness the principal lesson of a fateful choice made against the clear evidence provided by the long and difficult progress of science. The miasmatic atmosphere of some murky backwaters of nineteenth-century intellectual history should be a powerful reminder of the fact that choices in cosmology have an impact far beyond a particular science. SC 329-30

14. Oscillating Worlds and Wavering Minds

Locale: Europe, America (1900s)
Belief-system: Christianity (Roman Catholic and Protestant)

Finally we reach the age of electricity and radioactivity, the age of Einstein, and the debate on a linear versus a cyclic universe continues in the writing of MacMillan, Russell, Jeans, Lemaître, de Sitter, Hubble and Humason, and Eddington, who gave the Gifford Lectures in 1927 in which he "resolutely upheld the once-and-for-all unfolding of the cosmos as something far more meaningful than the prospect of endless repetitions." (SC 340) And though "the vocal prejudice among men of science in favour of a 'never-ending cycle of rebirth of matter and worlds' evidenced, indeed, a baffling oversight of the historical background of the question" (SC 341) Milne "warned about a formidable if not insuperable difficulty to be faced by oscillating models of cosmology: the gravitational collapse at a given degree of the cosmic compression of matter. In addition to grave scientific difficulties, the idea of an oscillating universe also implied for him something akin to a conceptual monstrosity." (SC 341) and Nernst angrily contented that "the infinite duration of time was a basic element of all scientific thought, and to deny this would mean to betray the very foundations of science." (SC 343)

Jaki goes on to examine the work of others including Abel Rey, Perrin, Tolman, Dicke, Whitrow, Öpik, and Dauvillier, who

> divided, and rightly so, the cosmological hypotheses into two main classes: one of them was that of a universe forever existing and evolving, or rather transforming. As the most ancient matrix of such a conception, Dauvillier named the Buddhist thought. ... The same view of the universe was taught... by the Greek philosophers... Dauvillier's account of the other main class of cosmological hypotheses was markedly different in tone. In reviewing it, he criticized from the very start instead of reporting first: "The Jewish and Christian thought postulated an unknowable world of supernatural powers, transcending ours beyond its space and time and having created it *ex nihilo*." (SC 352)

And yet:

> ...it is all too easy to profess reservations about a universe oscillating forever, and pour gentle scorn at the same time on the so-called Big-Bang theory, lampooning the idea of a creation out-of-nothing as well. It is anything but easy to provide proofs on behalf of a world-model that could only be saved if one were willing to heed Alfvén's request: "We beg leave to sidestep the question, 'What happened before then?'." But this is precisely what cannot be done in cosmology, be it scientific or philosophical. SC 353

21

15. Postscript: A Missing Mass and a Narrow Escape

Locale: Earth (1974-1986)

Jaki added an all-too-brief postscript to the 1986 edition of *Science and Creation*. By this point he had published a number of essays and several books including two translations: Lambert's *Cosmological Letters* and Kant's *Universal Natural History*; a massive study of an astronomical topic, *Planets and Planetarians: A History of Theories of the Origin of Planetary Systems*; two collections of lectures: *The Road of Science and the Ways to God: The Gifford Lectures 1975 and 1976*, and *The Origin of Science and the Science of its Origin: The Fremantle Lectures*; two somewhat smaller works: *Cosmos and Creator* and *Angels, Apes and Men*, as well as one on the papacy, *And on This Rock: The Witness of One Land and Two Covenants*, and his masterful biography of Duhem, *Uneasy Genius: The Life and Work of Pierre Duhem*.

But the postscript contains some important points which Jaki emphasizes elsewhere, especially the "Copenhagen interpretation" of the Uncertainty Principle and the resulting petty theft:

> The real guidance of the inflationary theorists was not so much the science of quantum mechanics as its fashionable philosophical interpretation mainly articulated by Bohr in his Institute in Copenhagen from the late 1920s on. The interpretation, whose essence is a denial through recourse to Heisenberg's uncertainty principle of ontological causality, rests on the fallacious inference that an interaction that cannot be measured exactly cannot take place exactly. Implied in this inference is an equivocation (pointed out as early as 1930) through which two different meanings of the word "exact," one operational and the other ontological, are equated. It was this equivocation which first made popular the intellectual theft through which the fractions of a proton mass or a few hundred electron volts of energy could be had without a cause. By the 1940s most scientific minds had become so accustomed to this petty thievery with matter and energy as to feel no abhorrence when the steady state theorists proposed the emergence out of nothing (and of course without a Creator) of entire hydrogen atoms at a steady rate throughout the universe. SC 365

Here is the final paragraph of his Postscript:

> To cultivate a science which has grown, in virtue of a viable birth, into a robust being, an explicit faith in Creation is not necessary. But since any such being lives in terms of the logic of its conception and birth, scientific blind alleys immersed in philosophical darkness will be in store for those who chart, intentionally or not, avenues whose sense is diametrically opposed to the most creative innovation in human thought, the *Christian* doctrine of creation of all out of nothing in the Beginning. SC 366-7

16. In Conclusion

...until the publication a few years ago of my *Science and Creation*, the sole monograph on the topic was a now almost two-hundred-year-old book, Jean-Sylvain Bailly's *Lettres sur l'origine des sciences et sur celle des peuples de l'Asie*.

SLJ, *The Road of Science and the Ways to God*, 5

Given the importance of this book within the field of the History of Science, and my own personal interests and shortcomings with respect to that field, it is hard (if not unjust) for me to attempt a conclusion. Fortunately Father Jaki has provided us with something rarely available, some personal comments about his own writing of this book, shedding light on his phrase "the stillbirths of science" (a phrase encapsulating the argument of chapters 1-6 and 9 of *Science and Creation*), the background, and a little of this book's effect.

It is not a pleasant task to call attention to the obvious. To make others appear to be shortsighted, let alone blind, may easily evoke resentment. But it had to be obvious and clearer than daylight that in none of those cultures, although they lacked no talent and ingenuity, did science become a self-sustaining enterprise in which every discovery generates another. In all those cultures the scientific enterprise came to a standstill. It is this phenomenon which I called the stillbirths of science. I could not help noticing that they are the most monumental and yet most studiedly ignored symptoms in the history of science. Further, it quickly became clear to me why historians of science shied away from the subject. Most of them simply did not want to face up to something that would have shaken their confidence in presenting science for the savior of mankind.

The putting of new labels, such as "stillbirths" and "viable birth," on well-known, though never really appreciated, phenomena, could seem innovative insofar as it put in a new, and perhaps disturbing light, something that has usually been shrugged off by historians of science and by historians of those cultures. Their nonchalance should reveal its hollowness as soon as one considers the possibility of a Galileo or of a Newton being a product of, say, ancient India. In that case ancient Rome might have been patrolled by Gurkhas and, *horribile dictu*, the tribal chiefs of the British Isles might have paid tribute not to Rome but to some maharajahs in Delhi. The scenario would include princely visits from India to those isles, with maharajahs landing where eventually Greenwich Observatory was to rise and setting up their tents on plots where much later Buckingham Palace was to loom large.

Or suppose that Newton had been a Chinese of old, who had given a scientific explanation of the working of the compass and of the trajectory of rockets, two instruments first devised in China. It is then tempting to imagine the Chinese of old venturing along the Aleutian Islands, colonizing what is now Alaska, and then spreading out all over the North American continent. After all, their ancestors did it, though with only bow and arrow in their hands. But now the colonization would have been carried out by a people that navigated with compass in hand, and with the science of ballistics in their head to make their rockets truly effective. Big and small cities in North America as well as in the South would now carry Chinese names. On landing on the shores of San Salvador, Columbus would have been in for a very different surprise, if he could have surprised its inhabitants at all. Political history would have been very different if the history of science had taken a different course.

Historians who often write on what might have been, even when they write up what had taken place, would have a great opportunity were they to focus on those stillbirths. They should take for a tell-tale sign the fact that not one but all major ancient cultures were dominated by a cyclic world view, and that none of them came up with a Newton, or rather with the three laws of motion that constitute the basis and backbone of exact science. The reading of the great classics of those cultures suggests more than a mere coincidence. All those cultures exude a tone of pessimism or dejectedness. None of them conveys a crisp idea of progress. At best their principal thinkers took the actual state of things for the highest that could be reached by human inventiveness. Aristotle emphatically stated this about his own times. Strange as such complacency may appear in a great mind, it revealed logic. Why make much effort to come up with innovations if the same would recur in every Great Year? That Year was the chronological specification of the rotation of the *swastika*, a Sanskrit word, which means, farcically enough, "being well." Could the prospect of the return of the same, again and again, be a cheerful prospect? Was it not rather conjuring up existence as caught up in a huge treadmill?

The reader may sense that I say all this in a way that betrays the excitement I felt as such questions forced themselves on me. I cannot hide my enthusiasm as I recall further steps of this intellectual journey of mine into the stillbirths and birth of science. For me this journey was into the unknown because when I had studied scholastic philosophy I heard no references to Aristotle's infatuation with the idea of eternal returns. Of course, he meant that things return only in a generic way. Peripatetics would return as a school, but not as individuals. And so with the Platonists. But other Greek sages held that each and every one would return individually. This could only generate fatalism, which incidentally decided the fate of the last stronghold of the Maya in the Yucatan peninsula, who were equally under the spell of eternal returns. In their defeatism they even told some Spaniards not to come until the fateful moment had struck for them according to their calendars.

There was another side to the coin, to which my reading of Duhem's *Système du monde* opened my eyes. Never one to mince words, Duhem put it bluntly: "The doctrine of the Great Year, held by all Greek philosophers and scientists, held by all the Rabbis of medieval times, and held by all Muslim philosophers as well, had to be first overthrown so that science might eventually rise. And this overthrow could only be effected by Christianity." But Duhem did not elaborate on two facts: First he did not explore the fate of science outside the Greek and Muslim ambience and even there he did not cast his net widely. Second, he did not explore the very special role which belief in Christ, as something much more than mere monotheism, played in this respect. To work this out fell to me, though I came to it

24

more than a dozen years after I wrote *Science and Creation*. Duhem merely hinted at the fact that the richness of a Christ-centered monotheism helped overcome man's poverty even in respect to science.

A devout Catholic and a great mind, Duhem was not a theologian. All he said about the background of Buridan's formulating around 1348 or so the idea of inertial motion, or Newton's first law, was that it related to Buridan's assertion of creation out of nothing and in time. But Duhem did not delve into the question: In what sense was that assertion for Buridan also a Christian dogma? Was that dogma for Buridan something specifically Christian, that is, directly and intimately relating to and rooted in belief in Christ as the only begotten Son of the Father? Could it be a Christian dogma if both Jews and Muslims also held it? Or was their monotheism less effective in prompting them to embrace emphatically the doctrine of creation out of nothing and in time? Did not cabalism, a characteristically Jewish preoccupation, cast a strange shadow on their belief in the Creator? Was not Averrhoism a typically Muslim phenomenon? As I was writing *Science and Creation*, I did not go beyond stating that such a Christian belief certainly played an explicit role in the Christian rejection of the idea of eternal returns, especially as that rejection was memorably articulated by Saint Augustine. But as I was to realize years later, the only viable birth of science took place in a matrix that was not merely monotheistic, but also christologically monotheistic. Further, it contained a specifically christological prompting for a firm espousal of the dogma of creation out of nothing and in time.

Meanwhile I took immense delight in enlarging my mind by delving into ancient Hindu, Chinese, pre-Columbian American, Egyptian, Babylonian, and Greek history, into a re-reading of biblical history and of patristic literature. They contained many indications that I was on the right track in unfolding a new vision of the history of science, not attempted beforehand. Some of the indications were a sheer delight to stumble on. I would not have found a waste all the effort that went into researching *Science and Creation*, if it had acquainted me with but one gem, a gem hidden in Moses Maimonides' *Guide for the Perplexed*. There the "great Moses," as Aquinas called him, sums up the futility of the speculations of Muslim sages about the physical world in a simile: the Creator rules nature in the same unpredictable way as a caliph decides on the spur of the moment whether he would turn right or left as he leaves his palace for an afternoon ride.

Writing *Science and Creation* forced upon me my first sustained study of the history of science during the Middle Ages and the Renaissance. The latter began to loom as a period as much antiscientific as scientific. There was a dark side to the Renaissance in the measure in which it stood for a reinstatement of the idea of the Great Year, with its periodic rebirths or renaissances. The rise of Newtonian science showed a decisive aversion to the idea of eternal returns, whereas 19th-century materialism tried to give it respectability, with potentially disastrous results for science.

During the 20th century the idea of an oscillating universe was seized upon by materialists who greeted it as something germane to the Great Year. Very recently the same perception propels the praises of the idea of an inflationary universe and, what it logically leads to, the idea of many universes, and the replacement of the idea of the Universe

25

with that of a Multiverse. There, to anticipate a point to be discussed later, even the word "cosmology" is no longer applicable. In its place inflationary theorists should introduce the term "cosmetology," or the art of sprucing up mere cosmic fiction with the semblance of science. All this further illustrates that the basic choices in cosmology are only two: cyclic or linear, or rather, chaos or order.

The reception of *Science and Creation* varied according to one's preference of any of those alternatives. Catholic historians of science should have been greatly pleased. But with the exception of one, who hoped that my book would start a debate, they did not seem to wish to jeopardize their academic reputation in the eyes of their secularist counterparts in leading universities by focusing on a feature that spoke well of Catholicism. The *Journal of Victoria Institute*, an association of believing scientists in Great Britain, was jubilant. And so were some Protestant missionaries in Japan. But the reviewer for the *British Journal for the History of Science* could hardly hold back his scorn.

Clearly, I must have touched some raw nerves in academe. No wonder. For most in academe the basic dogma is that science is the savior of mankind, and is already liberating mankind from that highest form of superstition, which is Christian belief in the supernatural. To them my thesis had to appear as nothing short of spitting on the flag. But the facts, told in over half a million words, could not be disputed. They could only be ignored in the manner in which ostriches behave when they feel threatened. So one of those prominent academic ostriches declared me to be the Number One enemy. Another, again a historian-philosopher of science, declined to review my next book with the remark that he (actually she) would not touch my writings even with a ten-foot pole. She also loved to parade as a Christian. But that was in Britain, the land where the calm toleration of contradictions passes for profundity of thought, for cultural harmony, and for human probity.

SLJ, *A Mind's Matter*, 52-57

III. The Scholium

1. Some Useful Terms

One of the more startling things a scientist will find in reading *Science and Creation* is that common technical terms of science appear much less often than a variety of odd philosophical "-ism" terms. I have paraphrased definitions from several sources, and tried to find suitable Jaki citations to aid in understanding how he used the terms.

Given this strange list of terms cataloging mostly heretical, anti-scientific, and even absurd ideas, one will quickly wonder what Jaki thought. Indeed, it is as GKC quoted an opponent: "I will begin to worry about my philosophy," said Mr. Street, "when Mr. Chesterton has given us his."[13]

What, then, is Jaki's take on all the -isms?
It's in the list under "moderate realism."

* * *

agnosticism: the doctrine that neither the existence nor the nature of God, nor the ultimate origin of the universe, is known or knowable. The term was coined by T. H. Huxley (SLJ, *Bible and Science*, 12), known as "Darwin's bulldog."

> Whatever philosophical loopholes he [Huxley] wanted to secure by coining the word agnosticism, he certainly did not want to weaken thereby faith in universal determinism. SLJ, "Determinism and Reality" in *Patterns or Principles and Other Essays*, 116.
>
> ...agnosticism is never free of one basic shortcoming: it can never outline with sufficient consistency the boundary line between what can and cannot be known. SLJ, *Brain, Mind and Computers*, 171
>
> Eddington is more agnostic about the material world than Huxley ever was about the spiritual world. SLJ, *Chesterton a Seer of Science* 40-41 quoting GKC, *The Well and the Shallows*, CW3:379.

animism: belief that all objects possess a natural life or vitality or are endowed with indwelling souls.

> Animism ... encourages an explanation which starts with empathy, intuition, and identification, and ends in quasi-mystical conjectures and a willful cultivation of inconsistencies. SC 262
>
> Both Buridan and Oresme introduced their discussion of the beginning of motion with a reference to souls, that is, to intelligences which in Aristotle's theory were the instrumental causes of the motions of stars and planets. To be sure, as Christians, Buridan and Oresme

---

[13] GKC, *Orthodoxy*, CW1:211, quoting *Outlook* for June 17, 1905.

could have retained those intelligences as identical with angels. But they refused to make room for angels in natural science. If there was to be a science of nature, then nature had to be liberated from all remnants of animism and for a simple reason. An *anima* or soul was not such if it did not have some measure of freedom of action. Now if a star or a stone had a soul, each could conceivably deviate from its predetermined path at any given moment and most unpredictably. If, however, this was possible, there could be no science which is strictly predictive about purely physical motion, even if it cannot be such about the motion of plants, animals, and human beings.

In other words, if science was to be born, nature had to be deanimized. Animism, which was always an essential feature of pantheism, had to retreat in the measure in which the monotheistic doctrine of creation was gaining ground. Animism was no match, in the long run at least, for the impetus of the doctrine of creation when the doctrine was taken in terms of the New Testament. Its doctrine on Christ as the "only begotten Son," in whom the Father created everything, put a damper on any flirtation with the idea that any other being might be a divine begetting in terms of an emanationism which always carries an animist touch. Animism – the entire history of philosophical learnedness in the Muslim world is a witness – held its own when confronted with the impetus with which the Koran carried the doctrine of creation. In sum, the whole question of why science was not born within the Muslim milieu, or the question of why the physics of impetus was not formulated there, is in the end a theological question, which can only be answered in terms of theology... SLJ, "The Physics of Impetus and the Impetus of the Koran" in *The Absolute Beneath the Relative and Other Essays*, 150-1

apriorism: the belief that the way things are can be deduced from certain fixed (*a priori*)[14] general principles. Especially to be noted in Plato and others in antiquity, and in some Muslim scholars. SC 210

...the great aim of cosmological apriorism, namely, the demonstration that the universe can only be what it is and therefore it is not contingent. SLJ, "The Metaphysics of Discovery and the Rediscovery of Metaphysics" in *The Absolute Beneath the Relative and Other Essays*, 50.

The real attractiveness of that world picture [of Aristotle] was not its superficial agreement with observations, but that it could also be deduced from a few basic postulates. It was one of the greatest lures ever presented to human reason which can all too readily fall prey to the mirage of self-explaining and final solutions. Apriorism means freedom from endless trial and error in the search for truth; it means a facile insertion of man and of his mind into a pantheistic whole and into its eternal rhythm going through forever the same patterns. ... Muslim scholars failed to perceive in the doctrine of contingency the

---

[14] *a priori* (Latin: from the former): reasoning which deduces consequences from definitions or principles regarded as self-evident; that is, reasoning from causes to effects. Opposed to it is *a posteriori* (Latin: from the latter): reasoning deriving propositions from observation, arriving at principles by generalization, hence designating what can be known only through experience.

very basis of a satisfactory formulation of scientific method. If the superlunary world, or the dominating part of the universe, was a necessary entity, then its laws too were to be thought of as eternally necessary. Apriorism then had its theological sanctioning with the simultaneous loss of interest in an experimental investigation of the universe. *SC* 208, 210

The valuable contributions to the scientific understanding of the world were made during the Renaissance by thinkers whose faith in the intelligibility of the world was rooted in a sincere attachment to the first article of the Christian creed. Most of them were also admirers of Plato but their faith saved them from becoming prisoners of the immanentism and apriorism of his interpretation of the world. SC 254

Eddington's fondness for that number[15] should appear very different when seen as a part of his penchant to derive from *a priori* considerations the major quantitative features of the universe. Apriorism, when cultivated consistently, never fails to invite solipsism, a stance that excludes a purpose propelling the subject beyond itself. SLJ *The Purpose of It All*, 99

atomism: the doctrine that the universe is composed of simple, indivisible and minute particles. Especially noted in Epicurus and Democritus, opposed by the Peripatetics and Stoics, and later by positivism. SC 118

...the soulless mechanism of atomism... SC 116

While Democritus' atomism knew no bounds as regards the application of the principle, "atoms in eternal motion," Epicurus frantically warned against attempts to demonstrate the validity of strict, unequivocal physical laws in heavenly phenomena. SC 119

Copernicanism: also called "heliocentrism" (as opposed to geocentrism): the *belief* that the Earth rotates once a day and that it and the other planets revolve in circles around the sun.

Kepler's argument that the orbit of Mars was elliptical made, for the time being, only more difficult the cause of Copernicanism. It was difficult to think of a dynamics that would account of the circular orbits of planets around the Sun. It was simply beyond any hope at that time to account for elliptical orbits. Not that this would have been Galileo's chief reason for ignoring Kepler's achievement. The reason was Galileo's Platonism which admitted only circular orbits, as befitting the presumed perfection of the heliocentric system. The system was not at all simpler than Ptolemy's, although for a Platonist it could look simplicity itself. Further, the clinching proof of heliocentrism should have been something quantitative to be observed and measured. Eventually the proof came, though many years later, through the work of Bessel and Fizeau, but by then nobody was inconvenienced by the thought of living on the surface of a rapidly rotating and orbiting earth.

---

[15] Eddington liked to seek out 137, which he believed was the exact value of the reciprocal of the "fine-structure constant" $\mu_0 ce^2/2h$. However, my 1981-2 edition of the *CRC Handbook of Chemistry and Physics* (page F-203) gives it as approximately 137.03604.

... Most Protestant scientists who endorsed Copernicanism during the seventeenth century were hardly believers in the sense in which Luther and Calvin meant believing. There were already then so many Protestant groups that it made little sense to ask whether Copernicanism clashed with Protestantism or not. A clash implies clearly definable contestants, and as far as Christian religion was concerned there was only one such contestant, the Catholic Church. SLJ, *Questions on Science and Religion*, 97-8, 102

For almost its first hundred years, Copernicanism stood for a spherical universe. SLJ, "Thomas and the Universe" in *A Late Awakening and Other Essays*, 240-1

Darwinism: (or evolutionism) the *belief* that the universe and all of its parts have no purpose, that life arose out of non-living matter, and that the environment and utterly purposeless "random mutations" acting over long time periods have caused the origin of every kind of living creature from others.[16] Nietzsche was "an ardent opponent of Darwinism." *SC* 320n98

[Darwinism] ... is not to be equated with the instrumentality of one species in the rise of another, and certainly not with the evolutionary perspective.

... The allegiance demanded by Darwinism was simply allegiance to the absence of all norms. It beckoned toward unfathomable whirls in which one was no more than flotsam hurled round and round by the blindest of blind fates. Such is not, strictly, an interpretation, but an experience. Many have felt what a biographer of Darwin, keen on psychological depths, described as the lasting effect of his reading of the *Origin*. What that book presented was not a philosophy, not even its camouflage as aggressive agnosticism, or militant atheism. What it inculcated rather was "a feeling of utter insignificance in the face of the unapprehended processes of nature...a sense of being aimlessly adrift in the vast universe of consciousness, among an infinity of other atoms, all struggling desperately to assert their own existence at the expense of all the others."

Every Darwinist is a living refutation of a philosophy, Darwinism, for which purpose is non-existent. For whatever the Darwinian claim that no biological organization can be shown to have developed for a purpose and under a directive agency, at least one organism or species, and hardly the least important, man, is engaged day in and day out in the most varied and most spectacularly purposeful activities.

The scientist investigating sound is as entitled to ignore aesthetic considerations as the composer is entitled to ignore the mathematical equations governing the propagation of sound. To ignore is one thing, to deny is another. By failing to heed this distinction Darwinists become Darwinian philosophers who revel in the denial of logic and values. They also remain blissfully unmindful of the fact that as a

---

[16] Given our context, this is not the proper place to argue the critical distinction between (on one hand) *evolution*, a valid and unobjectionable specialized branch of biology, and (on the other hand) *evolutionism*, a strange and irrational philosophy. There is plenty to be had on this topic in both Chesterton and Jaki, yet I will refrain from attempting to condense it here.

scientific theory Darwinism is just as incomplete and revisable as any other scientific theory. The pressure of environment and the slight genetic changes ever at work in every organism propagating itself, may or may not be sufficient to explain all steps in the transformation of one species into another, let alone of a family into another, to say nothing of phylae and kingdoms. Those who dogmatically give the affirmative answer are still lacking something essential to the scientific spirit.

...Darwin debunked thought itself, although he resorted to thought as the ultimate guarantee that the vast array of facts he marshalled did not speak falsely: "He who is not content to look, like a savage, at the phenomena of nature as disconnected, cannot any longer believe that man is the work of a separate act of creation." Darwin did not as much as suspect that this very ability of man, which is not possessed by the "savage" and makes science possible, was the irrefragable evidence that a special creation did indeed take place when it came to the mind of man. This is why the hostility of Christians to Darwin's hostility to Christianity should not appear unreasonable. Christians certainly cannot be made the principal carriers of unreasonableness when reasons given for siding with Darwinism reveal matters very distinct from reasoning.

...Huxley's description of meaninglessness... consists in assigning meaning to parts while denying meaning to the whole. Darwinism perfectly fits this description.

...Darwinism [is] a countermetaphysics...
SLJ, *Angels, Apes and Men*, which is rich on the topic. Also see "Critic of Evolutionism" in SLJ's *Chesterton a Seer of Science*.

deism: belief in a personal God as creator of the world and final judge of men, but in the interval remaining completely beyond the range of human experience.

[Leibniz] could hardly have guessed that his ideas and his philosophical optimism paved the way to deism and to the faith of the Enlightenment in an infinite progress in an infinite world. SC 289

Deism soon became a cover-up for atheism. ... Bailly's real failure had its source in his own efforts blindfolded by a deism suspicious of anything Christian in cultural history. ...the smug spokesmen of the century of Enlightenment. They not only felt far superior to the previous century – which for science was the century of genius – but viewed through thick filters the workings of the minds of all those geniuses. Thus they were unable to perceive that from Copernicus to Newton it was not deism but Christian theism that served as a principal factor helping the scientific enterprise reach self-sustaining maturity.

...the need to move from the universe to God was no longer felt once it was accepted that the universe could only be what it appeared to be, an infinite homogeneous three-dimensional extension. The pale God of deism, capable of creating but a Euclidean world, could readily be replaced with a cosmological infinity showing, on a cursory view, but pale or weak singularities. They were, as will be seen, not at all pale, but to see them for what they were demanded eyes still sensitive to the light of a metaphysics steeped in considerations about the singularity of existence. SLJ, *The Road of Science and the Ways to God*, 7, 10, 11, 263-4

31

To support the connection between the infinity of God's perfection and the infinity of his creation, Kant fell back on an argument characteristic of an aprioristic deism, which he embellished with specious references to science. SLJ, *The Paradox of Olbers' Paradox*, 135

...most of the Founding Fathers were Christians only in name. Their religion, including that of Washington, Madison, and Jefferson, was deism, a vague veneration of a Supreme Being who had nothing to do with man, whose sole rule was his inner moral conscience obeying immutable truths. SLJ, "The Parasitical Society and Its Parasite Families" in *A Late Awakening and Other Essays*, 151

Deism, in which the Creator was a pale image of his true self, proved no barrier to pantheism already advocated by Spinoza. It found favourable soil in German enlightenment and idealism, from Jacobi to Goethe, from Kant to Schelling, Hegel and beyond, parallel routes marked by miscomprehension of, and at times plain antagonism to science. On the French scene, Victor Hugo, who became a pantheist under the influence of Alexandre Weill, a Jewish cabbalist from Alsace, deserves special attention for having put in poignant terms that fissure and radical uncertainty which creation must evoke within pantheism...

Deism was no barrier to materialism, which from d'Holbach through Diderot to Moleschott and Engels produced no serious science. It rather ended in reinstating the ancient dogma of eternal returns, that chief nemesis of the scientific enterprise in all ancient cultures, including ancient Greece. As for deism professed by Comte, the father of positivism, it was part of those preconceived limits which Comte prescribed to science, especially to astronomy and physics, limits so narrow as to constitute a straitjacket. Nietzsche, the most animated mouthpiece in the nineteenth century of the idea of eternal returns, was no less effective in discrediting himself by what he wrote on science. All these, in many ways very disparate thinkers, were at one in denouncing the Christian dogma of creation out of nothing as the worst aberration of the human mind. They certainly deserve credit for being so consistent. SLJ, *Cosmos and Creator*, 82, 83

determinism: the belief that acts of the will result from determining (i.e. from physical) causes: "In its broadest sense *determinism* means that not only purely physical events but conscious human choices too are the inevitable consequences of their antecedent conditions." SLJ, "Determinism and Reality" in *Patterns or Principles and Other Essays*, 114

[Roger] Bacon was not the first, nor the last, to be trapped by the glitter of perfection, but his case has a particular moral. Admiration of an outstanding perfection can easily turn into sweeping generalizations and this is precisely what happened to him. The vista of the unfailing retracement of their courses by celestial bodies imposed on his mind the idea of an inexorable determinism of events. True, he did his best to safeguard man's freedom and moral responsibility. His prolific analysis of the influence of stars and planets could, however, easily undercut his otherwise sincere persuasion about man's uniqueness in the inexorable turnings of nature's great machinery. SC 227

...classical physics was based on the idea of absolute determinism in physical processes, that is, on the decisive importance of the initial conditions for the rest of the process in question. SC 317

It throws a sharp light on Nietzsche's wholly unscientific way of thinking that he never came to grips with the obvious conflict between the rigorous determinism on which rested his claim of identical returns and the complete willfulness in which he saw the ultimate feature of the universe. SC 324

Determinism, as I argued in my *Means to Message*, can never be a logical first step insofar as it is stated by man. For unless he states it freely, he merely parrots something without even remembering things past. SLJ, *A Mind's Matter*, 242

One chief victim of scientism was free will, whose vindication became a principal concern for Chesterton, partly through his debate with Blatchford, a champion of scientistic determinism. SLJ, "Chesterton's Landmark Year: The Blatchford-Chesterton Debate of 1903-1904" in *Chance or Reality and Other Essays*, 66-7.

See also SLJ, "Determinism and Reality" in *Patterns or Principles and Other Essays*, and "Chance or Reality: Interaction in Nature Versus Measurement in Physics" in *Chance or Reality and Other Essays*.

dualism: philosophical view that the universe has a twofold nature (mind and matter), to be contrasted with monism and pluralism; also theological view that the universe is under the dominion of two opposing principles, one good, the other evil; also belief that the human being has a dual nature, physical (body) and spiritual (mind), also that light has both wave and particle characteristics.

Darwinists for the most part still fail to recognize with T. H. Huxley in ethics something which should seem both an obvious fact and also an inescapable contradiction for Darwinism. On both counts ethical force, to recall Huxley's words, is "the checking of the cosmic process at every step" and a substitution for it of another – the end of which is not the survival of those who may happen to be the fittest...but of those who are ethically the best." Darwinists have no answer to this dilemma because the only answer – the recognition of a spiritual order in man who is more than mere matter – cannot come within their ken, a ken constructed to the specifications of strict materialism. Thus those who refuse to acknowledge the dualism of man are condemned to side with the dualism of the Manicheans of old who conjured up two ultimate and equal forces: one remorseless, another good – caught in eternal antagonism. The same contradiction, when translated into the dualism of blind versus purposeful, haunts the Darwinists no less while making them oblivious to another fact, although it is a fact within the reach of an elementary reflection on what they themselves are doing. Their work is a life-long commitment to the purpose of proving that there is no purpose. Every Darwinist is a living refutation of a philosophy, Darwinism, for which purpose is non-existent. SLJ, *Angels, Apes and Men* 62-3

On finding that a sensory impression of a given geometrical form produces on the cortical area an excitation pattern of entirely different shape, neurophysiologists will have a more serious metaphysical problem on hand than those scholastics who pondered over the number of angels that can be placed on a pinhead. That they do have on hand problems of metaphysical nature prompted a long array of prominent neurophysiologists to admit that dualism was still the most reasonable initial postulate in a scientific approach to the problem of mind and brain. SLJ *Brain, Mind and Computers*, 133

In fact, as soon as physics reached the layer of atoms, the evidence against the rigid, unitary concept of nature formed by mechanism began to grow by leaps and bounds. There had to come the recognition of the equal usefulness of such conflicting concepts as are waves and particles. But this was not the worst shock in store for the mechanistic creed. The wave and particle dualism shed further light on the fact that the absolute determinism and precision of which classical physics professed to know so much was not only unattainable but could not even be demonstrated to exist in nature. *TROP* 93

emanationism: (also emanatism) belief that created things are emanations of God (that is, particles of God's substance), opposed to creation from nothing. Closely connected to pantheism.

Within the Christian perspective the Son was not merely a Son, but the Only begotten Son, μονογενης [*monogenês*] or *unigenitus*. Both words may mean the only son of a father, but both words have another connotation as well. In the Greek philosophical corpus μονογενης [*monogenês*] is often synonymous with κοσμος [*kosmos*] and το παν, [*to pan*] or the universe. The Latin *unigenitus* also could be taken to mean *universum* or *mundus*. The reason for this is pantheism or pantheistic emanationism which dominated Greco-Roman thought. Emanationism received its broadest articulation in the *Enneads* of Plotinus, who flourished in the middle of the third century A.D. By then the view of the universe as *unigenitus* had been everywhere as the Romans carried far and wide Greek civilization in addition to the *ius Romanum*. SLJ, *Jesus, Islam, Science*, 26

To emphasize the orthodox doctrine of the essential difference between God and world, the expression 'to beget the world', already abused in support of emanationism, had therefore to be abandoned. ... the Jewish Cabbalistic lore where obscurantist mysticism left no opposition to cavorting with emanationism. SLJ, *Cosmos and Creator*, 71, 76

In all those cultures [ancient China or India] the world view was dominated by emanationism which invariably implies the growing absence of order and rationality as the chain of being extends farther and farther from the source of emanation, however divine. It was only with belief in that Word or Logos – as is clear from the writings of Athanasius who fully perceived in Arianism a potential backsliding into emanationism – that there came a categorical assertion about the full rationality of a world created by a fully divine Logos. SLJ, *Brain, Mind and Computers*, 297

encomium: warm or high praise, panegyric. This is one of Jaki's pet words, appearing eight times in *Science and Creation* and many dozen times in his other works.[17]

> Evaluations of his [Roger Bacon's] place in the history of science oscillate between lopsided encomiums and studied neglect. SC 226

eternalism: the belief that the universe is unending.

> ...Einstein's work was time and again invoked by fellow scientists in support of cosmic eternalism. Thus W. Nernst, on February 23, 1929, assured a distinguished audience that in addition to radioactivity as a "deteriorating process" there are also "great constructive energies at work in the universe, or else the universe would speed to its death. Radioactive destructive energies are counterbalanced by radioactive constructive energies." And as if to save this incredible declaration from ready objections, Nernst invoked the authority of Einstein as one who "has found a formula for these facts that alone would have sufficed to make that physicist immortal." Nernst must have thought that once cosmic immortality was on hand, a sort of personal immortality would be a cinch. His philosophical bravado was matched by plain irresponsibility in matters scientific: "According to his [Einstein's] formula we must suppose that cosmic masses may without emitting any rays submerge in the ether of light, which is the mother of all energy, there to condense and become a part of a new world system." The formula in question was the famous $E=mc^2$ which Nernst invested with magic powers. He had no excuse for forgetting that by then the ether had been laid to rest for twenty-five years through Einstein's work on special relativity that contained that very formula as its essential consequence. Had Einstein protested energetically, its echoes would have been remembered. His connivance with cosmic eternalism on pseudo-scientific grounds could not be of interest to most of his biographers, who as a rule portray him as an exemplary character without guile and without fault.
>
> ... scientific critics ignored the fact that the steady-state theory implied not only an eternal but also an infinite universe, with its consequent paradoxes. In addition to postulating a continual creation of matter out of nothing since eternity, the theory also implied the continual piling up of an infinite amount of matter just beyond the edges of the observable universe. The theory provided no explanation to the problem that all matter (particles or galaxies) passing through that edge could do so only by doing what is impossible, namely, by acquiring the speed of light and therefore becoming infinite in mass. Impossibilities of this kind were regularly encountered by those among modern scientific cosmologists who tried to ward off the specter of transitoriness by giving a scientific glitter to the cause of cosmic eternalism.
>
> A belief tied to a most obscure birth in an obscure corner of the globe may seem a mark of irrationality. The matter will look very different if one recalls the proverbial proclivity of Jewish and Muslim

---

[17] Every time I see it I smile and think of ENCOM, the company in "TRON" where Alan Bradley, Kevin Flynn, and Lora Baines worked, where the System was once dominated by the Master Control Program. (Maybe "encomium" is a transuranic they discovered in their quest to "digitize" matter.)

intellectuals towards pantheism and eternalism. Belief in creation out of nothing and in time, on which rests Buridan's reasoning about the inertial character of the motion of celestial bodies, remained intact and robust only within Christian monotheism. ... Eternalism is as old as paganism, crude or refined, unlearned or learned, unadorned by science or garbed in it. SLJ, *God and the Cosmologists*, 62-3, 66, 199, postscript

...the truth of the matter was that the Scholastics, Buridan and Oresme in particular, were very conscious of what they were doing. Moreover, their belief in God was not a belief in Jehovah but in the Father who revealed Himself in His only begotten Son, Jesus Christ. This is why, unlike their Jewish and Muslim counterparts among medieval students of Aristotle, the Christian Scholastics steered clear of Aristotle's pantheism and eternalism. The medieval Scholastics, precisely because they believed in Christian dogmas, held fast to the tenet that the universe was created out of nothing and in time. Herein lies the chief clue to Buridan's breakthrough toward the idea of inertial motion, or Newton's first law. SLJ, "Gilson and Science" in *Patterns or Principles and Other Essays*, 186

evolutionism: see Darwinism.

fatalism: the doctrine that all events are determined by necessity, or fate.

The background of frightening cosmic cycles with its debilitating fatalism undermined not only the chances of the Aztecs for meaningful cultural advances, but also destroyed their political future. SC 53

The Valentinians, Marcosians, Nicolaitans, Encratites, Borborians, Ophites, Sethians, and many others listed by Irenaeus, today are merely names familiar only to some specialists of church history. In Irenaeus' time they were at the peak of their influence. They were carriers of that religious syncretism and obscurantism which threatened with extinction whatever light the great philosophical schools of Greece succeeded in producing. Radical dualism and demonology, fatalism and reincarnation, emanationism and pantheism fused in those heresies with some Christian details, and were reinterpreted by an unbridled exercise in fantasy which barred any logic and consistency. The universe of those heretics was a maddening complex of demiurges and aeons that obeyed neither rhyme nor reason. SC 165

Medieval man, strong as many of them could be in faith, formed no exception to all this. As to the scientific understanding of the inexorable processes of nature they too were tempted by the mirage of fatalism. Its chief vehicle was astrology, the branch of speculation in which observation and vagueness found an alliance never matched in any other field. The vagueness of the dicta of astrology should suggest that it depends on and also fosters a state of mind for which the indefinable and inevitable are synonymous. Astrology claims a complete insight into the recondite intricacies of nature and human destinies, while at the same time it disdains a partial though reliable grasp of the workings of nature. Medieval investigators of nature fell short of their goals in the measure in which they fell under the sway of the fundamental tenets of astrology. SC 220

...when I had studied scholastic philosophy I heard no references to Aristotle's infatuation with the idea of eternal returns. Of course, he meant that things return only in a generic way. Peripatetics would return as a school, but not as individuals. And so with the Platonists. But other Greek sages held that each and every one would return individually. This could only generate fatalism, which incidentally decided the fate of the last stronghold of the Maya in the Yucatan peninsula, who were equally under the spell of eternal returns. SLJ, *A Mind's Matter*, 54

Chesterton's definition of a machine reveals its philosophical depth precisely because it can illustrate even the "machinery" of the mind without turning it into a machine. In addition to depth he also showed courage when long before the appearance of computers he labeled the expression "thinking machine" as a "baseless phrase of modern fatalism and materialism." SLJ, *Brain, Mind and Computers*, 286 quoting GKC, "The Blue Cross" in *The Innocence of Father Brown*, CW12:34

geocentrism: the belief that the Earth is motionless and at the center of all other celestial bodies, which revolve around it once a day, as specified by Ptolemy in his *Almagest*; hence it is called the geocentric, or Ptolemaic (as opposed to the heliocentric, or Copernican) system.

Kepler argued in the introduction to his *De stella Martis* (1609) that the Bible did not teach geocentrism. Geocentrism was not part of what the Bible taught to be necessary for salvation, although the Bible reflected the view that the earth, with man on it, was very much in the focus of God's attention. SLJ, *Questions on Science and Religion*, 97

Well before the advent of modern science, and indeed of heliocentrism, the contrast between that biblical world-tent and the world of Aristotelian-Ptolemaic geocentrism had to appear enormous. A universe bounded with the sphere of the fixed stars, with a spherical earth at its center, had a genuine scientific consistency. The measuring of a relatively short distance (from Alexandria to Syene along the Nile) on the earth's surface of a relatively minute part (the earth) of that universe could logically lead to quantitative estimates about the very size of that universe. Only a generation separates the measurement by Eratosthenes of Cyrene of the size of the earth from the computation by Aristarchus of Samos of the relative and absolute distances among the earth, the moon, and the sun. These great scientific achievements made around the middle of the 3rd century B.C. need not be reviewed here. Three centuries later they greatly helped Ptolemy calculate the minimum distance which, within that universe, the sphere of the fixed stars must have from the earth.

Biblicism almost succeeded in bringing irreparable discredit to the Counter-Reformers. This happened as they showed too much readiness to meet Lutherans and Calvinists on their own chosen ground, that is, biblical literalism. Perhaps partly because of this less attention was given to an all-important question about the authoritative ecclesial interpretation of the Bible as offered through the voice of a hierarchy centered on the bishop of Rome. The question was whether that hierarchy had ever put itself on record that geocentrism was a matter of faith. One aspect of the question was whether the Fathers had ever done so with convincing unanimity and, in particular, with explicit reference to Joshua's miracle.

Surprising as it may appear, patristic references to Joshua's miracle are few, and none of them shows the kind of scientific concern that one would expect to be on hand even within Ptolemaic geocentrism. Joshua's miracle was not mentioned when Oresme, bishop of Lisieux, proposed, around 1370, the earth's rotation as a convenient solution to the daily rotation of the heavens. Oresme referred only to the biblical parlance about the fixity of the earth, as a reason for making that proposal only tentatively. Copernicus made no reference at all to Joshua. The dubious distinction of dragging Joshua into the debates about Copernicus belongs to Luther who fulminated: "The fool [Copernicus] will turn upside down all astronomy, but as the Holy Writ shows, Joshua commanded the sun, and not the earth, to stand still." Melanchthon followed Luther, if not in tone at least in substance, in endorsing geocentrism.

Galileo took the Church by surprise by claiming that he had demonstrative (experimental) proof on behalf of the earth's motion, and that therefore the teaching of the Church had to be adjusted to the new situation. He did not have the proof, nor did he prove that the Church taught geocentrism as something to be believed. He simply took the Bible's parlance for Church dogmatics. SLJ, *Bible and Science*, 25, 111-2, 113

Hegelianism: a wacky, obscure, and ambiguous form of idealism, also called "a method and also a doctrine," which is "the dialectic" of "thesis, antithesis, and synthesis."[18]

Nature as seen through the lenses of Hegelian dialectic is a far cry from the Nature science presupposes. To be sure, Hegel was shrewd enough to make it appear that his dialectic would lead, say, to the elliptical orbit of planets and to the inverse square law of gravitation. In all appearance, he could not care less whether his dicta on space, time, matter, gravity, stars, planets, falling bodies, electricity, and chemical

---

[18] Apparently, like Tao (or is it Zen?) the absurdity of this Hegel thing is beyond definition, as witness the absurd entry in *A Dictionary of Philosophy*. The hilarity is incomparable. Jaki's sample of Hegel's definition of hydrogen as "the positive side of determinateness in opposition, or differentiated nitrogen" (Jaki, *Angels, Apes, and Men*, 37) reminds me of the debate of Professor de Worms:

"I don't fancy," he said, "that you could have worked out the principle that evolution is only negation, since there inheres in it the introduction of lacunae, which are an essential of differentiation." I replied quite scornfully, "You read all that up in Pinckwerts; the notion that involution functioned eugenically was exposed long ago by Glumpe."

(GKC, *The Man Who Was Thursday*, CW6:550).

Also: I could not find a clear distinguishing of the Hegelian "Right" from the Hegelian "Left" – even another reference work barely characterizes them, and Jaki leaves it vague – which leads me to think they are Tweedle-indistinguishable. (My neologism for such things, kind of what happens when you put Heisenberg through a Gödel-like mapping into Pauli's quantum states. Ahem. For the *locus classicus*, see Carroll, *Through the Looking Glass*, chapter four, for Tweedledum and Tweedledee, or the Daryls of "The Newhart Show" which were even more so.)

reactions would ring a bell with physicists and chemists. SLJ, *Angels, Apes and Men*, 37 *et seq.*

...Hegel's verbiage about astronomy, physics and chemistry. When the first instalment of that verbiage appeared in 1801, in the form of an essay on how many planets *ought* to be, the essay prompted the astronomer Von Zach to characterize it as the "*monumentum insaniae saeculi decimi noni*," or a monument to the madness of the nineteenth century. Further monuments of that insanity were the Hegelian Right and Left. They both showed marked hostility to science, which meanwhile made tremendous progress in unfolding the secrets of the *how* in which *things* work.

... Proponents in modern times of pantheism have invariably tried to bridge conceptually that difference between quantities and qualities. An egregious example of this is Hegel, who generated both the Hegelian right and left. While the Hegelian right could not establish itself politically, the Hegelian left did so. There, I mean communism in the former Soviet Union, it was claimed that if you pile quantities upon quantities you will produce quality. Such was the philosophical motivation to produce engineers in ever larger numbers. But the empiricists in the West fell into the same trap. Some of the early empiricists claimed that if you have many second-rate painters you will have some really great ones. It is equivalent to saying that if you pile many second-hand computers on one another, you will have a supercomputer. SLJ, "What God Has Separated... Reflections on Science and Religion" in *A Late Awakening and Other Essays*, 65-6, 72-3

The universe is at best a mere concept in various forms of idealism, Berkeleyan or Hegelian. Trust in the reality of the universe could but suffer through the fondness of many modern cosmologists for idealism. ... The Hegelian-left, which should be best called the Kantian-left, concurred with its celebration of an infinite eternal material universe as the ultimate entity, a dogma of a now defunct Marxist orthodoxy. SLJ, *The Limits of a Limitless Science*, 110, 113

heliocentrism: see Copernicanism

humanism: mode or attitude of thought centering upon distinctively human interests or ideals. (Also see "secular humanism" below).

...it was Socrates who initiated that trend which produced along with most of the literary and philosophical gems of Greek humanism a wholly misguided form of physical science. SC 105

In the new-fangled cultivation of classical antiquity, the external world could serve as the stage for the myths of Plato at best, or for the myths of the gods at worst, as can be seen in the fifteen books of the *De genealogia deorum gentilium* of Boccaccio, a trusted friend of Petrarch. In its final form, published in 1373, it became the sourcebook for all Humanists who for the next two centuries discoursed about the world in terms of allegories, in much the same, scientifically worthless, obscurantist manner, in which Porphyry, one of their antique idols, did in his *De antro nympharum*. Porphyry was a chief of Neoplatonists and whatever there was philosophical in the Rinascimento, it was largely a reaffirmation of Neoplatonism, and of its studied neglect of a reasoned investigation of the external world. SC 248

Only when the Renaissance tried to reinstate classical humanism, or the thesis that man is his own final judge, did Christian thinkers began to feel the necessity to prove in a systematic manner man's natural dependence on God. SLJ, *Why the Question: Is There a God?*, 64

Theological modernism was the deepest form of sheer humanism that brooked no interference from any factor above, whereas the Catholic Church represented in a most concrete way the view that such interference is a continuous, ubiquitous and daily process. SLJ, *Miracles and Physics*, 1

It is, of course, no surprise to me that the contingency of the universe is not pleasant news to a scientific humanism which claims that man is a mere accident, in no way subject to something transcendental to the entire universe. Such a humanism is more powerful in our times than it has ever been. This is why *Time* felt it natural to proclaim under Einstein's picture that everything is relative. The only message befitting Einstein's picture would have been a warning that the absolute is lurking everywhere beneath the relative. But *Time* is very human and so are our times, indeed all times. To this rather defective humanness of the times proper reflections on Einstein's work may bring a much needed corrective. SLJ, "The Absolute Beneath the Relative: Reflections on Einstein's Theories" in *The Absolute Beneath the Relative and Other Essays*, 13

In the midst of that wild flux, the mind naturally looks for some fixed point, some lodestar, or at least tries to construct one in order to coordinate those impressions into a coherent whole. All systems, indeed all fixed ideas, are so many witnesses to this natural urge in man. In the middle of the second century B.C. the Roman playwright, Terence, could still think that his dictum, *homo sum; humani nil alienum puto*, could raise no questions about the completeness of humanism. There must have been a great appeal to the view that man as a microcosmos was a condensation of the macrocosmos and therefore human nature comprised everything and was wholly sufficient to itself. ... The dogma defined at Nicaea was therefore, among other things, also a thorough corrective to the humanist perspective as capsulized in Terence's dictum. There was now on hand a human experience that demanded a rewriting of that dictum. In order to do justice to the completeness of his experience man henceforth had to say: *homo sum; humani divinique nil alienum puto*. SLJ, *A Mind's Matter*, viii-ix[19]

idealism: any theory which affirms the central importance of the mind, or the spiritual or ideal, in reality, such as (a) the theory that reality is essentially spiritual, or the embodiment of mind or reason; (b) the theory which identifies reality with perceptibility,

---

[19] The first Latin statement is Terence: "I am a man; nothing human is alien to me" (*Heauton Timorumenos* (Self-tormentor), I.i.23). The second is Jaki's "Nicean" extension, made possible by the incarnation of the Divine Word as the Son of Mary: "I am a man; nothing, human or divine, is alien to me."

or denies the possibility of knowing anything except the mental life.

The first major scientific discourse on the infinity of the universe came only with the *Principia* of Newton, and especially with the Scholium added to it in 1713. It was a step in which encouragement from Bruno's writings or memory had no part. Those whom Bruno really inspired were the chief representatives of German Idealism and *Naturphilosophie*. Their pantheism, antiscientific lucubrations, and infatuation with the idea of eternal recurrence will form another chapter of this story of the inner logic of some fundamental standpoints. SC 267

Nothing is more difficult than to speak of the brain-mind or mind-body relationship. It is a mysterious coin with two luminous sides. The only way to handle it is to follow the advice once given about a tax coin and render both mind and body their respective dues. In a sense the Thomistic doctrine of the soul as the form of the body states precisely this. It is a doctrine respecting facts, refractory though they may be to the impatience of reductionism. Lacking intellectual patience, Descartes from the start read his own mind into Scholastic terms. Had Descartes appreciated Thomas's doctrine of soul, he would have kept equal respect both for Thomas's emphasis on the priority of the sensory (thoroughly misunderstood by Locke and other empiricists) and for his simultaneous emphasis on the active role of the intellect (*intellectus agens*), mistakenly viewed by many nowadays as a vote by Thomas for idealism. Both emphases could but degenerate into shibboleths of empiricism and idealism once they were no longer considered as two sides of one and the same coin. ... A subtle indication of the anthropocentrism of Descartes' system can be perceived in the way it held over a generation or two. Ever since, the history of philosophy in the Western world has been a repetition of the same pattern: the transient glory of systems – idealism, positivism, existentialism – each duly buried by its successors.

Possibly he [Hegel] sensed that the ultimate unmasking of Idealism would come from the hands of science. To forestall this outcome science had to be turned into *Naturphilosophie*. Scientists and science were, however, much harder to crack than imagined by Hegel and Hegelians. In fact, as it turned out, even some scientists imbued with Idealism, were weaned from it simply by facing up to what they were doing as scientists.

The anthropic principle is the very opposite of anthropocentrism, precisely because it eliminates the most sophisticated form of subjectivism, embodied in a priori theories about man's knowing the world. This is not to suggest that there have been no cosmologists who, misled by idealist epistemologies, have not tried to turn the anthropic principle inside out. It is, however, one thing to pour idealism, Kantian, even Berkelian, into scientific cosmology; it is another to face the cosmic facts in their enormous singularity and specificity.

Causality could easily be sacrificed when the sense of reality had already been victimized by that subjectivism which is inevitably generated by pragmatism, positivism, and idealism, all variations of the philosophy to which members of the Copenhagen School subscribed. SLJ, *Angels, Apes and Men*, 19, 20, 36, 80, 93

immanentism: belief that God (or "spirit") pervades all things.

Kant's reducing Christ to a mere man, however exalted, whose resurrection (to say nothing of his miracles) was an illusion of his followers, did not turn him into an atheist or a materialist. But his studied ambivalence about creation could only be taken for a foil for an immanentism that differed only in name from an atheistic or materialistic position. Within the latter, it was possible to tolerate a religion that was a matter of mere sentiments, that is, the product of purely practical reason, on the basis of which no rational challenge could be posed to disbelief. SLJ, *The Savior of Science*, 123n8

There will, of course, be many who keep trying to shore up their Spinozean pantheism and immanentism by desperately claiming infinity for the universe along the parameter of time. Neither science nor scientific history will be their ready allies. SC 356

This book would not have been written except for my deep awareness of the fact that materialistic, immanentistic considerations play a heavy role in scientific research, and that facts unfavorable to those considerations are slighted or ignored time and again. SLJ, *God and the Cosmologists*, Postscript.

The complete autonomy of man as a rational being, or his radical immanence which it was Kant's chief aim to demonstrate, could not be disputed on the basis of "pure" reason by which the Age of Enlightenment set so great a store. SLJ, "Teaching Transcendence in Physics" in *The Only Chaos and Other Essays*, 206

Manicheism: religion founded by the Persian Mani in the 3rd century A.D, derived from Zoroastrian Dualism, Babylonian folklore, Buddhist ethics, and small superficial additions from Christianity, principally the theory that there are two eternal principles, good and evil, hence a form of religious dualism.

Had the world existed from eternity, souls too would have existed from eternity and also their ability to sin. This implied the idea of a fall since eternity which, in Augustine's eyes, suggested the Manichean idea about an eternal principle of evil rooted in matter. To such a notion Augustine, the former Manichean, was not to give even unwitting support. For him the material universe was beautifully ordered and radically good, and he clung to that conviction with utmost resolve. It was in this connection that he took issue with Origen who, according to him, pictured the world as a place created for the punishment of souls guilty of evil. For Augustine it was wholly baffling that "some even of those who, with ourselves, believe that there is only one source of all things, and that no nature which is not divine can exist unless originated by that Creator, have yet refused to accept with a good and simple faith this so good and simple a reason of the world's creation, that a good God made it good." SC 178

Darwinists for the most part still fail to recognize with T. H. Huxley in ethics something which should seem both an obvious fact and also an inescapable contradiction for Darwinism. On both counts ethical force, to recall Huxley's words, is "the checking of the cosmic process at every step" and a substitution for it of another – the end of which is not the survival of those who may happen to be the fittest...but of those who are ethically the best." Darwinists have no answer to this dilemma because the only answer – the recognition of a spiritual order in man who is more than mere matter – cannot come within their ken, a ken constructed to the specifications of strict materialism. Thus those who refuse to acknowledge the dualism of man are condemned to side with the dualism of the Manicheans of old who conjured up two ultimate and equal forces: one remorseless, another good – caught in eternal antagonism. The same contradiction, when translated into the dualism of blind versus purposeful, haunts the Darwinists no less while making them oblivious to another fact, although it is a fact within the reach of an elementary reflection on what they themselves are doing. Their work is a life-long commitment to the purpose of proving that there is no purpose. Every Darwinist is a living refutation of a philosophy, Darwinism, for which purpose is non-existent. SLJ, *Angels, Apes and Men* 62-3

Marxism: the socialism of Marx and Engels, based on the primacy of class struggle; the belief-system of the atheistic socialism known as Communism, also called dialectic materialism.

Marxism has grown into a giant political force, and its history amply shows what physical science can expect when scientism has the political power to impose its intellectual tyranny. That dialectical materialism was to rule science and scientific research was already intimated on the pages of *Das Kapital*. Marx not only compared his method to that used by physicists, but he also claimed to have discovered a basic set of rules unconditionally valid in both natural and social sciences. Of this method that was to provide the golden key to any puzzle under the sun, Marx stated that it "includes in its comprehension and affirmative recognition of the existing state of things, at the same time also the recognition of the negation of that state, of its inevitable breaking up."

Marxist dialectic, like Comtean positivism, was not hesitant about laying down a long array of regulations physics was supposed to comply with. That these rules were invariably erroneous was due in no small part to Engels' unbounded admiration for Hegel, a typical pitfall for thousands of amateur scientists in the nineteenth century. It was Hegel whom Engels echoed in claiming that the Newtonian theory of gravitation rested on taking attraction as the essence of matter. It should be no surprise that such mishandling of the facts of scientific history was but a step toward a wholly arbitrary account of the facts of nature. Beside attraction, Engels claimed with Hegel, one should assume repulsion as a basic law in nature. "Hegel is quite right in saying," Engels insisted, "that the essence of matter is attraction and repulsion." This was the a priori sway of scientism that came forth in brute force in Engels' dictum: "Attraction and repulsion are as inseparable as positive and negative, and hence from dialectics itself it can already be predicted that the theory of matter must assign as important a place to repulsion as to attraction, and that a theory of matter based on mere attraction is false, inadequate, and one-sided." If issues in physics are settled by dialectic, experiments will have, of course, to take second place.

That modern physics had refuted mechanical materialism, he [Lenin] readily admitted, but he was quick to insist with the limitless adaptability required of any good Marxist that "the destructibility of the atom, its inexhaustibility, the mutability of all forms of matter and of its motion, have always been the stronghold of dialectical materialism. All boundaries in nature are conditional, relative, movable, and express the gradual approximation of our reason towards the knowledge of master." TROP 481, 482, 485

Nothing is easier than to blame the "feudal" and "bureaucratic" society of pre-modern China for its failure to develop or assimilate science in a meaningful manner. Continual encomiums heaped on ancient Chinese contributions to science and endless allegations of unfavourable socio-economical factors, may easily turn into a self-defeating dialectic. Dialecticians, especially the Marxist brand, are distinguished by a sharp though one-way vision. In our case it is bafflingly insensitive to the distinctly different workings of the same socio-economical factors in feudal China and in feudal Europe. In the latter there was a burgeoning of universities and an intellectual ferment, the like of which China failed to match even remotely. Again, the more evidence, convincing or merely suggestive, is collected about the technological superiority of ancient and medieval China over the West, the more stumbling blocks are gathered for the contention that science is an inevitable result of using proper tools of production. The baffling fate of science in China should suggest that the explanation is far from being that simple. A reluctant admission of this comes from J. Needham himself, the leading Western historian of Chinese science, and an avowed Marxist.

Engels' deep attachment to the idea of eternal succession of worlds is also evidenced in the manner in which he vindicated it as an integral part of the socialist, that is Marxist, *Weltanschauung*.

In view of the highly activist, revolutionary career of Blanqui, which covered a good part of nineteenth-century French history, his startling excursion into cosmology and philosophy of science should come as a surprise to anyone thinking of Marxism as a purely economico-social theory. SC 40, 313, 314

materialism: any theory which considers the facts of the universe to be sufficiently explained by the existence and nature of matter.

the ship of science ... run aground on the shallows of pantheistic presumptions about man's introspective capacity to penetrate the inner workings of a universe made not by human hands. No wonder that Bacon felt greater sympathy with Democritus' approach to nature than with that of Plato and Aristotle. But one wonders how some recent students of Bacon could find in this a revival of materialism by Bacon, who took pains to warn about the difference between the philosophical materialism of Democritus and the usefulness of his ateleological approach to the particular phenomena of the material world... ...the enunciation of the principle of the conservation of energy by Mayer, Joule, Helmholtz, and others. While Moleschott, Vogt, and Büchner tried to forge from the principle an unassailable foundation for their "scientific" materialism, perceptive scientists discovered a most far-reaching aspect of energy transformations. SC 282, 294

The reason for Engels' animosity toward Clausius is not difficult to identify. Clausius, entropy, and the heat-death of the universe meant one and the same thing for Engels. They represented the most palpable threat to the materialistic pantheism of the Hegelian left for which the *material* universe was and still is the ultimate, ever active reality Engels made no secret about the fact that the idea of a universe returning cyclically to the same configuration was a pivotal proposition within the conceptual framework of Marxist dialectic. He saw the whole course of science reaching in Darwin's theory of evolution the final vindication of the perennial recurrence of all, as first advocated by the founders of Greek philosophy. SC 312

...[Nietzsche's] early advocacy of materialism almost certainly turned his attention to F. A. Lange's *History of Materialism* of which the second and vastly revised edition from 1873 discussed the question of eternal returns with references to Epicurus, Lucretius, and Blanqui. SC 320

From the mid-1850s on, a materialism preached in the name of science and of an infinite universe began to produce runaway bestsellers as if never to be discredited again. ... The first stage of the lesson is provided by the fact that all the early phases of the universe appear to be the very opposite to that nondescript homogeneous stuff out of which the actual universe had, until recently, been claimed to have developed. The claim received its most popular form when Herbert Spencer turned Laplace's nebular hypothesis from an explanation of the origin of the solar system into a genesis of the entire universe. As such, the nebular hypothesis became a mainstay of bourgeois as well as bolshevik materialism. The alleged homogeneous starting point of the universe assured countless superficial minds that such a point was so simple as to make unnecessary further questions about it. ... The confidence of the promoters of that search [for extraterrestrial intelligence] had its chief source in what should be called – and right at the outset – integral Darwinism. According to it life and intelligence are the necessary and inevitable outcome in a world in which particles of matter and their physical characteristics (forces) are producing ever new situations and configurations in immense varieties whose succession is a limitless flux. Within this strictly materialistic perspective nothing is more natural than to claim that "we are not alone" and to look, if not for advanced civilizations, at least for evidences of lower forms of life even in our own planetary backyard. ... Rationally speaking, so Kant insisted, man was alone; he could in no rationally respectable way go to that "outside" that constitutes the universe. Nor was it rational, according to Kant, for man to infer from his inner world to the existence of a moral Lawgiver. It could not be known, in terms of Kant's third and fourth antimonies, whether man was free or not, and therefore morally responsible or not. If such was the case, his purposeful acts had to appear as illusions, to say nothing of their moral horizons. The trend of this intellectual strategy toward plain materialism and atheism was fully known to Kant and he stuck by it. ... The chief target of the *Notebooks* [of Darwin] is man's mind, the "citadel," in Darwin's words, which was to be conquered by his evolutionary theory if its materialism were to be victorious. In Germany David Strauss, busy in weeding all miracles out of the Bible, hailed Darwinism as the definitive answer to miracles. The last in Germany to oppose Strauss would have been Ernst Haeckel, the first major German champion of Darwin. In his *History of Creation* man was turned so outspokenly into a product of an exclusively materialistic evolution that for a while Darwin thought that there was no reason for him to write the *Descent*. SLJ, *The Savior of Science*, 92, 106, 120, 122-3, 126, 142

maximalism: usually said with reference to some idea or action, taking that idea or action in its widest, most extensive sense. Also see minimalism.

I wrote an essay on "Newman and Miracles." I did so because I found him to be an enthusiastic advocate of the reality of miracles. Putting it bluntly, I found him a maximalist. ... ...focusing on Newman's maximalist stance on miracles, the second chapter in [my] *Newman's Challenge*. Already in his time which took the Great Exhibition of 1850 in the Crystal Palace for a display of true miracles brought about by science and technology, that maximalist stance had to appear jarring. SLJ, *A Mind's Matter*, 195, 213

It seems that more justice is done to the record by assuming a middle position between Duhem's maximalism and a minimalism harking back to the virulent antimedievalism of the Enlightenment for which everything before Galileo was dark, as far as science was concerned. SC 232

medievalism: the belief and general character of the Middle Ages.

I do not think, however, that I have even yet brought out the greatest contribution of medievalism to the formation of the scientific movement. I mean the inexpugnable belief that every detailed occurrence can be correlated with its antecedents in a perfectly definite manner, exemplifying general principles. Without this belief the incredible labours of scientists would be without hope. It is this instinctive conviction, vividly poised before the imagination, which is the motive power of research: – that there is a secret, a secret which can be unveiled. How has this conviction been so vividly implanted on the European mind?

When we compare this tone of thought in Europe with the attitude of other civilisations when left to themselves, there seems but one source for its origin. It must come from the medieval insistence on the rationality of God, conceived as with the personal energy of Jehovah and with the rationality of a Greek philosopher. Every detail was supervised and ordered: the search into nature could only result in the vindication of the faith in rationality. Remember that I am not talking of the explicit beliefs of a few individuals. What I mean is the impress on the European mind arising from the unquestioned faith of centuries. By this I mean the instinctive tone of thought and not a mere creed of words.

In Asia, the conceptions of God were of a being who was either too arbitrary or too impersonal for such ideas to have much effect on instinctive habits of mind. Any definite occurrence might be due to the fiat of an irrational despot, or might issue from some impersonal, inscrutable origin of things. There was not the same confidence as in the intelligible rationality of a personal being. I am not arguing that the European trust in the inscrutability of nature was logically justified even by its own theology. My only point is to understand how it arose. My explanation is that the faith in the possibility of science, generated

46

antecedently to the development of modern scientific theory, is an unconscious derivative from medieval theology.
(All this is from A. N. Whitehead, *Science and the Modern World: Lowell Lectures, 1925* (New York: The Macmillan Company, 1925), pp. 17-18, quoted at length in SC 230-1.)

minimalism: usually said with reference to some idea or action, taking that idea or action in its narrowest, most specific sense. Also see maximalism.

The bishops, theologians, and laymen who urged and welcomed the declaration of infallibility were seen by Renan as representatives of that craving for at least a minimum of stability. Indeed, though not all of them were minimalists, they came up in the end on the pope's extraordinary magisterium with a decree which is a classic in minimalism. According to that decree the pope is infallible *only* in matters of faith and morals; *only* when he speaks *ex cathedra*; and *only* the very core of his solemn utterance is within the range of his infallibility. SLJ, *And On This Rock*, 111-2

Opinions about their localization [memory in the human brain] run the whole gamut of possibilities. On the one extreme are the minimalists who in effect smear out over the whole organism the physiological foundation of each memory. On the other extreme are the advocates of special memory centers and memory cells. SLJ, *Brain, Mind and Computers*, 103

moderate realism: (or methodical realism) The only reasonable and rational philosophical system which is in harmony with both science and religion, since it proceeds from things-which-are to thoughts. See Gilson, *Methodical Realism*, with an introduction by Jaki.

A reasonable approach to the universals, of course, can be had only on the basis of that moderate realism which Gilson characterized in another context in words that cannot be reprinted often enough: "The first step on the path of realism is to recognize that one has always been a realist; the second is to recognize that, however much one tries to think differently, one will never succeed; the third is to note that those who claim that they think differently think as realists as soon as they forget to act a part. If they ask themselves why, their conversion is almost complete." SLJ, *The Road of Science and the Ways to God*, 327n44

According to that thesis, [in SLJ's Gifford Lectures, printed in *The Road of Science and the Ways to God*] all great creative advances in science were achieved in terms of what is best called an epistemological middle road between empiricism and idealism. This middle road is often called moderate realism, but I would prefer to call it "methodical realism," an expression of Gilson's. If there is any epistemology in the Bible, it is the epistemology of moderate and, therefore, metaphysical realism. SLJ, *A Mind's Matter*, 88, 155

The moderate realism which characterizes Aquinas' theory of knowledge, and the analogy of being which forms the essence of his metaphysics, proved to be the classic stance of balance in reasoning. His resolve to give reason its due in the highest possible measure meant, however, in the actual context, an overly generous acceptance of the Aristotelian system, the epitome of rational explanation of the world at that time. In this search for conceptual stability, Aquinas was also motivated by the sad predicament of Muslim theologians and philosophers and by their highly unsettling impact on a Christian Europe going through its birthpangs. SC 225

monism: the doctrine that there is only one kind of substance or ultimate reality, as mind or matter; the doctrine that reality is one unitary organic whole with no independent parts. Also see dualism.

The true need of philosophy consisted in vistas pointing far beyond the confines of pantheistic monism, however ancient its pedigree could be in the history of man's speculations about the universe and his destiny in it. SC 229

The most startling feature of his [Tyndall's] voluminous monograph, *Heat a Mode of Motion*, which in the 1860's went through four editions, was its author's silence about the Second Law of thermodynamics. Those familiar with the monism of Tyndall's famous address given before the British Association meeting in Belfast in 1874, can easily surmise the key to Tyndall's cultivated silence. For the one who saw in the First Law of thermodynamics the very foundation of an eternal universe, the Second Law must have been a bitter pill, not to be swallowed if possible. Tyndall clearly tried to chase away the ghost of entropy as he described in his book on heat a universe derived from only the First Law: "The energy of Nature is a constant quantity, and the utmost man can do in the pursuit of physical truth, or in the applications of physical knowledge, is to shift the constituents of the never-varying total, sacrificing one if he would produce another. The law of conservation rigidly excludes both creation and annihilation. Waves may change to ripples, and ripples to waves – magnitude may be substituted for number, and number for magnitude – asteroids may aggregate to suns, suns may invest their energy in florae and faunae, and florae and faunae may melt in air – the flux of power is eternally the same. It rolls in music through the ages, while the manifestations of physical life as well as the display of physical phenomena are but the modulations of its rhythm." The smallness of the last word was in inverse proportion to its significance in Tyndall's cosmological views. This was recognized by a no less literate advocate of scientific monism at that time than Herbert Spencer. He noted with satisfaction that "after having for some years supposed myself alone in the belief that all motion is rhythmical, I discovered that my friend, Professor Tyndall, also held this doctrine." The word doctrine could not have been better chosen. For Spencer the doctrine of the rhythmic nature of every motion was a fundamental tenet in the sense of a metaphysical or religious doctrine. SC 295

Materialists and idealists represented the two chief possible options of a monistic approach to the question of the mind-body relationship, an approach which was one of the alternatives within the perspectives of realism. The other was dualism, of which the Cartesian version was meant to be "scientific," whereas the Aristotelian-Thomistic version remained content being plainly philosophical. SLJ *The Road of Science and the Ways to God*, 254

naturalism: action, inclination, or thought based on natural desires and instincts alone; the doctrine denying that anything in reality has a supernatural significance, specifically, the doctrine that scientific laws account for all phenomena, and theological conceptions of nature are invalid; loosely, materialism and positivism; denial of the miraculous and supernatural in religion, and the rejection of revelation as a means of attaining truth.

Celsus, in line with the best Greek philosophical tradition, could conceive of religion only as an ennobled form of naturalism. In his eyes nature was the supreme being outside of and above which nothing could exist. Nature was eternal and for ever recurring. SC 172

...the naturalism, which liberalism demands from the theologian, is also evident in the claim of one such biblical expert that while his critical reason forbids him to see a divine being in Jesus, he accepts his divinity on faith. Such a distinction between faith and reason is however, the very dynamics which turns faith into a subjective sentiment which does not strictly depend on supernatural grace.

...a prominent Barthian, whose name I am not at liberty to divulge, disclosed to me his suspicion that naturalism is the real outcome of Protestantism. Naturalism is also the chief harm which liberalism is producing in Catholic theology. The optimist view of human nature which is fostered in liberalism forces the liberal theologian to be silent on hell. If he speaks of heaven he describes it as a place into which everybody would slide almost naturally and almost insensibly.

Naturalism has always been the chief threat to Christianity, which is about the purpose of existence, but today the threat is particularly pervasive. There are many who take natural science for the redeemer and healer of man's nature.

As a champion of the study of the thought of Thomas Aquinas, Leo XIII had most articulate views on the support which man's fallen nature has to take from the supernatural in order to cope with the natural order. Those views are most timely parts of his Encyclical at a time when Catholic theological, philosophical, and socio-economic discourse is cavorting with sheer naturalism. A pivotal part of that naturalism is the denial of original sin.

SLJ, *The Gist of Catholicism and Other Essays*, 76, 77-8, 225-6, 240

Naturphilosophie: a pseudo-scientific view of nature especially in the work of Kant, Schelling and Hegel.

The "critical" viewpoint which Kant implemented for metaphysics (*Critique of Pure Reason*) and extended to ethics (*Critique of Practical Reason*), esthetics (*Critique of Judgment*), and afterwards to pedagogy and theology, had to be spelled out in detail also for the sciences if "critical" philosophy was to obtain its ultimate touchstone of truth. The result was sheer horror, *Naturphilosophie*, about which Neo-Kantians preferred the strategy of silence. Planck, and this should be indicative of his uncritical Neo-Kantianism, never referred to that aspect of Kant's system, nor did he refer to *Naturphilosophie* as practiced by Kant's successors, Schelling, Hegel, and others, although it was the target of very critical and well known remarks by such prominent German physicists as Gauss and Helmholtz. SLJ, "The Impasse of

Planck's Epistemology" in *The Absolute Beneath the Relative and Other Essays*, 28

...Kant's legislation, on the basis of the first critique, on the exact sciences. The legislation is antiscience throughout, the kind of counterscience which first raised its head in *Naturphilosophie*. *Naturphilosophie* is antiscience because it is sheer subjectivism. Subjectivism of the weaker, superficial kind is founded on the sentiments. The real threat is posed by a subjectivism of the intellect. Such is the subjectivism of Kantian philosophy. Its springs are not in the sentiments but in the intellectual pride which was a distinctive feature of Kant's mental physiognomy.

In 1818 *Naturphilosophie* reigned supreme and its dévotés wanted not only the control of the philosophical faculties but also of the faculties of science. Some German scientists despaired indeed of their very future. Hegel himself pressed the cause of *Naturphilosophie* relentlessly. Between 1817 and 1831, the year of his death, he brought out his *Encyclopedia*, the quintessence of the obscurantism of *Naturphilosophie*, in three editions, each considerably larger than the last. Possibly he sensed that the ultimate unmasking of Idealism would come from the hands of science. To forestall this outcome science had to be turned into *Naturphilosophie*. Scientists and science were, however, much harder to crack than imagined by Hegel and Hegelians. In fact, as it turned out, even some scientists imbued with Idealism, were weaned from it simply by facing up to what they were doing as scientists. SLJ, *Angels, Apes and Men*, 32, 36

necessitarianism: the doctrine that results follow by invariable sequence from causes, especially that the will is not free.

For devout Jews it was clearly an anathema that "the Universe came into existence, like all things in Nature, as the result of the laws of Nature." The biblical account demanded a middle course between the more or less overt occasionalism of the Mutakallimun and the pantheistic necessitarianism of Aristotle endorsed by the Mutazalite tradition. SC 214

Aristotle had his share of critics long before the medievals, but the pantheistic necessitarianism of his synthesis had never received a broad and effective challenge before Christianity developed into an all-pervading cultural matrix during the Middle Ages. If, therefore, the primacy of a mental outlook over the bare facts of sensory evidence is worth defending when it comes to the analysis of the development of science, then the faith of the Middle Ages in a personal, transcendental, providential, and rational Creator should appear of paramount importance. It was a faith shared enthusiastically by most of those who functioned as teachers in a culture with truly novel features. It was a faith generating a sense of confidence, purpose, and guidance with respect to the fundamental issues about man's place in the universe. It was a faith fully aware of the rights of reason. If it insisted on going beyond the immediate range of reason it was because of an honest willingness to consider the credentials of the greatest factual claim made in human history, the claims of the Rabbi from Nazareth. Such a faith certainly represents a mental outlook and can be taken lightly by any professedly non-positivist historian of science only at the risk of grave inconsistency. SC 236

...the eighteenth-century infatuation with the presumed presence of intelligent beings on almost every celestial body will appear astonishing only if one overlooks the overpowering impact which a commonly shared philosophical presupposition can have on thinking about matters scientific. In this case the philosophical presupposition was the principle of plenitude, according to which the created realm has to reflect in every possible way the plenitude of God. Since God's life is intellect, life and intellect must be everywhere in the universe. This necessitarian and *a priori* character of the principle of plenitude should make it clear that its origin is not Christian, whatever its injudicious endorsement by many a Christian thinker. SLJ, *Cosmos and Creator*, 127

I doubt that Chesterton ever read Book Lambda of *Metaphysics*, where the pantheist Aristotle roundly declared that the universe is a house without a master, or an army without a commander. [Aristotle, *Metaphysics*, 1074b-75b. Such was both the capstone and very source of that cosmic necessitarianism which put science into a straitjacket for almost two thousand years; that is, until some basic points of Aristotelian cosmology were rejected by medieval Scholastics, guided by the dictates of their Christian faith in creation out of nothing and in time.] Chesterton's universe explicitly had a captain and a "divine captain" at that, and this is why it had a Flag. SLJ, *Chesterton a Seer of Science*, 98 and note 27

Neoplatonism: philosophy of a group of thinkers of the early Christian era, endeavoring to reconcile the teachings of Plato and Aristotle with Oriental conceptions; also similar teachings in more recent times.

Damascius (Nicolas of Damascus), one of the last of Neoplatonist philosophers (fl. 510) ... Porphyry was a chief of Neoplatonists... SC 98, 248

Enthusiasm for Plato was one thing, casting one's mental lot with Neoplatonism was another. The former did not start with Ficino. Grosseteste and other leading figures of medieval science had already found in the Platonic philosophy of numbers fruitful inspiration, but their Christian faith in the Creator enabled them to see the difference between genuine gold and that of fools. The Plato which proved itself scientifically productive during the Renaissance was the continuation of the Platonism of medieval thought which carefully avoided the syncretistic morass exuding from Ficino's thought and from the Neoplatonism of his Academy. Diacceto's Neoplatonist paganism came from the very core of that morass and it certainly was not a negligible aspect of his thinking. What it represented was rather the very matrix out of which emerged an interpretation of the world which became increasingly alien to considerations that constituted the real progress of science during the Renaissance. SC 254

In the medieval context reason meant Aristotle. Byzantium largely skirted the issue by withdrawing its orthodoxy into a lofty supernaturalism steeped in Neoplatonism. In such a framework there was no room either for science or for natural theology. ... For them [Averroës and for his followers] the world was strictly eternal and in no need of a creation. Their natural theology followed closely, though shrewdly, Aristotle's pantheistic natural theology, or its Neoplatonic version, known as the "theology of Aristotle." That theology was as barren of unambiguous words about God as a transcendent being as Aristotle's physics was barren of meaningful science. SLJ, *The Road of Science and the Ways to God*, 35-6

obscurantism: a mode of thought aimed at hindering the progress or spread of knowledge.

...the difference between the two major works of Ptolemy, the *Almagest* and the *Tetrabiblos*. The latter shows a thinker completely lost in the labyrinths of astrology, while in the former no magic or obscurantism taints the long, sustained geometric account of the motion of planets. ... Much, though rather misplaced, admiration is still accorded by some obscurantist authors to the all-over masterplan that determined the construction of pyramids. One of the early proponents of the special significance of the ancient Egyptian cubit was none other than Sir Isaac Newton, whose great mind had become trapped in the latter half of his adult life in cabbalistic speculations. ... In this latter respect he [Oresme] certainly was no worse than Copernicus, or Kepler, or a Galileo who kept casting horoscopes, or a Newton whose obscurantist proclivities are only beginning to come to full light. ... ... the antiscientific obscurantism of Ficino, Diacceto, Paracelsus, Bruno, and of many smaller figures, such as Palingenius, Telesius, and Campanella. SC 17, 79, 236, 267

Armed with the massive evidence which Yates presented about Bruno's pantheistic obscurantism, I found the study of his *Cena* quite rewarding. It quickly became clear to me that that Bruno was interested in Copernicus only as the destroyer of the clear contours of a geocentric universe as if this had justified Bruno's resolve to eliminate all clear contours and structures from the cosmos. No wonder that unlike Kepler and Galileo, who sang the praises of geometry, Bruno resented whatever he found contrary to this in Copernicus' work, because he saw threatened his radical animization of the universe by what he called Copernicus' use of the "file of geometry." ... About Kant, let me recall here a remark of E. Rommel, the son of the "Desert Fox," who, as Mayor of Stuttgart, once complained to a scholarly gathering there about the fact that Kant had made obscure diction *de rigueur* for German academics. Herr Rommel would have hit his target better had he pointed out that Kant set a standard for academic excellence by promoting obscure thought through convoluted phraseology. SLJ, *A Mind's Matter*, 42-3, 44

occasionalism: the claim that all events, physical or mental, are strictly disconnected.

Needless to say, occasionalism was not referred to when computers were given the first opportunity, in connection with machine translation, to prove that they embody some intelligence, even if purely "artificial." Advocates of AI, who hardly ever demonstrate a serious concern for basic philosophical problems, let alone their very long history, would not, of course, be embarrassed on that score. They are determined to go about those problems *ambulando*, that is, in Diogenes' way of coping with one of Zeno's paradoxes or sophisms. Nevertheless, the philosophical presupposition that language is decomposable into strictly separate units has always been a cardinal tenet in the ideology underlying AI programs including machine translation. The ideology reveals its Ockhamist character by the very fact that those units, artificial to be sure, resist efforts aimed at grouping them into a coherent intelligible whole, such as any plain discourse. Those disdainful of wider views would do well to recall four chief advocates of occasionalism, al-Ashari, Ockham, Malebranche and Sartre. Being so widely separated from one another in time and space (and culture), their identical options should seem to represent a pattern of the inner force of logic. That science and the making of machines are not germane to occasionalism is amply illustrated by the virulently antiscientific dicta of al-Ashari and Sartre. That Ockham and Malebranche were keen on science has not failed to give headaches to those students of theirs who easily overlook the ineradicable call of human nature for intellectual coherence. SLJ, *Brain, Mind and Computers*, 254-5

Christian Ockhamists usually fail to ponder how close Ockham's philosophy is to occasionalism, Moslem and Malebranchian, and how little justice it does to biblical utterances declaring God's radical unchangeability. SLJ, *The Road of Science and the Ways to God*, 42n42

Malebranche, a most acute and enthusiastic Cartesian, tried to shore up matters by postulating occasionalism, a doctrine according to which all interactions between all physical things, not only between mind and body, are inscrutable. SLJ, *Cosmos and Creator*, 92-3

operationalism: the doctrine that the meaning of a concept is given by a set of operations; it is related to logical positivism.

The word "faith" was an ugly word for most of those who in those years and until very recently posed as the supreme interpreters of science and were accepted as such. I have in mind the neopositivists and the operationalists. There is, of course, much that can be said in favor of operationalism and of logical positivism. When, however, taken as the fundamental and exclusive theories of science, they display a serious shortcoming. Operationalism and logical positivism do not square with the facts of scientific creativity. In our times this was emphasized by such creative personalities of physical science as Einstein, Born, Schrödinger, and many others. SLJ, "The Role of Faith in Physics" in *Chance or Reality and Other Essays*, 150-1

Bridgman's book had before long become a bible for operationist psychologists. This was hardly a development to Bridgman's liking. As a matter of fact, he resolutely protested against being considered the originator and authentic exponent of operationism. "I believe," he wrote ten years after the publication of *The Logic of Modern Physics*, "that I myself never talked of 'operationalism' or 'operationism,' but I have distaste for these grandiloquent words which imply something more philosophic and esoteric than the simple thing that I see." That simple thing was that, whenever a concept is defined in physics, the observational operations implied in it should be clearly kept in mind. One must, however, admit that Bridgman at times articulated that "simple thing" in a rather sweeping manner. Thus he flatly declared that "the concept is synonymous with the corresponding set of operations," and that "the attitude of the physicist must therefore be one of pure empiricism." SLJ, *Brain, Mind and Computers*, 169

...the physicist's study of the history of his field will guard against his considering theories as mere artificial creations of the mind, suitable today and useless tomorrow. History will show him that although theories may quickly replace one another, all that was valuable in one will be incorporated into the next one, and as new theories are adopted, the observational data will be classified in an increasingly more comprehensive manner. Thus the conviction of the physicist will be strengthened that physics is making progress in learning more about the physical world and that physical theory is not just a construct having no real relation to the physical reality. For strict operationalism is just as much an extreme as mechanistic realism, and the smugness and despair they generate respectively can create only an intellectual atmosphere that will widen further the gap between science and the humanities. TROP 515

pantheism: the doctrine that the Universe is God
...[Bruno's] pantheism, as well as later that of Robert Fludd and of others, was too mixed up in Hermetist and cabbalistic lore to make it immediately appealing. Bruno began to come into his own only with the coming of pantheism in the guise of German idealism. ... ...the definition [by Vatican I] that God is absolutely different from the world and can be recognized with certainty from the contemplation of things visible. The stated target of the definition of God's existence as absolutely different from the universe is pantheism, which is, of course, a logical consequence of idealism, German or other. ... As to the prophetic character of the definition which had pantheism for its target, this should seem abundantly clear in view of the deification of the earth and of the universe which is turning into a vogue nowadays. ... As to the prophetic character of the definition which had pantheism for its target, this should seem abundantly clear in view of the deification of the earth and of the universe which is turning into a vogue nowadays. ... By the time of Vatican I, Laplacian cosmogenesis had become a chief vehicle of pantheism, especially through its recasting by Herbert Spencer. According to it, the universe had its origin in a supposedly homogeneous fluid, a primordial nebula Scientists knew only one thing about it, namely, that it was nebulous, but then as now such defects in scientific parlance were readily overlooked by the public increasingly eager to be saved by science. ... The cosmic meaning of το παν [*to pan*, "the all"] survived with particular effectiveness in the word "pantheism," or the idea that the world or universe is the ultimate or divine entity. SLJ, *Universe and Creed*, 7, 15-6, 18, 41

Platonism: the philosophy of Plato, especially his doctrine that things are but copies of ideas, and these are objects of true knowledge. Related to idealism, Hegelianism.
Duhem, famed for his insistence that the method of physics consists in hewing to the Platonic dictum, "to save the appearances," or the phenomena. ... It would have been foolish to endorse either the vitalism that plainly vitiated Aristotle's physical science, or the mechanistic philosophy that so badly served the great attainments of classical physics. All the great successes of modern physics could not make me blind to the untenability of Pythagoreanism or Platonism which some modern physicists saw embodied in quantum mechanics. At that time

already I found significant the fact that Einstein himself groped for a middle ground in epistemology. SLJ, *A Mind's Matter*, 84, 163

...the rule which should seem basic to all philosophy with a claim to a minimum of consistency: No form of philosophy, not even idealism (let alone its Kantian brand), can assert less than the means whereby it is communicated to others. Otherwise philosophy degenerates into a non-communicable love of wisdom, a sort of radical self-centeredness. Among those means is such an indispensable, material factor as the vibrations of the air, produced by flesh-and-blood tongues (and not merely by their critical ideas). Those air-waves must impinge on real ears in order to initiate an argument. The point can be made with even greater force about books as carriers of philosophical arguments. Unlike evanescent air-waves, books remain tangibly present even after the arguments fell silent together with the disputants. Such considerations should make *prima facie* suspect two kinds of discourse about the Universe. One is riveted on the claim of Platonists, old and new, that mere ideas can generate real matter, including its totality, the Universe. The erstwhile version of this Platonism need not detain us. It has, however, today a novel appeal dressed as it is in esoteric references to world-lines, zero-point oscillations in the quantum mechanical vacuum, and the like. Because of their scientific glitter, these expressions are apt to be taken for factors that can generate material reality and its totality as well, or the Universe. Unfortunately, credence is given even to that crudest renewal of primitive Platonism which makes some modern scientific cosmologists claim, as has been seen, that by scribbling complicated equations they can literally create universes out of nothing. Only by falling head over heels for that glitter will one find less convincing the starting point riveted in real matter. SLJ, *Is There a Universe?* 109-10

positivism: system of philosophy originated by Comte which excludes everything but the natural phenomena or properties of knowable things, together with their relations of coexistence and succession.

Positivist scientists and philosophers of science, like Mach, Ostwald, and Stallo, turned their opposition to atoms into the touchstone of the truth of their contentions. Their radical views had often been seized upon by thinkers like Nietzsche, who saw in the doubts besetting the conceptual foundations of late classical physics a confirmation of their own attitude extolling the subjective and the irrational. Nietzsche was hardly a disciplined thinker sensitive to the fine points of the anti-atomism of positivism, and he was certainly poles apart from the thinking of the great majority of physicists about physical reality and its lawfulness. ... [There is] the steadily growing realization that the man of science, no less than his counterpart in religion, lives ultimately by faith. With the mirage of positivism now being unmasked, it is easier to recognize that the scientific enterprise rests on a conviction which presupposes far more on man's part than the mere juxtaposition and correlation of the data observation. The conviction in question is nothing short of a faith which, like religious faith, consists in the readiness of going beyond the immediately obvious. The step is not simply a glib conjecture about a deeper layer. It is rather a recognition of the indispensable need of such a layer if the scientific enterprise is to make any lasting sense. It is in that deeper layer that notions like the intelligibility, simplicity, and lawfulness of nature are taking on a meaning which demands absolute, unconditional respect and acceptance. It is that deeper meaning which science must command if its laws should be considered not merely clever manipulations of terminology and data, but a concrete encounter with the real structure of nature. SC 325, 356

Planck's longest address of a non-technical nature was devoted to the defense of the freedom of the will against the claims of the Monistic League, that tried to sell the public on a world outlook (*Weltanschauung*) based on purely scientific grounds. For Planck, the basic shortcomings of attempts of this type consisted in ignoring the fact that the determinism of the scientific method is inapplicable when it comes to the innermost core of the personality where human decisions have their ultimate roots. He repeated this conviction seven years later in a lecture that dealt with the concept of external reality as conceived by positivism. In doing so, he made no digression from the subject of his lecture. For, as Planck had clearly seen, in both monism and positivism, taken as general philosophical explanations, freedom of the will, moral responsibility, ethical autonomy, and the like are "meaningless questions." To the dangers and consequences of such a position, Planck called attention in a most resolute manner: "It is a dangerous act of self-delusion if one attempts to get rid of an unpleasant moral obligation by claiming that human action is the inevitable result of an inexorable law of nature." Freedom of the will, or individual responsibility, constituted in Planck's eyes a point "where science acknowledges the boundary beyond which it may not pass, while it points to farther regions which lie outside the sphere of its activities." To recognize in such a manner the limits of the range of physical science was in Planck's view anything but a partial renunciation of the rights of scientific method. On the contrary, he stressed that such an acknowledgment of the limitations of science "gives us all the more the confidence in its message when it speaks of those results that belong properly to its own field." TROP 383

rationalism: the practice of guiding one's opinions and actions solely by what is considered reasonable; the theory that reason is a source of knowledge in itself, superior to and independent of sense perception; an explanation of apparently supernatural events according to reason.

A classic target of sophomoric rationalism and vicious bias which often parade in the cloak of science, the first chapter of Genesis is, in fact, a most lucid expression of that faith in the rationality of the universe without which the scientific quest in man could not turn itself into a self-sustaining enterprise. The story of Genesis 1 has, of course, been often presented as a feeble derivative of Babylonian and other creation myths. The bias implied in such an evaluation of the biblical account of creation is characteristic of that rationalism which cannot go beyond the immediate wording of the story and catch sight of its monumentally simple structure and highly elevated message. The structure is patterned after the logical procedure followed in every construction work: first comes the framework, and afterwards the details of each major section. Whereas the sober compliance with this straight pattern sets Genesis 1 markedly apart from other ancient cosmogonies, there is nothing original in the list of the principal parts of the world and their embellishments as given in Genesis 1. The list would have been much the same in any part of the land stretching from the Nile to the Euphrates and beyond. ... One may or may not agree with the extraordinary claim which the Master from Nazareth made about himself. Many millions have been deeply touched by his humaneness, uncounted others still find distasteful his emphatic other-worldliness. Yet, only the councils of rigid rationalists and dogmatic Marxists would deny that anyone ever changed the world as much as he did, and for the better. His immediate disciples were impressed by him to the point of according him divine honours. But their worship of him was only matched by the magnitude of their and their master's concern, lest any crack, however slight, be made in the edifice of the jealously strict monotheism of the Covenant. ... In that "physics" [of Tycho] the sun, the earth, the planets, and the four elements stood in the same animistic correlation that was believed to exist among the various organs of the human body. That Tycho did not get wholly trapped in the morass of that "physics" was due to his commitment to observational and mathematical astronomy, in which he saw a most exquisite service to the Creator. When such a faith was lacking, the safeguards of reason also vanished rapidly. The classic case is that of Giordano Bruno. His vision of an infinite universe composed of an infinitely large number of "worlds" or planetary systems, is mentioned on the pages of a legion of modern works, whose authors seem to demonstrate only their second-hand knowledge of Bruno, or their own bent on propagating a dubious brand of rationalism. SC 146, 157, 262

realism: the doctrine that universals exist outside the mind. (Opposed to nominalism). Also, the conception that objects of sense perception are real in their own right, existing independently of their being known or related to mind. (Opposed to idealism.)

Uncertainty and vagueness about the facts of nature was a typical feature of the times of William of Auvergne. Thus, it was all too easy to supplement meager information about facts with speculations that could readily go over into sheer phantasy. Yet, even in such cases the ramifications of the Christian belief in the Creator could provide some precious guidelines for reasoning about phenomena. ... Obviously, what was needed was an unremitting search coupled with an unconditional respect for some guidelines marking the major pitfalls in reasoning about nature, a contingent entity. These guidelines could be formulated in several ways. One of them was exemplified in the gigantic effort of Aquinas to bring reason and faith into a stable synthesis. The moderate realism which characterizes Aquinas' theory of knowledge, and the analogy of being which forms the essence of his metaphysics, proved to be the classic stance of balance in reasoning. His resolve to give reason its due in the highest possible measure meant, however, in the actual context, an overly generous acceptance of the Aristotelian system, the epitome of rational explanation of the world at that time. In this search for conceptual stability, Aquinas was also motivated by the sad predicament of Muslim theologians and philosophers and by their highly unsettling impact on a Christian Europe going through its birthpangs. SC 224-5

A Christian can only be a realist, even if he does find much of value in Plato. A chief case in point is Augustine, who often, unbeknownst to himself, poured baptismal water on Platonism which the latter badly needed. Long before Christians knew much about Aristotle, they were realists when they were philosophizing. And this happened because for centuries Christians philosophized for the sole reason of understanding better the propositions of the various credal formulas, all of which are about reality, natural or supernatural. In our times Gilson was the one who elaborated on this in the most sustained way. He also gave it a capsule formulation by speaking of "Christian philosophy." SLJ, *A Mind's Matter*, 185

...it was precisely the Christian doctrine of creation out of nothing which was the mainstay of Christian realism and which forced (together with the dogma of Incarnation) some patently idealist Christian philosophers to reassert the truth of flesh and blood reality in at least a roundabout way. ... The call by Leo XIII for a return to the Christian philosophy of Thomas Aquinas, a philosophy of realism, was inevitable because the recognition by the human mind of the existence of the Creator by means of created things implies a philosophical framework which makes no sense unless there is a totality of things, real, orderly, and contingent, which is the notion of a universe proclaimed by the dogma of creation and claimed by science as well. ... Part of the truth of Thomas' metaphysical realism, the only proper label of a genuinely Thomistic 'epistemology', lies in its consistency. This will not appear a small matter if one recalls Chesterton's poignant observation that 'No sceptics work sceptically; no fatalists work fatalistically; ... no materialist, who thinks his mind was made up for him by mud and blood and heredity, has any hesitation in making up his mind'. SLJ, *Cosmos and Creator*, 74, 86, 101, quoting GKC's *St. Thomas Aquinas*, CW2:542

Romanticism: movement reasserting of imagination and sentiment and emphasizing individualism in thought and expression as against the restrictive formality of classicism.

Most modern forms of pseudoscience have their roots in the rise of Romanticism. Various features of Romanticism are all too evident, for instance, in the basic assumptions as well as in the vagaries of *Naturphilosophie*. *Naturphilosophie* looked for its theoretical justification in the works of Fichte, Schelling, and Hegel, chief representatives of German Romanticism and Idealism. Common to their thinking was a theological orientation with distinctly pantheistic colouring, and this also meant a heavy emphasis on the priority of subjective consciousness over the external world. For Fichte, Schelling, and Hegel the external world was ultimately the emanation of the subjective Spirit, or Ego, which unfolded itself through the circular process of thesis, antithesis, and synthesis. SC 306

Since the rise of science, but especially during the last hundred years, there have been many evidences of a one-sided approach toward resolving this problem. One of these is to turn man into a machine, on the ground that man has reliable knowledge only about quantities. Hume claimed this, Voltaire too, and another figure of the

Enlightenment, Baron d'Holbach, authored the famous phrase: "all errors of man are errors in physics." The other one-sided approach is primitive romanticism, ready to discard machines, and busy creating suspicion about the value of science. The classic originators of this approach were the Luddites and Jean-Jacques Rousseau. SLJ "The Last Century of Science: Progress, Problems, and Prospects" in *The Absolute Beneath the Relative and Other Essays*, 167-8

Edmund Burke was not too far from the truth as he wrote: "The age of chivalry is gone. The age of sophisters, economists, and calculators has succeeded, and the glory of Europe is extinguished forever." Romanticism was an effort aimed at recovering that glory, or rather that hope and purpose. It was also an effort which showed little comprehension of science, for which great, spectacular triumphs were in store. SLJ "Science and Hope" in *The Absolute Beneath the Relative and Other Essays*, 167-8, 219

Scholasticism: the dominant Christian philosophy of the Middle Ages, chiefly expounded by St. Albert the Great, Duns Scotus, St. Bonaventure, and St. Thomas Aquinas.

Scoffing at the intellectualism of medieval scholasticism usually goes hand in hand with insensitivity to the religious ideals proclaimed in the rules of Saint Dominic and Saint Francis. Yet, there ought to be food for thought in the fact that intense evangelical fervor was a basic and undisputed characteristic of the foremost scholastics, Albert, Aquinas, Bonaventure, and Scotus. If scholasticism as an intellectual movement spread like wildfire, it was partly because it was carried by the contagiousness of an evangelical spirit of which it could be a natural component. It is in such a perspective that one should look at scholastic intellectualism, which had become a pervasive cultural matrix, a fact grudgingly acknowledged even by some notable antagonists and critics of Christianity in general and scholastic philosophy in particular. Condorcet's statement mentioned in chapter 1 (see n. 12 there) has been the pattern of many similar ones since. SLJ, *The Road of Science and the Ways To God*, 134n1

...one might be struck by the modesty which characterizes official declarations of Christian theism such as that "it is impossible to notice a strong similarity between Creator and creatures without being forced to note an even stronger dissimilarity between them" and that "in the present condition of humanity, revelation is morally necessary in order that everyone might arrive in fact at the full and certain knowledge of God." The first of those declarations was made by the Fathers of Lateran IV (1215) in the heyday of a scholasticism steeped in the notion of analogy, the second by the Fathers of Vatican I (1870), the time of the first infiltration of idealism into Roman Catholic theology. SLJ, *The Road of Science and the Ways To God*, 140n68

secular humanism: modes of belief which reject all forms of the supernatural, found in some modern academic systems, the Media, Communism, Marxism, Darwinism, modernism, etc.

Bloom's slighting of the Christian and especially Catholic intellectual and moral tradition on absolutes is hardly an accident. It reveals something of the systematic crusade whereby many agnostic and religious Jewish writers try to turn into a negligible factor the Christian cultural presence, as if it deserved mention only when it can be castigated for its "crimes" against humanity. This crusade finds a ready ally in non-Jewish protagonists of secular humanism – the creed that sets the dominant tone of an academic world to which many Catholic colleges and universities have for some time been eager to cozy up. Their thinking may be conditioned by the Chardinian abolition of original sin. In its light one can imagine that there is already on hand the kind of Utopia wherein the lamb can lie down with the lion.

...questions could be raised on the basis of the doctrine of separation of church and state, or rather the doctrine that forbids state support to any religion. But if prayers, let alone classes of religion, have no right in public schools, why should it be legal to teach there the religion called Darwinism or secular humanism? SLJ, *The Savior of Science*, 188, 207

What Duhem unearthed among other things from long-buried manuscripts was that supernatural revelation played a crucial liberating role in putting scientific speculation on the right track. But then the claim, so pivotal for the secularist anti-Christian interpretation of Western cultural history – that science and religion are in irreconcilable conflict – could only be deprived of its prima facie credibility. It is in this terrifying prospect for secular humanism, for which science is the redeemer of mankind, that lies the explanation of that grim and secretive censorship which has worked against Duhem (and his few allies) by two principal means: One is the prevention of major scholarly evidence in favor of Duhem's perspective to appear in print or at least to be printed by "prominent" publishing houses. The other is selective indignation in scholarly societies and their journals – allegedly devoted to universal truth regardless of race, religion, and politics. SLJ, "Science and Censorship: Hélène Duhem and the Publication of the *Système du monde*" in *The Absolute Beneath the Relative and Other Essays*, 185

socialism: a political and economic theory of social organization based on collective or governmental ownership and democratic management of the essential means for the production and distribution of goods.

...This fully otherworldly perspective sets the tone of Christ's two great sermons, of which one, the Sermon on the Mount, with its eight somber beatitudes, marks the beginning of his teaching mission. The other great sermon of his, the one on the final judgment, brings that mission to a close. It is a sermon full of social consciousness, though with nothing socialistic or even humanistic about it. He did not conjure up earthly rewards for feeding the poor and clothing the naked. He offered for reward only an eternal union with him. SLJ, *Bible and Science*, 68

Of the many reactions prompted by *Mater et magistra* there was one which is better remembered than the others possibly because it received a pregnant formulation, *mater si, magistra no*, a variation on the then popular battlecry, *Cuba si, Yankee no*. The voicing of *mater si, magistra no* in circles of well-to-do conservative American Catholics represented something new and something old. The new was the vocal defiance on the part of Catholics of papal teaching, a rather novel phenomenon compared with the uniform respect for papal teaching earlier in this century. The old, and this is the important point here, was the reappearance of a misunderstanding about the real gist and thrust of those great papal encyclicals. According to that old, heavily ingrained, and almost stereotyped misunderstanding, those encyclicals are a defense of labor unions and therefore by implication of socialism. Nothing could be further from the truth. Of course, those encyclicals, especially the one by Leo XIII, view the socio-economic situation more from the perspective of the working man or proletariat than from the perspective of business or capital. But this is only so because those encyclicals, which are the authoritative modern formulations of Catholic teaching on the economic life of society, want to turn as many wage earners as possible into capitalist businessmen. ... That those encyclicals, which form an organic sequence, are not a narrow defense of labor can already be surmised from their subtitles. Reference to labor occurs only in the subtitle of *Rerum novarum* "on the condition of labor," but not in those of the other two, which are respectively, "on reconstructing the social order" and "Christianity and social progress." Clearly, what these encyclicals aim at is a formulation of a broad set of directives valid for society as a whole and not only for a particular group such as labor. If labor is considered more in detail in those encyclicals, it is only because laborers represent in modern industrial society by far the broadest segment whose condition is often a matter of severe injustice. Redressing that injustice was to be done along tenets in which socialists or rather Marxists would not recognize any part of their basic philosophy. The encyclicals reject time and again the Marxist principle of the absolute priority of the society over the individual with the words: "Man is older than the State." To be sure, the classic capitalist principle, that the sole justification of the growth of wealth is wealth itself, is unqualifiedly rejected, but private property as the basis of wealth and even the need for its growth within limits is most categorically endorsed: "The essential reason why those who engage in any gainful occupation undertake labor, and at the same time the end to which workers immediately look, is to procure property for themselves and to retain it by individual right as their own." SLJ, "The Business of Christianity and the Christianity of Business" in *Catholic Essays*, 133, 134

subjectivism: the theory which limits knowledge to conscious states and elements; a theory which attaches great or supreme importance to the subjective elements in experience

...mysticism is certainly a field where preferences of the individual thinker, of his subjectivism in short, can readily take the leading role. ... ...[the Renaissance,] an age that witnessed a hardly concealed desire on the part of many to bring about a "re-naissance" of classical paganism. Man's longing for science, buttressed by the Christian faith in the Creator, prevented that desire from becoming more than an interlude. The desire itself was in part caused by that shift which consisted in a heavy preference for feelings and in a weariness of the rationality of scholasticism. In many cases the process ended in rank subjectivism. ... Schelling's philosophy of nature was imbued with pantheism and with its natural ally, idealistic subjectivism. SC 204, 268, 308

61

Obscurity, length and pedantry were partly responsible for the assent of many to Kant's basic contention that critical reflection on knowledge could be the first step in philosophy. He and countless others failed to see that criticism presupposes knowledge itself. To emphasize such an error may seem to some a matter of pedantry. Yet is the most colossal and portentous error one can commit in philosophy. Most colossal in proportion, because it leads to sheer subjectivism, nay solipsism, which cuts one off from the rest of the universe. Most portentous in consequence because on its basis man can believe he is his own master in the strictest and most fundamental sense. ... Kant's avowed aversion to sentiment may have been a defense mechanism designed to mask a thorough subjectivism in his thinking, the deepest form of entrapment by sentiment. ... *Naturphilosophie* is antiscience because it is sheer subjectivism. Subjectivism of the weaker, superficial kind is founded on the sentiments. The real threat is posed by a subjectivism of the intellect. Such is the subjectivism of Kantian philosophy. Its springs are not in the sentiments but in the intellectual pride which was a distinctive feature of Kant's mental physiognomy. No one can be assumed to be without a strong touch of hubris who at the age of thirty, with no training in Newtonian physics, believed that he had said that very last word on the physics of cosmogony of which Newton despaired. It was the same hubris that made Kant believe 25 years later that he had put metaphysics in its final form after millennia of futile efforts by a galaxy of geniuses. ... A glance at the table of contents of the *Encyclopedia* [by Hegel] was often enough to make a scientist suspicious of it. To verify his suspicions he had only to read the paragraph in which Hegel summarized the message of the *Encyclopedia*. There he painted in quick strokes the deployment of the Idea through gravity into the "free heavenly bodies," in which it achieved the first stage of its "externality." The latter then shaped itself into "individual unities" through physical movement and chemical processes. Organic life arose when gravity was released "into members possessing subjective unity." Thus was the stage set for the grand conclusion: "The aim of these lectures is to convey an image of nature, in order to subdue this Proteus: to find in this externality only the mirror of ourselves, to see in nature a free reflection of spirit: to understand God, not in the contemplation of spirit, but in this His immediate existence." Whatever the reaction of a practicing scientist to the sheer pantheism of this passage and its rank subjectivism and apriorism, he must have realized that it cannot be germane to an experimentation aimed at fathoming, in a laborious way, some of Nature's secrets. The interiorized mind knows, if Hegel is right, through reflecting on its own dialectic, what Nature is like. Nature as seen through the lenses of Hegelian dialectic is a far cry from the Nature science presupposes. SLJ, *Angels, Apes and Man*, 30, 31, 32-3, 36-7

syncretism: the reconciliation or union of conflicting beliefs, especially religious beliefs.

The Valentinians, Marcosians, Nicolaitans, Encratites, Borborians, Ophites, Sethians, and many others listed by Irenaeus, today are merely names familiar only to some specialists of church history. In Irenaeus' time they were at the peak of their influence. They were carriers of that religious syncretism and obscurantism which threatened with extinction whatever light the great philosophical schools of Greece succeeded in producing. Radical dualism and demonology, fatalism and reincarnation, emanationism and pantheism fused in those heresies with some Christian details, and were reinterpreted by an unbridled exercise in fantasy which barred any logic and consistency. The universe of those heretics was a maddening complex of demiurges and aeons that obeyed neither rhyme nor reason. SC 165

A p.c. [politically correct] religion will have no problem being integrated with science, though the relation may not amount to more than a convenient cohabitation that can be initiated, acted out, terminated, resumed, and reinterpreted on short notice. Cohabitation is always a dissimulation of the true identity of a rapport, an identity crisis in short. The religious side of that cohabitation can only function as religious syncretism. Thus no real difference will be claimed between nature worship and a worship steeped in that supernatural which is a Creator free to create or not to create what is called Nature writ large, that is, a universe. Within that syncretism every form of religion can be accommodated. There polytheism, with its worship of idols, will not appear too distant even from a worship that forbids the making of graven images of God. And when God and nature are fused to the extent in which this is done in pantheism, not only can one's religion not be identified, but even one's own identity diminishes to the vanishing point. In no form of pantheism has there ever been a place for that personal immortal soul which alone makes one's identity (and one's religion) meaningful and raises it above the lowlands of mere aestheticism. SLJ, "Science and Religion in Identity Crisis" in *The Limits of a Limitless Science*, 163-4

utilitarianism: the doctrine that the useful is the good, and that the determining consideration of right conduct is the usefulness of its consequences.

Bruno's advocacy of Copernicus was a largely utilitarian attitude. Copernicus was for him a welcome ally only so long as heliocentrism helped discredit the closed world of Aristotle. Once Aristotle was out of the way, so were Copernicus and science. SC 263

Following his early aborted attempts at geometry, Hume opted instead to become the Copernicus of moral philosophy. All he achieved in that respect was a sustained plea for utilitarianism. It undoubtedly represented a radical turn, although in a direction which was the very opposite to the epistemological stance of Copernicus, who, to recall Galileo's famous words, chose "to commit a rape of his senses." The utilitarianism of Humean ethics was a logical sequel to that dismemberment of man into a heap of sensations which is the hallmark of Hume's *Treatise on Human Nature*. The inner logic leading to such an outcome has often been told, not always deplored, and hardly ever viewed against the hallowed shibboleth that Hume carried on in the spirit of Newton. That shibboleth is as patent absurdity. Newton's work is impossible to grasp on the assumption that the cause-effect relationship, which physics must assume as long as it is a study of physical reality, can only be the object of a study of the physicist's imagining such reality. Physics, be it of Newton or of Einstein, presupposes far more than a projection of our slowly-formed and still-forming habits into the study of matter. Also, Hume's own work is impossible to grasp on strictly Humean grounds. In no way could Hume persuade his readers that there was at least one world, the world represented by Hume, writing to them, existing independently of their sensations of it. ... Utilitarianism, as the ultimate bedrock of an ethical behavior for which no strict justification can be given, is presented unequivocally in the conclusion of Hume's *An Inquiry concerning the Principles of Morals*: "I cannot, *at present*, be more assured of any truth which I learn from reasoning and argument, than that personal merit consists entirely in the usefulness or agreeableness of qualities to the person himself possessed of them, or to others who have any intercourse with him" (Library of Liberal Arts edition, Indianapolis: Bobbs-Merrill, 1957, p. 98). The context is all the more notable because there Hume is taken aback by the contrast between a lack of consensus in matters of morality in spite of the benevolence infused into all human hearts (p. 92) and the subjection, as revealed by science, of heavenly bodies "to their proper laws" (p. 98). Hume failed to realize that his philosophy in no way assured validity to the recognition, scientific or not, of such laws. That in the same breath Hume credited science even with the reduction to calculation of "the infinite itself," only revealed the amateur in him in matters scientific. SLJ, *Angels, Apes and Men*, 24-5 and note 40

voluntarism: any theory which conceives the will to be the dominant factor in experience or in the constitution of the world.

The only way of knowing that the world was ordered, or, to be specific, that the starlight was due to stars, must therefore come from revelation about the ordained power of God, to use Ockham's favorite expression. Some admirers of Ockham saw in this a redeeming feature because it witnessed to his resolve to do justice to the voluntaristic aspect of the God of the Bible. Whatever that aspect, the feature in question is neither redeeming nor biblical, and it certainly does not redeem Ockham the philosopher. It was to soften the shock of his epistemology that he resorted to a distinction between the absolute and the ordered will of the Creator, a distinction which, by implying an ordered state for all created things, furtively brought the universals back into the real world. SLJ, *The Road of Science and the Ways to God*, 42

Beneath the logical defect of taking Heisenberg's principle for a refutation of causality, there is the emotional ground for taking it for such a refutation. It is still to be widely realized that Heisenberg had denied causality for some years before he formulated his principle in 1927. He was still in his late teens when he denied causality under the influence of the vitalism he encountered in the philosophy of the so-called Student Movement (*Jugendbewegung*). A few years later he found that some prominent older physicists had been denying causality for similarly non-logical reasons. Ultimately, all such reasons rested on that voluntarism which Kant had generated by his subjectivism. This voluntarism has become a distinctive feature of modern Western culture. It is as much alive in totalitarian ideologies as it is in various forms of pragmatism that support the ideology of Western democracies. In none of them is there room for a proper respect for free will. Disrespect for free will had for some time been promoted by prominent scientists before computer theorists and champions of artificial intelligence became emboldened to ignore free will for all practical purposes. As they freely go about their implicit and at times explicit denial of freedom, they resemble the Darwinists whom Whitehead once dismissed with a devastating phrase: "Those who devote their lives to the purpose of proving that there is no purpose, constitute an interesting subject for study." The same applies to those who freely deny free will. They still have to learn the elementary fact that no materialist is reluctant to make up his mind and no determinist argues deterministically. Such are Chesterton's remarks.[20] Poincaré voiced the same elementary truth when he remarked that "*c'est librement qu'on est déterministe.*" SLJ, "Computers: Lovable but Unloving" in *The Limits of a Limitless Science*, 41. Earlier in that book (p. 9) he translates Poincaré's French as "Even a determinist argues non-deterministically"; a literal version is "It is freely that one is deterministic."

---

[20] Jaki omitted the reference to GKC's *St. Thomas Aquinas*: "No sceptics work sceptically; no fatalists work fatalistically; all without exception work on the principle that it is possible to assume what it is not possible to believe. No materialist who thinks his mind was made up for him, by mud and blood and heredity, has any hesitation in making up his mind. No sceptic who believes that truth is subjective has any hesitation about treating it as objective." CW2:542-3

2. Some Foreign Terms

Annäherung	(German) contraction (Zöllner in *Über die Natur der Cometen*)
annus magnus	(Latin) great year
a priori	(Latin) from the former
archê	(Greek) principle, beginning
bara	(Hebrew) make (in Genesis, used only with God)
bereshit	(Hebrew) in the beginning (First word of the Book of Genesis)
caveat	(Latin) Let him beware
circulus vitiosus deus	(Latin) defective circle god (Nietzsche, *Beyond Good and Evil*)
cosmos	(Greek) the creation, or entire universe[21]
creatio ex nihilo	(Latin) creation out of nothing
da capo	(Italian) from the head, beginning
deus ex machina	(Latin) a god from a machine (i.e. an artificial solution)
dunamis	(Greek δυναμις) power
ekpyrosis	(Greek) dissolution into fire
electiones	(Latin) elections, choosings
Entfernung	(German) expansion (Zöllner, *Über die Natur der Cometen*)
ex nihilo	(Latin) out of nothing
Ex nihilo nihil fit.	(Latin) Out of nothing, nothing is made.
experimentum crucis	(Latin) crucial experiment (Descartes)
finita	(Latin) ended, determined
hexis	(Greek) tension
Homo sapiens	(Latin) Man, the wise (the taxonomic genus and species of human beings)
id quod substat	(Latin) a thing which stands firm, stands below (Schelling, *The Ages of the World*)
in actione et passione	(Latin) in cause and effect (Grosseteste, *De Lineis*)
in se	(Latin) in itself
interrogationes	(Latin) questionings
katabolê	(Greek) deterioration
kinetikê dunamis	(Greek) kinetic force
Naturphilosophie	(German) the philosophy of nature (Schelling)
ouranos	(Greek) imperishable superlunary world (the "heavens")
pantokratôr	(Greek παντοκρατωρ) universal ruler
pax Romana	(Latin) Roman peace
physikoi	(Greek) scholars who study nature
praxis	(Greek πραξις) action
raison d'être	(French) reason for being
terminus [a] quo	(Latin) the end from which, the starting point
tonikê kinesis	(Greek) tensional motion
tour de force	(French) a feat of strength or skill
Umtrieb	(German) cycle (Schelling, *The Ages of the World*)
Weltanschauung	(German) world-view

---

[21] "This distinction between the perishable sublunary world (cosmos) and the imperishable superlunary world (ouranos) is important to note..." (SC106). Anciently the Greek, κοσμος (*kosmos*) meant the "corruptible world" (Earth and all things "below the moon") while ουρανος (*ouranos*) meant "the heavens."

3. Some Major Sources

There are several books one ought to be aware of in reading *Science and Creation*, not merely as reference works, but as major items in the historical context.

Almagest: Ptolemy (2nd century A.D.). Originally called *Mathêmatikê syntaxis*, became known as *Megalê syntaxis*, or *Great Collection*, which became known as *al-Majisti* in Arabic. a technical work on astronomy using trigonometry, the "definitive account of the Greek achievement in astronomy according to Hipparchus, with some additions of Ptolemy's own." [*Oxford Classical Dictionary*, 746]

> ...the difference between the two major works of Ptolemy, the *Almagest* and the *Tetrabiblos*. The latter shows a thinker completely lost in the labyrinths of astrology, while in the former no magic or obscurantism taints the long, sustained geometric account of the motion of planets. SC 17

The City of God (*De civitate Dei*): St. Augustine of Hippo, (413-426).

> Systematic analysis of such questions [having philosophical and scientific ramifications] could only be done in scholarly treatises of which, in patristic times, the most monumental in scope and breadth was *The City of God* by Saint Augustine. It moulded more than any other book by a Christian author the spirit of the Middle Ages. Its pages were as many wellsprings of information and inspiration for the emerging new world of Europe about the meaning of mankind's journey through time. What the medievals learned in that book was, above all, the proposition that the physical universe and human history both had their origin in the sovereign creative act of God, which also established a most specific course and destiny for both. The intelligibility of human and cosmic existence portrayed in that framework represented a compactness and consistency the like of which had never before appeared on the pages of any book. *The City of God* had, indeed, become the intellectual vehicle for a confidence which centuries later made possible the emergence for the first time of a culture with a built-in force of self-sustaining progress. SC 177-8

The Consolation of Philosophy: Boethius (520s). Written while in prison, having been accused of conspiring against Theodoric, Ostrogoth ruler of Rome, finally executed without trial.

> To see the strength of optimism exuding from a firm belief in the Creator a brief look at Boethius will not be amiss, as his influence on the intellectual formation of the medievals was only second to the one exerted by the Bishop of Hippo. Boethius' tragic fate extinguished not only a great political vision, but also put an early end to his gigantic cultural plan, the translation into Latin of all the works of Plato and Aristotle. Nevertheless, his elementary treatises on geometry, arithmetic, astronomy, and music served, together with his translations

of Aristotle's works on logic, as the main source of learning until the 12th century. His philosophical interests were matched by some fine theological treatises, but above all by his stature as a Christian. From his *The Consolation of Philosophy* the medievals could learn how the Christian faith in the Creator gave meaningfulness to dark situations and courses of events as behind them the Source of all reason and benevolence was believed to be weaving an intelligible pattern. SC 183-4

De Genesi ad litteram libri duodecim: St. Augustine (400s). His important commentary on the book of Genesis. See part 5, below.

Cosmologische Briefe: Lambert (1760). See Jaki's translation, *Cosmological Letters on the Arrangement of the World-Edifice*.

Lambert, the most prominent contemporary of Kant among German scientists, wrote his famous *Cosmologische Briefe* with no knowledge of Kant's work published six years earlier. Unlike Kant's universe Lambert's cosmos was finite and basically static, in the sense that Lambert paid no detailed attention to such problems as evolution and decay of planetary systems, stars, and galaxies. Lambert's brief reference to the Platonic Year was rather innocuous. In his hierarchical arrangement of galaxies and of some five hundred higher orders of systems of galaxies everything rotated around an immensely massive, dark, central body. It was, therefore, natural for Lambert to ask the question about the period of rotation of our sun around that mythical centre. Was it equal to the Platonic Year or only a mere fraction of it? To this question Lambert did not profess to know the answer though he did not hesitate to speak positively about equally problematic points of his hierarchical world order. With Lambert the hierarchical world order reflected a design pointing to a Supreme Architect assuring stability and purpose for the cosmic clockwork. SC 290-1

Dialogue Concerning the Two Chief World Systems – Ptolemaic and Copernican: Galileo (1632). This was the book which got him in trouble.

The crucial obstacle in the way of Copernicanism was, in addition to an increasingly stiff theological attitude, the fact that the Newtonian science of motion and gravitation was still more than a century away. Even Galileo, armed for some time with the law of free fall, had to rest content with the position that no experiment performed on the earth could prove or disprove its daily and annual motions. [As is well known, Galileo contradicted himself when in the Fourth Day of his *Dialogue* he presented the tides as a combined effect of the earth's daily rotation and orbital motion around the sun.] Pre-Galilean physics was simply no match to the task although the study of motion made some progress during the Renaissance. SC 261, note 82

The Elements: (Στοιχεια, *Stoicheia*) Euclid (c. 300 BC). The great compendium of Greek geometry, the chief source and text of geometry until the 19th century.

The very beginning of the Hellenistic period of Greek science saw the publication of one of the greatest books written in history, the *Elements* of Euclid, containing propositions the content of which was fully grasped only by nineteenth-century geometry and mathematics. ... Thus Euclid's *Elements*, published around 300 B.C., represented to a great extent the concluding phase of the spectacular emergence of scientific geometry to which no less than sixty known Greek geometers contributed during the previous four or five generations. What is true of geometry holds also of algebra, as its cultivation remained throughout the Hellenistic times distinctly geometrical in character. SC 102, 103

The Guide of [or *for*] *the Perplexed*: Maimonides (1190). His chief work on religious philosophy.

...Maimonides' great philosophical work, the *Guide for the Perplexed* written in Arabic, was not to change the hopeless course which Muslim thought was following. Not that devout Arabs could not have read with tremendous intellectual profit Maimonides' penetrating critique of the abuse of reason by official Muslim theology, which followed closely the tenets of the Mutakallimun and leaned heavily toward occasionalism. What Maimonides offered was a careful balance between faith and reason, between Bible and science, a balance which never became a reality within the medieval Muslim world where scientist-philosophers came under the sway of necessitarianism. As a result, science among the Arabs largely remained, apart from some minor though valuable modifications, in the stage in which they found it in the old Greek and Syrian manuscripts. SC 213

Another great medieval attempt to show by philosophical and scientific arguments the reasonableness of faith, *The Guide of the Perplexed* of Moses ben Maimon, dwells also at great length on a comparison between the cosmos and the purposeful functioning of the human organism and personality. To see the universe as a living being was for the Great Moses, as Aquinas referred to him, "indispensable... for demonstrating the unity of God; it also helps to indicate the principle that He who is One has created only *one* being." TROP 36

Opus Majus: Roger Bacon (1267). Prepared on request of Clement IV embracing treatises on grammar, logic, mathematics, physics, philology, and philosophy.

Bacon's impetuous crusading to secure the service of science on behalf of the Christian faith has much of the boldness and drama that became the hallmark of Galileo's career. Within ten years of the composition of the *Opus majus* in 1267 he was imprisoned on suspicion of holding novel views. Friar Roger was certainly not censured for his emphasis on the basic unity, interconnectedness, and interdependence of all branches of learning. There could be nothing wrong about his reasoning that since the Creator was one and there was only one creation, its understanding too had to form one single body of truth. ... According to him, the temperament of the individual was completely determined by the influence of stars while single decisions were not. Collective actions, such as battles, represented a general trend that could be strictly predicted together with its outcome. And so were the relative fortunes of religions. Not surprisingly, the *Opus majus*

69

contains a section on the application of astrology to Church government. By this Bacon not only meant the forestalling of disastrous projects such as the Children's Crusade through the casting of accurate horoscopes, but also the recognition of great cycles in the history of religions. SC 226, 227

Although not reluctant to conjure up the vision of vehicles running at high speed across land and under the seas, Friar Roger saw the chief benefit of experimental science in the possibility of ending warfare with hardly any bloodshed. SLJ, *The Road of Science and the Ways to God*, 305-6

Philosophiae naturalis principia mathematica: Isaac Newton (1687, second edition with scholium 1713).

The first major scientific discourse on the infinity of the universe came only with the *Principia* of Newton, and especially with the Scholium added to it in 1713. It was a step in which encouragement from Bruno's writings or memory had no part. ... Newton greeted with obvious satisfaction Bentley's efforts to indicate the role of the Creator against atheism and deism on the basis of the main conclusions of the *Principia*. On his part, Newton most explicitly endorsed the notion of a Creation once and for all as the only sound framework of natural philosophy. This he did as he added the Scholium to the second (1713) edition of the *Principia* and as he kept enriching the subsequent editions of the *Opticks* with further Queries. The universe for Newton was a clockwork constructed by the Creator out of basic components created out of nothing. It was also the Creator who kept, according to Newton, this world mechanism in good repair by preventing it from a too early unwinding through His repeated interventions. Again, it was the Creator who secured the ultimate transition of this world into its final transformed condition at the end of time. SC 267, 286-7

The Refutation of All Heresies: St. Hippolytus (230 A.D.).

There are, however, some details worth recalling in the other great compendium of heretical doctrines written around A.D. 230, *The Refutation of All Heresies* by Hippolytus, a disciple of Irenaeus. Unlike Irenaeus, Hippolytus emphasized that the conceptual vagaries of the heretics were an elaboration, or rather distortion, not of scriptural themes, but of the ideas and systems of philosophers and of sundry astrological doctrines and practices. Thus, in Hippolytus' work one finds an informative compendium of the doctrines of the Ionians, Pythagoreans, and the atomists with many interesting details about the later penetration of Babylonian, Persian, and Hindu thought into the Hellenistic mentality. Few developments appeared to Hippolytus as disconcerting as the practically complete harnessing of astronomy into the devious objectives of astrology. He grieved in particular that Ptolemy had not lived when the Tower of Babel was erected. By Ptolemy's calculations of celestial distances the maddening project to reach the heavens could have been nipped in the bud. Space does not allow us to summarize even briefly the many bizarre "cosmologies" surveyed and criticized by Hippolytus. Most of them were variations on the idea of the eternity of a divine world revolving through infinite aeons. SC 166

Republic: Plato (300s BC). generally recognized as his greatest work, a search for justice in the construction of an ideal state.

> This perfect number giving the length of the perfect year, or, as it was later called, the Great Year, had an importance in Plato's cosmological thought that cannot be stressed enough. He assigned to it a supreme role of causality, admitting that even his ideal state was no exception to the general law of periodic dissolutions and restorations. The inevitable decay of a well-governed state was due, according to him, to the fact that the revolutions of celestial orbs defined a period of fertility and barrenness, of healthy and defective breeding for each living species. "Not only for plants that grow from the earth but also for animals that live upon it there is a cycle of bearing and barrenness for soul and body as often as the revolutions of their orbs come full circles, in brief courses for the short-lived and oppositely for the opposite." SC 108-9 quoting *Republic*, 546

Le Système du Monde: Duhem (1910-1916).[22] His greatest work, ten volumes on the history of science, revealing the medieval origin of science at the Sorbonne under John Buridan. See Jaki's books on Duhem for details, in particular on the struggle of Duhem's daughter to bring the last five volumes to publication.

> All modern discussions of medieval science stand in debt to Pierre Duhem's *Le système du monde: Histoire des doctrines cosmologiques de Platon à Copernic* (Paris: Hermann, 1913-55), in ten volumes.
> ... Duhem offered the last five volumes of his monumental opus as proof of the proposition that modern science "was born, so to speak, on March 7, 1277 from the decree issued by Monseigneur Étienne, bishop of Paris." By this Duhem meant that the decree decisively reinforced, mainly at the University of Paris, a train of thought leading ultimately to the formulation of a new (classical) physics. SC 220n9, 230n52

Tetrabiblios: Ptolemy in the 2nd century A.D., a work of astrology; see his *Almagest*, above.

Thus Spake Zarathustra: Nietzsche (1883-1892)

> ...1881, the very same year when he had undergone the most decisive experience of his life. This consisted in his being captivated with a dramatic suddenness by the idea of eternal recurrences. In his autobiographical *Ecce Homo* written in 1888 Nietzsche gave the following account of the event: "I now wish to relate the history of *Zarathustra*. The fundamental idea of the work, the *Eternal Recurrence*, the highest formula of a Yea-saying to life that can ever be attained, was first conceived in the month of August, 1881. I made a note of the idea on a sheet of paper, with the proscript: 'six thousand feet beyond man and time.' That day I happened to be wandering through the woods alongside of the Lake of Silvaplana, and I halted not

---

[22] These dates are when the ten volumes were written. However, the last five volumes were not published until the 1950s: for details see SLJ's essay "Science and Censorship: Hélène Duhem and the Publication of the *Système du monde*" in *The Absolute Beneath the Relative and Other Essays*.

far from Surlei, beside a huge rock that towered aloft like a pyramid. It was then that the thought struck me." The work to which Nietzsche referred in the foregoing passage is his famous *Thus Spake Zarathustra*. Its four books written in four very short periods of time between 1883 and 1885 bespeak not only the extraordinary vehemence of inspiration by which the idea of eternal recurrence kept Nietzsche's mind and moods in a permanent grip. They also give some clue about Nietzsche's familiarity with the idea of eternal recurrences prior to August 1881. Zarathustra (Zoroaster), the ancient religious leader of the Iranian highland, is mentioned next to Heraclitus in Nietzsche's essay on "Philosophy during the Tragic Age of the Greeks," written in 1873. SC 319

Utopia: St. Thomas More (1516)

This overtly astrological buttressing by Machiavelli of his interpretation of history was a pattern present also in other Renaissance supporters of the cyclic nature of history. Revealingly, none of them had been part of the growth of the scientific movement during the sixteenth century. As Bacon was later to observe, their cyclic theory of history sapped precisely that confidence in steady progress which the scientific enterprise needed if it was to prosper. Long before Bacon made this comment based in part on the wisdom of hindsight, a small book, the *Utopia* of Thomas More, the finest Humanist of Renaissance times, proclaimed the basic principles which [Francis] Bacon outlined in detail in his *New Atlantis*. Wisely enough, More implied in the very title of his book the basic unattainability of the ideal set forth there. Yet, its very writing evidenced the confidence that it was worth working toward at least a partial realization of that ideal. The identification of the deepest source of that confidence should be no problem with a Christian of More's stature. The "natural" religion of the Utopians is not an idealized reconstruction from some historical precedent, but a studied "naturalization" of Christian faith and morals. This should be clear from the firm resolve by which More's Utopians held fast to such tenets as the immortality of the soul and its eternal reward or punishment. By this latter point More set a great store. The hope rooted in eternal life was for him the only sound foundation on which society and its cultural pursuit could securely be based. Distinctly Christian is also the set of principal features which More put forward to describe the faith of the Utopians in the Creator of all. He is one, eternal, far above the reach of human mind, everywhere present in the universe, but as More carefully adds with his Christian instinct, the omnipresence in question is not a physical diffusion, but an influence of power. The same instinct is also evident in More's emphasis on the image of the Creator as the Father of all and the source of all beginnings, changes, and ends. Existence, personal, social, and cosmic, was for the Utopians, a once-and-for-all process, designed and directed by a personal, supreme Benevolence. Not surprisingly, More also took pains to note that the universe could not be carried along by chance. SC 257

4. On the Famous Quote from the Book of Wisdom

On page 170 of *Science and Creation* appears the first of Jaki's many citations of a very famous line in scripture. Here is how it appears there:

> As to the punishments, [of the Israelites] it is pointed out that God's power could have inflicted the damage in one single devastating blow, but such would not have been in line with the procedure typical of God who interacts in history in the same manner as He rules the cosmos: "They could have dropped dead at a single breath... But no, you ordered all things by measure, number, weight." [Ws 11, 20-21] The passage is worth noting not only because it instances the ready assimilation of a typically Greek philosophical or scientific idea. The real importance of the passage is in its subsequent impact. The ordering of all things by measure, number, and weight served as inspiration and assurance for those who in late antiquity assumed the role of champions of the rationality of the universe.

In the reference, the symbol "Ws" stands for the deuterocanonical book of Wisdom.[23] I have here put his footnote in brackets since there is something curious to be noted about this phrase which occurs in many of Jaki's books.

This is by no means meant to be a criticism, but simply a clarification. As Cicero puts it, "even Homer nods," and one can find instances where Jaki quotes this verse as "ordered all things *in* number" or "*arranged* all things" – or where he permutes the order of the three "dimensions":

> ...both mind and reality are the products of the One who disposed everything according to "weight, measure, and number"...[24]

This is also unusual as he does not give the biblical citation.

However, in many other cases he gives the citation as Wisdom 11:20. Having examined a fair amount of Jaki's work at an intimately literal level, I have seen cases where he cites his own citation.[25] This may save time, but can lead to inaccuracies. Note that in the earlier excerpt, the biblical quote begins with "They could have..." which is the first part of verse 20. However, in virtually all other cases he only cites the phrase "but You ordered..." which is the concluding part of verse 21.

---

[23] Footnote 2 on page 153 of *Science and Creation* states that all its biblical quotes are from the *Jerusalem Bible*, (London and Garden City, N.Y. 1966).

[24] Jaki, *The Road of Science and the Ways to God*, 259

[25] It may be a case of "Physician cure thyself" given what Jaki says: "There is no substitute to the perusal of primary texts, which, incidentally, hardly ever fail to reveal something that has not yet been noticed by others. Engrossment with the secondary literature can readily trap one's vision along tracks that have little in common with the thrust of the primary sources." *A Mind's Matter*, 5-6.

All this, as I said, is for the sake of clarification. But there is something very important about the quotation which deserves to be cited, appearing as it does in a footnote:

"Every reader of medieval Latin texts knows that few Bible verses are so often quoted and alluded to as the phrase from the Wisdom of Solomon, 11:21, *omnia in mensura, numero et pondere disposuisti*," was noted by E. R. Curtius in his magisterial monograph, *European Literature and the Latin Middle Ages*, translated from the German by W. R. Trask (London: Routledge and Kegan Paul, 1953), p. 504.[26]

The book cited is by Ernst Curtius, (1886-1956), whom he cites as "a foremost Protestant specialist of Medieval literature."

I think this piece of scripture is one of the two most important citations given by Father Jaki, one which deserves some deep meditation.[27] It would be easy enough to write an essay on it, which would hopefully avoid fielding the issue of its deuterocanonical context, but which would rather link to the profundity of St. Paul's reference to Jesus Christ, "In Whom are hid all the treasures of wisdom and knowledge" (Col 2:3), or to his demand (Rom 12:1) for λογικη λατρεια, "reasonable service," which translation needs to be understood as "logical worship" (*logical*, hence *rational, reasoned*, and not merely "suitable") – or to St. Peter's command, "But sanctify the Lord Christ in your hearts, being ready always to satisfy every one that asketh you a *reason* (λογον, whence "logic") of that hope which is in you." (1 Pet 3:15)

Indeed, for that verse of Wisdom is one of the unprovable axioms upon which Science Writ Large is founded, and without which no Science is possible.

---

[26] Jaki, *Cosmos and Creator*, 47n36, or *The Savior of Science*, 88n10.
[27] The other citation is treated in the very next section of this book.

5. On the Quote from St. Augustine's Commentary on Genesis

In opening the topic of science and religion the most common whine to be heard arises from two topics, which we may catalog as "Galileo" and "Darwin" – but in reality they both come down to something else: the question of exactly what one believes (and what one *must* believe) as far as the statements of Holy Scripture are concerned. To put it another way: is the Bible *literally* true, or not?

Of course it is easy enough to demonstrate that the Bible *cannot* be taken literally: the phrase "there is no God" appears in the Psalms (14/13:1). As *foolish* as that sounds, it ought to alert us to the real issue at stake. After all, there is such a thing as *context*.

For at least the first 1500 years of the Christian era, this was never a difficulty. In fact, it was obvious that some parts of the Bible were clearly meant literally, and others were clearly not literal at all. No one had difficulty thinking the Earth was not flat, but round, as had been shown by the Greeks. The problem arose relatively recently in two cases, with respect to the motion of the Earth and heavenly bodies ("Galileo"), and with respect to the origin of living creatures ("Darwin").

While Jaki has quite a lot to say about both these topics, spending at least an entire book, *Genesis One Through the Ages*, on the topic, he provides the ultimate and conclusive answer in *Science and Creation*, an answer given by no less than St. Augustine some 1600 years ago. He frames it in his chapter, "The Leaven of Confidence," and here is the complete context:

> Augustine's appreciation of quantitative relationships had, of course, no immediate consequences for the emergence of scientific method. His main concern went far beyond the acquisition of numerical data in particular and learning in general. What interested him most was the quest for happiness, and this implied far more than marshaling bookish details, a point well to remember in this age threatened by the tyranny of sheer learning and by the voracious storing of information. Possibly, he underestimated the role of man's mastery of nature by knowledge in the process of securing happiness. He took the view that the knowledge of natural sciences, astronomy in particular, could not help one much in understanding the biblical message, as it concerned not man's natural skill but his supernatural destiny. [*On Christian Doctrine*, in *The City of God and Christian Doctrine*, p. 550 (Book II, chap. 29).] On the other hand, he wanted no part of a study of the Bible which purposely ignored the well-established results of scientific studies. He put the matter bluntly: **"It is often the case that a non-Christian happens to know something with absolute certainty and through experimental evidence about the earth, sky, and other elements of this world, about the motion, rotation, and even about the size and distances of stars, about certain defects [eclipses] of the sun and moon, about the cycles of years and epochs, about the nature of animals, fruits, stones, and the like. It is, therefore, very deplorable and harmful,**

and to be avoided at any cost that he should hear a Christian to give, so to speak, a 'Christian account' of these topics in such a way that he could hardly hold his laughter on seeing, as the saying goes, the error rise sky-high." Such a performance, Augustine remarked, would undercut the credibility of the Christian message by creating in the minds of infidels the impression that the Bible was wrong on points "which can be verified experimentally, or to be established by unquestionable proofs." [*Sancti Aureli Augustini De Genesi ad litteram libri duodecim*, edited by J. Zycha, in *Corpus Scriptorum Ecclesiasticorum Latinorum*, vol. XXVIII, Sec. III, Pars 1 (Vienna: F. Tempsky, 1894), pp. 28-29 (Book 1, chap. 19).]

While ignorance on the part of Christians was reprehensible, not every detail of knowledge about nature possessed, as Augustine was quick to note, the same measure of certainty. Beside incontrovertible facts there were probable hypotheses and simple conjectures. When some statements of the Bible collided with the latter, Augustine urged caution. A case in point was the question whether celestial bodies, stars in particular, were animated or not. As reason and observation provided no decisive evidence, nor did the Scriptures seem to be explicit, the matter was open to further inquiry.[*Ibid.*, p. 62 (Book II, chap. 18).] When, however, a question appeared to be settled in a convincing manner by scientific reasoning, Scriptures had to be reinterpreted. Clearly, the biblical phrase about God stretching out the firmament as a tent (skin) clashed with the sphericity of the earth. This naturally demanded a spherical covering, which was also suggested by the motion of the planets and stars. Augustine was not reluctant to give reason its due: "The Bible contradicts those who affirm something which is false; for that is true which is asserted by divine authority and not that which is conjectured by human frailty. However if perchance, they [the heathen] should prove it [the sphericity of the heavens] with evidences that cannot be doubted, it remains to be shown that what is spoken of as a tent, does not contradict those true demonstrations." [*Ibid.*, p. 46 (Book II, chap. 9).]

For Augustine the overriding issue invariably remained the dignity of the Bible as the outstanding embodiment of the supreme form of knowledge leading to eternal happiness. This is what reverberates in his analysis of another topic touching both on science and theology. The question concerned the reconciliation of the immobile firmament of the Bible with the rotating skies of astronomy: "For if the firmament stands firm, the stars, which are believed to be fixed therein, go around from east to west, those more to the north describing smaller circles around the pole, so that the skies would appear rotating like a sphere (assuming that there is another celestial pole), or like a discus (if there is no other celestial pole). My reply... is that it would require much subtle and laborious reasoning to perceive which is the actual case, but to undertake and discuss these matters I have no time, nor is it needed by those whom I wish to instruct for their own salvation and for the benefit of the Church." [*Ibid.*, p. 47 (Book II, chap. 10).] [28]

---

[28] Jaki, *Science and Creation*, 200-201, emphasis added and Jaki's footnotes in brackets. Confer Augustine's final words with the famous phrase in Galileo's "Letter to Grand Duchess Christina" which Jaki notes "contains the phrase, formulated by Cardinal Baronius, possibly under the influence of his reading of Augustine's commentaries on Genesis, that *the Bible teaches man not about how*

Elsewhere Jaki heaps ridicule on those who disregard the great Bishop of Hippo, especially those literal-minded folks who take issue with Foucault's pendulum and Bessel's parallax (these establish the rotation of the Earth and its revolution about the sun). One of the funniest is his little tale about the "firmament" of Genesis 1:6-8, which even St. Augustine knew wasn't real:

> I have already given easily a hundred or so lectures all over the United States, Europe, and Australia on Genesis 1 and I hardly ever failed to get some objections from creationists. They turn up in most unexpected places and times. The word "Genesis" attracts them from as far afield as pollen does honeybees. Usually it is effective to undercut their credibility by calling their attention to the firmament and ask: do astronauts wear helmets in order to protect their heads as they go through the firmament into outer space? For the firmament of the Bible is something very solid indeed. Some creationists are so hardheaded that if put on such a journey they would not have to wear hardhats.[29]

But there are plenty of other things which could be cited if one bothers to hunt through the Bible looking for things which obviously are not meant as literal truth.[30]

Augustine's brilliant distinction is emphasized by an ancient formula[31] on the four distinct meanings possible to Holy Scripture:

> *Lettera [sic; littera?] gesta docet*
> *Quid credas allegoria,*
> *Moralis quid agas,*
> *Quo tendas anagogia.*

Or in my rough translation,

> The Letter teaches things accomplished, (i.e. events)
> Allegory what you should believe,
> Moral what you should do,
> Anagogy what you should tend towards.

indicating a division into a literal and a spiritual sense, which is further divided into allegorical, moral, and anagogical (that is, the prophetic) senses.

---

the heavens go but how to go to Heaven." This is from Jaki, "The Catholic Church and Astronomy" in *The Gist of Catholicism and Other Essays*, 207, and the Galileo quote may be found in *Discoveries and Opinions of Galileo*, translated with an introduction by S. Drake (New York: Doubleday, 1957), 186.

[29] Jaki, *A Mind's Matter*, 151.

[30] Such as the question: does God's "right hand" (mentioned many times in the Psalms) have fingernails and hair and sweat glands and fingerprints? I will forgo making a list, except for one particularly interesting item very few will notice: according to the Bible (1 Kings/3 Kings 7:23), π is *exactly* three: "He made also a molten sea, of *ten cubits*, from brim to brim, round all about; the height of it was five cubits, and a line of *thirty cubits* compassed it round about." Note that the diameter is 10 and the circumference is 30, hence $\pi = 3$. Truly a cause for sky-high laughter.

[31] Quoted in *Catechism of the Catholic Church*, §115.

6. On Olbers' Paradox, or, Why is the Night Sky Dark?

This question sounds odd, but it is at the heart of a significant topic in astronomy and physics, that is, is the Universe infinite or not? Since Jaki spends over 300 pages on this topic in his *The Paradox of Olbers' Paradox*, it would be futile to attempt to condense it here, but then it comes up in *Science and Creation*. In fact, just as the ubiquitous pagan "Great Year" posits an infinity of *time*, there is a corresponding belief in the infinity of *space*.

But here we have a paradox, known as Olbers', for both the gravitational and optical situation argues against such an infinity, which thus conclusively settles the matter. The universe is *not* infinitely large, with infinitely many stars; it is of finite size, with finite contents.

And yet, as Jaki notes, "The relatively few scientists who showed awareness of the gravitational and optical paradox of the infinite universe took the matter in stride mainly because of the conviction that intelligibility and infinite meant one and the same thing." (SC 315) Jaki's *Paradox* has more on this – in particular, the failure of major researchers to do adequate research about the topic. For our purposes here, it is enough to indicate the paradox as it arises in *Science and Creation*.

Jaki quotes Kelvin (1824-1907) as insisting "with baffling naiveté" that it was "impossible to conceive a limit to the extent of matter in the universe; and therefore science points rather to an endless progress, through endless space, of action involving the transformation of potential energy into palpable motion and thence into heat, than to a single finite mechanism, running down like a clock, and stopping forever."[32]

In the same timeframe Nietzsche (1844-1900) "had no inkling" of the gravitational and optical paradoxes, as he was never a scientist, yet his writing has had an impact on society and on scientists. He was arguing from an assumed finiteness in space to an infinity of time:

> The extent of universal energy is limited; it is not 'infinite': We should beware of such excesses in our concepts! Consequently the number of states, changes, combinations, and evolutions of this energy, although it may be enormous and practically incalculable, is at any rate definite and not unlimited. The time, however, in which this universal energy works its changes is infinite – that is to say, energy remains eternally the same and is eternally active: – at this moment an infinity has already elapsed, that is to say, every possible evolution must already have taken place. Consequently the present process of evolution must

---

[32] SC 325-6, quoting Kelvin "On the Age of the Sun's Heat" (1862), in *Popular Lectures and Addresses* (London: Macmillan, 1891), vol. I, pp. 349-50.

be a repetition, as was also the one before it, as will also be the one which will follow. And so on forwards and backwards! Inasmuch as the entire state of all forces continually returns, everything has existed an infinite number of times.[33]

Just to make things even more confusing, Jaki has a footnote (120) on that "had no inkling":

The two problems [the gravitational and optical paradoxes] were referred to with sufficient frequency during the latter part of the 19th century. J. C. F. Zöllner, professor of astrophysics at Leipzig, to whom Nietzsche made numerous references, and whose book, *Über die Natur der Cometen* (Leipzig: W. Engelmann, 1872), Nietzsche had in his library, pointed out in detail in that book, long before the advent of relativistic cosmologies, that a four-dimensional, closed universe with a finite mass, provides a logical solution to the problem.

* * *

At this point I feel I ought to add a comment, for you may be wondering, "Well, so what *is* the universe, then: finite, or infinite?" or at least, "All right, so what does Jaki believe about it?"

No, no. That is part of the reason why the study of the History of Science in general, and Jaki's books in particular, are so important. The unspoken point is this: *that is not how Science works*, or should work. Science, inasmuch as it is a study of Reality, does not depend on one's belief in that fashion.[34] One does not say, "I believe the universe is ___ " and then quote the evidence for it, and ignore the evidence against it. Not only is that non-scientific, it is poor scholarship. As GKC writes in his *Chaucer*, "Nobody can read St. Thomas's theology without hearing all the arguments against St. Thomas's theology." It is all the funnier when one reads the next sentence: "Therefore, even when that sort of faith produced what many would call ferocity, it always produced what I mean here by fairness; the almost involuntary intellectual fairness of one who cannot help knowing that *the universe is a many-sided thing*."[35]

So, if you want to know the truth of the universe, be ferocious *and* be fair. Go read what the scholars of the past *actually discovered* about it, not just what they thought. And then *get busy, get to work, go exploring* – there's plenty waiting to be done – but be careful to remain HUMBLE IN THE FACE OF REALITY, and do not make assumptions about it based on your own thoughts about how it "should" be.

---

[33] *SC* 357 quoting Nietzsche, "Eternal Recurrence," in *Works*, vol. XVI, p. 237, aph. 1.

[34] It *does* depend upon certain beliefs, specifically, a belief that the universe is rational and consistent, that in general the mind is rational, the senses are reliable, and so on. In lieu of a book I hope to write eventually, I suggest Jaki's essay "Gilson and Science" in *Patterns or Principles and Other Essays*, or Gilson's *Methodical Realism*, reprinted with an introduction by Jaki, and GKC's *Orthodoxy*.

[35] GKC, *Chaucer*, CW18:367. Emphasis added.

7. Why All Those Non-scientists in the Last Four Chapters?

Actually, that is just the flip side of the usual complaint made against Jaki's books: "why does Father Jaki drag in all this Catholicism and Christianity into studies of Science?" [36]

The simple fact is that scientists are human, and like it or not, the environment in which they learn and live and work has an effect on their thinking. This effect can be good or bad, and the stunning thing is that most writers on the history of science try to make out how *bad* Judaism and Christianity have been for Science – but in reality, it is Paganism, ancient or modern, which is bad. Jaki argues this in countless places beginning with our text, and especially in subsequent works such as *The Savior of Science, Cosmos and Creator, The Purpose of It All, Is There a Universe?*, and so on.

To put it briefly, Christianity "freed" God from the cosmos, by asserting that Christ was the Μονογενης (*Monogenês*), *Unigenitus*, the Only-Begotten Son[37] – and *not* the universe... but let me quote Chesterton on this very topic:

> ...the ancient world was exactly in our own desolate dilemma. The only people who really enjoyed this world were busy breaking it up; and the virtuous people did not care enough about them to knock them down. In this dilemma (the same as ours) Christianity suddenly stepped in and offered a singular answer, which the world eventually accepted as *the* answer. It was the answer then, and I think it is the answer now.
>
> This answer was like the slash of a sword; it sundered; it did not in any sense sentimentally unite. Briefly, it divided God from the cosmos.[38] That transcendence and distinctness of the deity which some Christians now want to remove from Christianity, was really the only reason why any one wanted to be a Christian. It was the whole point of the Christian answer to the unhappy pessimist and the still more unhappy optimist. As I am here only concerned with their particular problem, I shall indicate only briefly this great metaphysical suggestion. All descriptions of the creating or sustaining principle in things must be metaphorical, because they must be verbal. Thus the pantheist is forced to speak of God in all things as if he were in a box. Thus the evolutionist has, in his very name, the idea of being unrolled like a carpet. All terms, religious and irreligious, are open to this charge. The only question is whether all terms are useless, or whether one can, with such a phrase, cover a distinct *idea* about the origin of things. I think one can, and so evidently does the evolutionist, or he would not talk about evolution. And the root phrase for all Christian theism was this, that God was a creator, as an artist is a creator. A poet is so separate from his poem that he himself speaks of it as a little thing he has "thrown off." Even in giving it forth he has flung it away. This

---

[36] Cf. the complaint against GKC's work in GKC's *The Thing* CW3:227-9.

[37] See John 1:14 and the great Creed of the Council of Nicea (325).

[38] On this division see Jaki's discussion of the Hebrew verb *bara* (to divide or hack, translated as "to create") in his *Genesis 1 Through the Ages*.

80

> principle that all creation and procreation is a breaking off is at least as
> consistent through the cosmos as the evolutionary principle that all
> growth is a branching out. A woman loses a child even in having a
> child. All creation is separation. Birth is as solemn a parting as death.[39]

Because Jesus Christ (NOT the cosmos) is asserted to be God's Only-Begotten Son, the so-called "heavens" (the sky, the sun and moon, the planets, and the stars) could NOT be "divine." Hence, they *could* be studied in the same way as *any* "sublunar" (merely earthly) objects. Moreover, by also asserting that this same Jesus Christ suffered, died *and rose* once and for all in a most singular and unrepeatable act, Christianity formally excluded any possible hint of the "Great Year" and its dull and unending repetitions.

But now there is something besides the old pagan fascination with the animism of the universe, the Great Year and all that which motivates people. Christ Himself even predicted that opponents of Him, His work, and His followers would arise... and so they have, and it is not surprising that they have turned into neo-Pagans, just as infatuated with the Great Year as the ancient Pagans were.

It is therefore especially important for scientists and scholars of our times to note the effect of these recent pagans: Darwin, Kant, Engels, Marx, Nietzsche, Hegel, Spencer, Fichte, Schelling, and their ilk on recent scientists... and this is what Jaki has done in the final four chapters. Few indeed of modern scientists will know of any of these writers (except, of course, for Darwin) in any "scientific" context, but the effect of their writing, as non-scientific as it is, is pervasive in society.

Oh but we are doing *science*, you say; we never even *heard* of Hegel or Fichte or Nietzsche, and we surely don't read *them*!

Yes, quite likely, but as you will see from our text, they had their effects on major scientists: on Einstein, Planck, Bohr, Heisenberg, and so on – and that same effect is still being propagated in writers like Asimov, Sagan, Hawking, Gould, Dawkins...

But really, you say: *does it matter?* Science has already come to a "viable birth" (SC 131) and is now a "self-sustaining enterprise" (SC 146) – how can paganism harm it, or us, now?

Well... it can, and it does. There are less and less people who study Science Writ Large these days, and few who bother with things like Engineering, which can be even harder. Even as recently as the 1950s and 60s young men were buying jalopies, tinkering with them, improving them, and driving them. Now, fifty years later, there's very little one can do to a car unless one is certified by the manufacturer. And that's mechanics – gears and cams and

---

[39] GKC, *Orthodoxy*, CW1:280-1

pistons – it's even more hopeless to speak about getting into electronics, where everything is on a chip, and the ever-more dumb INTERNET with its so-called "search engines" enables people to know ever-more *less* about computers, not more.

Then there is the hilarious "STEM" idea, a feel-good "let's wish and maybe it will happen" game, entertaining the kids with fun while freeing the teachers from the necessity of imparting knowledge, especially trying to convince girls[40] to like these subjects by doing tricks (scientific in appearance but mindless in reality, always completely excluding anything truly technical) – like dropping eggs from helicopters, making "slime," or building bridges with uncooked spaghetti. Never any math, of course. Fun things, like arts-and-crafts, because real science is slow,[41] boring, and difficult – and as that famous talking doll said, "Math is hard!"[42]

Parallel to this is the Amish/Luddite exaltation by tiny orthodox academies, each with its own website, even to the point of providing the smartphones of the parents with near-real-time status of their children, but where the coursework is restricted to Latin, the Trivium and Quadrivium, Latin, poetry, Shakespeare, and Latin. But Science? No – *absit!* – lest they get too close in appearance to the public schools while pretending to be in the Middle Ages... But five of the seven Liberal Arts are mathematical, and in the Middle Ages they were too catholic to divide Arts from Sciences.[43] Moreover, no Scholastic would have stood for such absurdities; they were too intent, as GKC said, on getting things done.[44]

Neither Amish/Luddite nor STEM is helping, since schools, public, private, and orthodox, are terrified of Science and especially of Mathematics. So hard, so boring... They don't dare teach chemistry, since someone might build a bomb, or make drugs. They don't dare teach physics, as somebody might build a bomb. They don't dare teach biology, as somebody might make drugs, or worse, they might have to confront the matter of where babies come from, and hence *when* life begins, not to mention *how* life begins. All the public schools ever teach in the way of "science" is how wicked those big companies are for polluting, and yet one can watch inner-

---

[40] Yes, I said girls. These are always aimed at girls. They don't care very much about boys. Yet in every one of my math and science classes through 12th grade the girls did well, including Calculus, Organic Chemistry, and Nuclear Science.

[41] To the medievals, the classic line *Ars longa vita brevis* ("Art is long, life is short") included *scientia* as an "art."

[42] See the discussion in my *The Problem With "Problem-Solving Skills"*.

[43] See the discussion in my *A Twenty-first Century Tree of Virtues*.

[44] "I revert to the doctrinal methods of the thirteenth century, inspired by the general hope of getting something done." GKC, *Heretics*, CW1:46

city students climb out of cars, or get off schoolbusses, and toss their snack food wrappers on the sidewalk as they go into school to be babysat by their laptops.[45] So effective.

As a result, those cool smartphones every kid walks around with are actually not something technical, not even something which can be studied and thus known about, but something *magic*: no one knows anything about how they work. Invoke the spell, and behold!

Yes, but that's what Arthur C. Clarke told us, isn't it? "Any sufficiently advanced technology is indistinguishable from magic."[46] (You know Clarke, that modern pagan who wrote *2001*. He wrote so many books on science, and he ought to know.)

This is *dangerous*. Dangerous because nobody seems to know enough about Science, or even about Philosophy, to provide a rebuttal.[47] And so these wonderful tools are taken to *be* magic.

Even more dangerous is the idea that no one knows how electricity works, and all its related background: the mining and refining of copper and other metals, the building of generating stations, transmission lines and so on – or the making of the splendid integrated circuit "chips" in those ubiquitous smartphones and laptops. And we have not yet mentioned the parallel issues in chemistry and biology, where people actually think a "cure for cancer" will be found in a Brazilian rainforest, or possibly the INTERNET will evolve an "app" for handling it.

This is a whole new form of agnosticism... or rather it is the same one as found in all the ancient cultures. Juvenal was right about *panem et circenses*, that is, bread and circuses, though now he would call it "foodstamps and smartphones."

A little personal note, by way of explanation. My father fought in World War II, and saw such horrors he wanted to do something when he got home after it was over. And so he opened a small bookstore, intent on selling *good* literature, not even just *Catholic* literature, for he knew that bad ideas cannot be eliminated by war.

It takes a good idea to evict a bad idea from men's minds.

---

[45] If spending hours with their electronic toys grants these children credentials as computer scientists, does their daily ride on a schoolbus make them automotive engineers?

[46] Apparently Clarke said this in his "Profiles of the Future" (1961).

[47] My own rebuttal (in *The Horrors in the Attic*) begins: "It's false, and easily disproven. There is a fundamental difference which provides an unfailing means of distinguishing the two. Any technology, no matter how advanced, possesses a well-known path leading from the purely sensory study of nature, by a series of completely rational – moreover, completely teachable – steps, to that technical tool or mechanism or device or method. It is necessarily true – for technology is merely Greek for 'the study of art' – and art is a thing that is done by Man."

Thus, Jaki's work, not just in the concluding portion of our text, but his entire corpus, is his attempt to supply such good ideas.

I must mention one more thing. I obtained my first Jaki book, this book, *Science and Creation*, at my father's store.

8. Why Are There So Many Footnotes?

That is not the right question. It really should be more like the criticism received by the great J. R. R. Tolkien. As he declared in a preface to his three-volume *The Lord of the Rings*, the complaint he most often had was that his work was *too short*. In a similar mode, then, one can hardly say that Jaki's work has *too many* footnotes.[48]

Footnotes, besides being a mark of scholarship, serve in two ways. A good footnote points outward, to a source which the writer has used, and to which one may turn for additional information. The larger the subject, the more footnotes one should expect. There are even great "review" volumes: these huge, incredibly valuable, topic-spanning studies have thousands of references. Of course every good doctoral dissertation or well-written journal article demands a "review of the literature," where one expects to see pointers to both the relevant and the helpful, no matter how these may later be debunked, corrected, or extended. This is not only traditional in academics, it is the Scholastic style, the style of great works like the *Summa Theologica* of Aquinas, in which a proposed question is always considered from every aspect, since its purpose is the search for truth.

And that brings us to the second way a footnote serves. Footnotes bring the dignity of humility to scholarship. A footnote proclaims, in no uncertain terms, that *the author does not know everything*: he has turned to others, friends and foes, supporters and opponents, scholars of long ago as well as contemporary, in an almost desperate search to learn what he could from other masters of the discipline. This is good for the author, and helpful for the reader, since if (by some chance) the author has erred, he may present a good defence: "At least I did my homework."

Now, there is another point to be made about Jaki's footnotes, as he himself points out in his "intellectual autobiography":

> There is no substitute to the perusal of primary texts, which, incidentally, hardly ever fail to reveal something that has not yet been noticed by others. Engrossment with the secondary literature can readily trap one's vision along tracks that have little in common with the thrust of the primary sources. ... historical research implies the reading of original sources which in turn are an inexhaustible source of novelty. Satisfying as it does an inveterate sense of curiosity, the flow of ever new details into one's ken can but delight one's mind. There is further the excitement of finding data that have been ignored beforehand, at times a long chain of documents and data that generations of scientists (and historians of science) failed to notice, or if they did, they passed them up. SLJ, *A Mind's Matter*, 5-6, 31

As a cautionary tale he gives a notable example of a failure:

> ...it was one thing to describe idealism as mystical, and another to equate empiricism with reason and science. Revealingly, [John Stuart] Mill did not try to evaluate idealism and empiricism against the standards of science but in relation to political and social theory. It was a curious bypassing of the principal issue, a tactic paralleled by Mill's

---

[48] E.g., the tale of how Newton "wasted precious time on erasing references to Descartes from his manuscripts" has no footnote. SLJ, *The Savior of Science* 48.

treatment in the *Logic* of the true features of science as it grew into full maturity during the century following Copernicus. Mill was not willing to see in that process any trace of metaphysics, a fact which should nowadays discredit his logic in the eyes of those historians of science who cultivate their discipline on the basis of reading the original sources. According to Mill, Kepler's establishing the ellipticity of planetary orbits was not even a case of induction by enumeration. Since astronomers long before Kepler had observed that "planets periodically returned to the same places" (so Mill presented his reading of scientific history) "there was no induction left for Kepler to make, nor did he make any further induction." Clearly, Mill did not bother to plod through the laborious pages of Kepler's *Astronomia nova de stella Martis*. There he would have met face to face the heroic groping of a great man of science with facts, with ideas, with perspectives, and not least with the need to arrive at a law which enabled the prediction of planetary positions with the greatest possible accuracy. Nothing of this was intimated in Mill's account of what had happened. The account had actuality only in Mill's positivism in which even the most complex and herculean inductions performed by the mind had to appear as simple, matter-of-fact self-organization of observations. SLJ, *The Road of Science and the Ways to God*, 152

Jaki also admits to a similar failure:

...I was careful to verify any quotation, which I found in secondary sources, against its original provenance. Out of the thousand or so references in *The Relevance* I failed to do this in three cases, trusting secondary sources that did not give the context of the passages I quoted. In two of those cases my use of those quotations gave them a thrust which, in their own context, they certainly did not have. SLJ, *A Mind's Matter*, 5

Just to help prove my point, consider this, taken from a book on the history of chemistry, comparable in some ways to Jaki's own work:

In this [second] edition the original intention of the book is fulfilled; for not only is an account given of the "lives" of the chemists (which constituted the first edition), but, in addition, a detailed account of their "work," with copious references to the original literature, is now offered (pages 241-458). Formidable as this task seems when one considers the extensive literature which had to be consulted, it hardly seemed so during the time (some five years) when the book was gradually being put into shape; because, for my own part, I know of nothing quite so exhilarating as to read and re-read the original papers of the masters of our science. Let the reader himself try the experiment by making use of some of the references in the book. For example, turn to volume 69, page 556, of the *Journal of the Chemical Society* (London) and read Perkins' own account of the origin of the coal-tar industry; or turn to volume 186, page 187, of the *Philosophical Transactions* and read Rayleigh and Ramsay's account of their isolation of argon, "a new constituent of the atmosphere"...

Harrow, *Eminent Chemists of Our Time*, v.

It's worth reading that line again: "I know of nothing quite so exhilarating as to read and re-read the original papers of the masters of our science." Hence the need for footnotes to point to those papers.

IV: Dramatis Personae

Note: this list does not include authors cited only in bibliographic notes. Some dates and data from *Webster's New Biographical Dictionary*, 1988 edition.

Abd-al-Rahman. (III, an-Nasir) (891-961) headed Umayyad caliphate of Spain.

Abraham. (early 2nd millennium BC; see Gen 11:26 ff) father of Ishmael and Isaac.

Abu-Mashar, or Albumasar. (fl. 870), the most famed of Arab astrologers, studied under Al-Kindi.

Abu-al-Wafa. (940-998) Persian astronomer, invented secant and cosecant, devised sum of sines: $\sin(\alpha + \beta) = \sin\alpha\cos\beta + \sin\alpha\cos\beta$.

Adelard of Bath. (12th century) English traveller, philosopher, author of *Quaestiones naturales*, Latin translation of Arabic version of Euclid's *Elements*.

Ailly, Pierre d'. (1350-1420) French prelate and theologian, made a qualified defense of astrology in his *Tractatus contra astronomos*.

Akhenaton, (14th c. BC) 18th dynasty king of Egypt (1379-1362). Forced his monotheistic worship of Aten the sun-god on the country.

Albert of Saxony. (1316-1390) German scholastic philosopher, bishop of Halberstadt.

Albertus, Magnus, Saint. (c. 1200-1280) Theologian, philosopher, scientist. Doctor of the Church, patron saint of the sciences. The *CRC Handbook of Chemistry and Physics* credits him with the discovery of arsenic.

Albumasar. See Abu-Mashar.

Alcmeon. (6th century BC) Greek physician and Pythagorean philosopher, first known to have made anatomical dissections of humans.

Alexander of Aphrodisias. (fl. c. 200 A.D.) Greek philosopher, head of Lyceum in Athens, wrote commentaries on Aristotle and works including *On Fate*, against Stoics, *On the Soul*.

Alexander the Great. (Alexander III, 356-323 BC) King of Macedonia, tutored by Aristotle, conquered much of known world.

Alfvén, Hannes (20th century) Physicist, Nobel laureate for work on plasma physics, "an unabashed eternalist." SLJ, *God and the Cosmologists*, 82

Alhazen Ibn-Khaldun. (Abu Ali al-Hasan ibn al-Haytham, 965-1039) Arab mathematician and physicist, studied reflection, discovered spherical aberration, wrote 7-volume "Book About Optics," first to explain vision as effect of light from object to eye.

Ambrose, Saint. (339-397) Roman prelate, bishop of Milan, converted Augustine.

Amenophis IV. See Akhenaton.

Anaxagoras. (c. 500-c. 428 BC) Greek philosopher.

Anaximander. (610-c. 547 BC) Greek astronomer and philosopher.

Anaximenes. (c. 380-c. 320 BC) Greek rhetorician and historian.

Anytus (5th-4th century BC) Athenian politician, accuser with Meletus of Socrates.

Apollodorus of Seleuca (fl. 120 BC) Stoic philosopher.

Apollonius of Perga. (c. 262-c. 190 BC) Greek mathematician. "The Great Geometer," wrote 8 books on conic sections; introduced terms ellipse, parabola, hyperbola; eccentric and epicyclic motions later used by Ptolemy.

Aquinas, Thomas, Saint. (1247-1274) Scholastic theologian and philosopher, Doctor of the Church.

Arago, François (1786-1853) French physicist.

Archimedes. (c. 287-212 BC) Greek mathematician and inventor.

Archytas. (fl. 400-350 BC) Greek Pythagorean philosopher, scientist, mathematician.

Aristarchus of Samos. (fl. c. 370 BC) Greek astronomer. First to maintain the Earth rotates on its own axis and revolves about sun; estimated relative distances to moon and sun.

Aristotle. (384-322 BC) Greek philosopher; studied under Plato at Academy in Athens. He is to be read with a great deal of caution, since Jaki says that he "put physics and cosmology into a straitjacket for almost two thousand years." *Chance or Reality*, 165, with "his sweeping and usually wrong generalizations about nature." SC 195.

Arrhenius, S. (1859-1927) Swedish physicist and chemist, 1903 Nobel laureate in chemistry.

Aryabhata.(476-c. 550) Indian mathematician and astronomer.

Ashari, al-, (873/4-935/6) Muslim Arab theologian and mystic.

Asoka. (c. 269-238/232 BC) King of India. (c. 265-238 or 273-232 BC) Convert to Buddhism, making it the state religion.

Athenagoras. (2nd century A.D.) Greek Christian apologist.

Augustine, of Hippo, Saint. (354-430) Church Father and philosopher. Originally a Manichean, converted in 387.

Augustus Caesar. (63 BC-14 A.D.) Roman emperor.

Averroës, or Ibn-Rushd (1126-98) Arab philosopher and ophthalmologist. Known as the "Commentator" for his writings on Aristotle.

Avicenna, or Ibn Sina. (980-1037) Arab philosopher. His "Canon" was the standard Arab medical text for centuries.

Avitus. (d. 456 A.D.) Roman emperor of the West (455-456).

Bacon, Francis, Lord Verulam. (1561-1626) English philosopher.

Bacon, Roger. (c. 1220-1292) English philosopher and scientist; Franciscan monk. Wrote *Opus majus* on request of Pope Clement IV.

Banu Musa (fl. c. 850) wrote book on balance.

Barnes, E. W. (1874-1953) Mathematician, Anglican Bishop of Birmingham.

Basil, Saint. (c. 329-379) Church Father, Doctor of the Church; brother of St. Gregory of Nyssa.

Basilides. (2nd century A.D.) Syrian mystic and heresiarch, founded a Gnostic sect.

Battani, al-. (877-918) Arab scholar, derived trigonometric formulas

$$\sin a = \frac{\tan a}{\sqrt{1+\tan^2 a}} \text{ and } \cos a = \frac{1}{\sqrt{1+\tan^2 a}}$$

Benedetti, G. B. (Castiglione) (c. 1616-1670) Italian painter.

Bentley, Richard. (1662-1742) English (Anglican) clergyman, scholar, critic.

Berossos (fl. c. 290 BC) Babylonian priest, authored history of Babylonia in Greek.

Bessarion, Cardinal. (1403-1472) Byzantine theologian and humanist, translated Aristotle's Metaphysics, collected library of Greek manuscripts.

Biruni, al-, (973-1048) Arab scholar, corresponded with Avicenna, studied and wrote on culture of India.

Blanqui, Louis Auguste. (1805-1881) French socialist and revolutionary.

Boccaccio, Giovanni. (1313-1375) Italian writer, father of classic Italian prose.

Bodin, Jean. (1530-1596) French political philosopher.

Boethius. (c. 480-524) Roman philosopher, among other things translated and wrote commentaries on Aristotle; most famous for *On the Consolation of Philosophy* written while in prison awaiting execution.

Bohr, Neils. (1885-1962) Danish physicist proposed model of atom based on Planck's quantum theory.

Boltzmann, Ludwig. (1844-1906) Austrian physicist, worked on statistical mechanics and thermodynamics.

Boyle, Robert. (1627-1691) British physicist and chemist, described Boyle's Law that gas volume varies inversely as the pressure.

Brahe, Tycho. (1546-1601) Danish astronomer, showed that the nova of 1572 was a star, amassed records of most accurate observations made to date in Europe.

Brethren of Purity. (*Ikhwan al Safa*) A quasi-monastic fraternity, compiled a classic summary of Arab alchemy and an encyclopedic summary of knowledge, the *Rasa'il*.

Bruno, Giordano. (1548-1600) Italian philosopher, critic of Aristotelian logic, champion of Copernican cosmology, advocate of obscurantist writings attributed to the mythical Egyptian priest Hermes Trismegistus. Arrested by Inquisition and burned at the stake for heresy. See SLJ's translation of his *The Ash Wednesday Supper*, essay "Giordano Bruno's Place in Science" in *Numbers Decide and Other Essays*, and booklet *Giordano Bruno: a Martyr of Science?*

Büchner, Ludwig. (1814-1899) German physician and philosopher, wrote on determinist materialism in *Kraft und Stoff* (*Force and Matter*) (1856) which "became overnight the Bible of that crude materialism for which E. Haeckel served from the 1870's as the chief spokesman in Germany." [SLJ, *Brain, Mind and Computers* 33n59]

Buddha (Gautama Siddharta). (c. 563-c. 483 BC) Indian prince, founder of Buddhism.

Buridan, Jean. (1300-1358) French scholastic philosopher, wrote *Summulae Dialectica, Quaestiones super quattuor libris de caelo et mundo*, and notably a commentary on Aristotle's *Physics*, in which he stated what is now called Newton's First Law. SC 232

Calippus. (4th century BC) Greek astronomer, devised Callippic cycle of 76 years, or four Metonic cycles less one day, to harmonize solar and lunar cycles.

Campanella, Tommaso. (1568-1639) Italian philosopher, Dominican monk, imprisoned for heresy, wrote *La Citta del Sole* (on a utopian state like Plato's *Republic*) and *Apologia pro Galilaeo*.

Carneades. (214?-129? BC) Greek skeptic philosopher, founded New/Third Academy in Athens.

Carnot, Sadi. (1796-1832) French physicist and engineer, studied heat in relation to motion, developed what became the Second Law of Thermodynamics.

Cato (the Elder) (234-139 BC) Roman politician, noted orator, champion of anti-Carthaginian policy, fought Hellenistic influence.

Celsus. (2nd century A.D.) Roman or Alexandrian philosopher, a Platonist, author first notable attack on Christianity, *True Discourse*, (c. 178) which was famously answered by Origen in his *Contra Celsum*.

Censorinus. (fl. 240 A.D.) Roman scholar, only extant work *De die natali* (238).

Charles V. (1337-1380) King of France (1364-80), enthusiastic patron of learning.

Charlier, Carl Vilhelm Ludvig. (19-20th century) Mathematician and cosmologist. Professor of astronomy at the University of Lund from 1897 to 1927. Wrote on Olbers' Paradox; monistic in religion. See SLJ's *The Paradox of Olbers' Paradox*.

Chrysippus. (c. 280-c. 206 BC) Greek Stoic philosopher, considered with Zeno the founder of the Stoa academy at Athens.

Chrysostom, John, Saint. (c. 347-407) Syrian prelate, called "Chrysostom" (Greek: "golden-mouthed") after his death. Doctor of the Church.

Chu Hsi. (12th century A.D.) Chinese scholar, wrote on fossil oyster shells found on high mountains. SC 34.

Cicero, Marcus Tullius. (106-43 BC) Roman orator, statesman, philosopher.

Clagett, Marshall. (20th century) Historian of science, published critical edition of Oresme's *De configurationibus qualitatum et motuum* in his *Nicole Oresme and the Medieval Geometry of Qualities and Motions*, author of *The Science of Mechanics in the Middle Ages.*

Clarke, Samuel. (1675-1729) English philosopher, disciple of Newton.

Clausius, Rudolph. (1822-1888) German mathematical physicist, summed up the Second Law of thermodynamics in the now famous statement: "The entropy of the universe tends towards a maximum."

Cleanthes. (331/330-232/231 BC) Greek philosopher, succeeded Zeno as head of Stoic school.

Clement of Alexandria, Saint. (c. 150 – between 211 and 215) Major Christian apologist of the second century.

Cleomedes. (c. 150-c. 200 A.D.) Astronomer.

Condorcet, M. J. (Marie-Jean Caritat) (1743-1794) French mathematician, philosopher and revolutionary. SLJ says he was "a most dedicated apostle of unlimited progress on the basis of a resolute and exclusive application of sciences and mathematics... It is no longer the mark of undisputed scholarship to repeat with Condorcet that *the triumph of Christianity was the signal for the complete decadence of philosophy and the sciences.*" SC 292-3

Confucius. (K'ung Ch'iu) (551-479 BC) Chinese philosopher.

Copernicus, Nicolaus. (Mikolaj Kopernik) (1473-1543) Polish astronomer, wrote *De Revolutionibus orbium coelestium* advancing heliocentric theory and earth's diurnal rotation.

Crombie, Alistair C. (20th century) Historian of science, wrote *Medieval and Early Modern Science* and *Robert Grosseteste and the Origins of Experimental Science, 1100-1700.*

Ctesibius. (2nd century BC) Greek physicist and inventor.

Cusanus, Nicolaus. (Nicholas of Cusa) (1401-1464) German prelate and philosopher, author of *De docta ignorantia* on learning, anticipated Copernicus, conducted botanical experiments, collected manuscripts.

Curtius, Ernst. (1886-1956) German historian of medieval literature. Author of *European Literature and the Latin Middle Ages* (1948).

Cuvier, Georges. (1769-1832) French naturalist.

Damascius, see Nicolas of Damascus

Darwin, Charles. (1809-1882) English naturalist

Dauvillier, A. (20th century) French astronomer, director of the Observatory of Pic du Midi in the Pyrenees, "another articulate advocate of a universe going through cycles without end."

Democritus. (c. 460-c. 370 BC) Greek philosopher, extended atomistic theory of Leucippus.

Descartes, René. (1596-1650) French mathematician and philosopher.

Diacceto, Francesco Cattani da, (late 1400s) Renaissance Platonic philosopher, leader of the Florentine Academy, " a most devoted disciple of Ficino"

Diáz del Castillo, Bernal. (1492-1581?) Comrade-in-arms of Cortés, wrote *Historia verdadera de la conquista de Nueva España* on the conquest of Mexico.

Dicke, Robert H. (20th century) Physicist and cosmologist, studied Big Bang theory.

Didacus de Stunica, see Zuñiga

Dingle, Herbert. (1890-1978) English astrophysicist.

Diogenes. (d. c. 320 BC) Greek philosopher, founded philosophy of the Cynics. The legend is told that he went through the streets with a lantern "looking for an honest man."

Diophantus. (3rd century A.D.) Greek mathematician, introduced symbolism into Greek algebra, studied number theory and the "Diophantine" equations (those having integers as roots).

Duhem, Pierre. (1861-1916) French thermodynamicist and historian of science, author of ten-volume *Le Système du monde* and many other works See SLJ's *Uneasy Genius: The Life and Work of Pierre Duhem* and *Scientist and Catholic: Pierre Duhem*.

Dühring, Eugene. (fl. 1875) Convert to socialism, authored *Cursus der Philosophie als streng wissenschaftlicher Weltanschaunug und Lebensgestaltung*, condemned by Engels.

Eddington, Arthur Stanley. (1882-1944) English astronomer.

Einstein, Albert. (1879-1955) American physicist, studied photoelectricity, Brownian motion, formulated theories of Special and General Relativity. See esp. SLJ's "The Absolute Beneath the Relative: Reflections on Einstein's Theories" in *The Absolute Beneath the Relative and Other Essays*.

Empedocles. (c. 490-430 BC) Greek philosopher and statesman, developed theory of Four Elements govern by Love and Strife, reputed founder of rhetoric; traditionally said to have hurled himself into the crater of Mt. Etna to convince people he was a god.

Engels, Friedrich. (1820-1895) German Socialist, admirer of Hegel, associate of Karl Marx, after Marx's death completed his *Das Kapital*, edited and published his works.

Epictetus. (c. 55-c. 135 A.D.) Greek Stoic philosopher.

Epicurus. (341-270 BC) Greek philosopher, emphasized pleasure is the only good and the end of all morality but that the genuine life of pleasure must be life of simplicity; adopted atomistic theory of Democritus.

Erasistratus. (fl. 250 BC) Greek physician and anatomist.

Eratosthenes. (c. 276-c. 194 BC) Greek astronomer, geographer, mathematician, measured obliquity of ecliptic, calculated circumference of Earth, devised "sieve" method of finding prime numbers.

Euclid. (fl. 300 BC) Greek geometer; drawing on other workers authored *Stoicheia* (*Elements*).

Eudoxus. (c. 400-c. 350 BC) Greek mathematician and astronomer.

Eusebius (of Caesarea) (c. 260-c. 339) Bishop of Caesarea, author of *Historia ecclesiastica*. and *Praeparatio evangelica*. [Note: there are several men of this name. Unfortunately Jaki mentions "Eusebius" several times in his works but without qualification; from the context "Eusebius of Caesarea" seems intended]

Farabi, al-. (c. 878- c. 950) Muslim philosopher, wrote commentaries on Aristotle, became known as "Second teacher" (after Aristotle).

Faraday, Michael. (1791-1867) English chemist and physicist.

Faustus. (fl. 400s) Famous Manichean, "an African by race, a citizen of Mileum," against whom St. Augustine wrote his *Contra Faustum Manichaeum*.

Fichte, Johann Gottlieb. (1762-1814) German philosopher, ardent disciple of Kant, exponent of a pantheistic and voluntaristic system of a transcendental idealism.

Ficino, Marsilio. (1433-1499) Italian philosopher, Platonist; became head of Platonic Academy of Florence, promoted the translation and printing of obscurantist works ascribed to the mythical Egyptian priest Hermes Trismegistus.

Fludd, Robert. (1574-1637) English physician and Rosicrucian, advocate of "the astrological tradition and the pantheistic animism" and fought against by Father Marin Mersenne, who called him "the evil magician." SC 284

Franciscus de Marchia. (?) SC 242 states that he wrote a commentary on the *Sentences* of Peter Lombard. [I was not able to find anything on this man. Curiously, in *Uneasy Genius*, 430 Jaki does mention someone named Francis of Meyronnes, also called Franciscus de Mayronis, (c. 1285-after 1328): a French Franciscan monk and Scholastic philosopher who wrote commentaries on Aristotle *and* on the *Sentences*. Moreover, it appears that Pierre Duhem wrote a journal article on this man: "*François de Meyronnes O.F.M. et la question de la rotation de la terre*" in *Archivam Franciscanum Historicum* (1913) 6: 23-25.]

Friedmann, Alexander. (1888-1925) Russian mathematician and physical scientist, one of the first to postulate a "big-bang" model of the universe, a founder of dynamic meterology. [Note, SC has the spelling *Friedman*.]

Galen. (129-c. 199) Greek physician, considered founder of experimental physiology, demonstrated that arteries carry blood, believed in theory of the "four humors" of the body.

Galileo, Galilei. (1564-1642) Italian astronomer, mathematician, physicist.

Gama, Vasco da. (c. 1460-1524) Portuguese navigator.

Gamow, George. (1904-1968) American physicist, studied nuclear physics, stellar processes, and cosmology.

Geminus, of Rhodes. (fl. 75 BC) Greek astronomer. Wrote *Isagoge* (an introduction to astronomy). Mentioned in SLJ's *The Milky Way*.

Ghazzali, al-, (al-Ghazali) (1058-1111) Islamic jurist, theologian, philosopher, author of *Tahafut al-falasifah* ("Incoherence of the Philosophers") – a critique on the use of reason. This was rebutted by Averroës' *Tahafut al-tahafut* ("Incoherence of the Incoherence"). SC 208

Goethe, J. W. von. (1749-1832) German poet, wrote on optics and other topics. See SLJ's "Goethe and the Physicists" in *Chance or Reality and Other Essays*.

Grant, Edward. (20th century) Historian of science, edited translation of Nicole Oresme's *De proportionibus proportionum* and *Ad pauca respicientes*.

Grosseteste, Robert. (c. 1168-1253) English theologian and prelate, bishop of Lincoln, chancellor of Oxford.

Guericke, Otto von. (1062-1686) German physicist, invented air pump, first electrical generating machine (a rotating ball of sulfur), discovered electroluminescence.

Hakim, al-. (985-1021?) Fatimid caliph of Egypt, astronomer, established an institute of higher learning in the new city of Cairo in 966.

Hakim II, al-. (961-76) Amassed more than 300,000 volumes for the library in Cordoba.

Hammurabi. (d. 1750 BC) King of first dynasty of Babylon, known for his code of laws.

Harun-al-Rashid. (763 or 766-809) Fifth caliph, idealized in *Thousand and One Nights*.

Hegel, G. W. F. (1770-1831) German philosopher.

Heine, Heinrich. (1797-1856) German poet and critic.

Heisenberg, Werner. (1901-1976) German physicist, known for studies of quantum mechanics and development of the principle of indeterminacy, also called the "uncertainty principle."

Helmholtz, Hermann L. F. von. (1821-1894) German physicist, anatomist, physiologist, a founder of the principle of the conservation of energy.

Heraclitus. (c. 540-c. 480 BC) Greek philosopher, claimed fire as principal element and the whole is a manifestation of *logos*.

Hermes Trismegistus. Mythical Egyptian priest, reputed to be the author of a third-century collection of mystical, magical, and cabbalistic writings. Ficino, Paracelsus and Bruno were his chief advocates during the Renaissance. He "allegedly travelled as far as Saturn to gather the true science of the heavens." SC 262, 207

Herodotus. (c. 484-between 430 and 420 BC) Greek historian, "Father of History," traveled most of known world.

Heron. (Hero) (1st century A.D.) Greek scientist, devised first steam-powered engine, Hero's formula for area of triangle.

Herophilus. (c. 335-c.280 BC) Greek anatomist and surgeon, one of first to conduct post-mortem examination, describe ventricles of brain, the liver, spleen and genital organs, distinguish motor and sensory nerves, time the pulse.

Herschel, William. (1738-1822) British astronomer, discovered Uranus.

Herschel, J. F. W. (1792-1871) British astronomer, continued father's work, first to apply "positive" and "negative" to photographic images.

Hesiod. (fl. 800 BC) Greek poet.

Hipparchus. (fl. 146-127 BC) Greek astronomer, discovered precession of equinoxes, compiled first catalog of some 850 stars, developed trigonometry, devised method for terrestrial location based on latitude and longitude.

Hippolytus, Saint. (c. 170-c. 235) Christian theologian, wrote The Refutation of All Heresies (c. 230), Father of the Church, martyr.

Ho Shen. (1750-1799) Chinese courtier.

Hobbes, Thomas. (1588-1679) English philosopher.

Hölderlin, J. C. F. (1770-1843) German poet, befriended in youth by Schiller, insane from 1802 except for brief periods.

Hooke, Robert. (1635-1703) English scientist, propounded Hooke's law of elasticity, applied the term "cell" to shapes seen in his microscopic studies of cork, discovered diffraction, anticipated Newton's inverse square law.

Hoyle, Fred. (20th century) British astrophysicist who " struck atheistic views whenever opportunity arose." SLJ *Questions on Science and Religion*, 56

Hsia (c. 2193-c. 1752 BC) Traditionally the first Chinese dynasty.

Hsiang, Hsiu. (3rd century A.D.) With Kuo Hsiang wrote commentary on *Chuang Tzu*, the second most important book of Taoism, put together around 300 BC.

Hsun Chhing. (fl. 250 BC) Confucian, wrote against Taoists.

Hsun Tzu. (3rd century BC) Leading Confucian.

Hu Hsi. (4th century A.D.) Chinese astronomer.

Hubble, Edwin. (1889-1953) American astronomer, demonstrated some nebulae are galaxies, classified them by shape, discovered red shift due to receding galaxies, deduced Hubble constant for expansion of universe.

Humason, M. L. (20th century) Astronomer, worked with Hubble on recession of galaxies.

Humboldt, Alexander von. (1769-1859) German naturalist, traveler, statesman, published 23-volume work on his American travels, studied climatology, discovered decrease in Earth's magnetic field from poles to equator.

Hume, David. (1711-1776) Scottish philosopher and historian.

Hunayn, ibn-Ishaq. (c. 809-877) Arab scholar, translated many of Galen's works.

Huygens, Christiaan.(1629-1695) Dutch mathematician, physicist, astronomer, first to use pendulum for clocks and determine acceleration due to gravity.

I-Hsing. (8th century A.D.) Chinese mathematician.

Iamblichus. (c. 250-c. 330) Greek philospher, traditionally credited with transforming Neoplatonism of Plotinus into a theology of magic and mystery.

Ibn-Rushd, see Averroës

Ibn-Sina, see Avicenna

Ibn-abi-al-Mahasin. (fl. 1265) Arab physician, wrote *Kitab al-kafi fi al-Kuhl*, a treatise of ophthalmology.

Ibn-al-Haitham, see Alhazen Ibn-Khaldun

Ignatius of Antioch, Saint. (d. c. 110 A.D.) Bishop of Antioch, a Father of the Church, martyred under Trajan.

Ikhwan-al-Safa, see Brethren of Purity

Irenaeus, Saint. (c. 120 to 140-c.200-203) Greek prelate, martyr, wrote against Gnosticism.

Jeans, James H. (1877-1946) English physicist, astronomer, author.

Jerome, Saint. (c.347-419/20) Latin Church Father, translated Bible into Latin.

Joule, James P. (1818-1889) English physicist, determined mechanical equivalence of heat.

Juan Yuan. (1764-1849) Chinese scholar, wrote *Chhou Jen Chuan* in 1799, giving biographies and accomplishments of some hundred Chinese and of some two dozen Western mathematicians.

Julius Caesar. (100-44 BC) Roman orator, writer, general and statesman, effected many reforms including calendar (46 BC), murdered in 44 by group of nobles.

Justin the Martyr, Saint. (c. 100-c. 165) a Father of the Church, martyred in Rome.

Kang, Yu-Wei. (1858-1927) Chinese scholar and reformer.

Kant, Immanuel. (1724-1804) German philosopher, wrote *Allgemeine Naturgeschichte und Theorie des Himmels* (1755) available as SLJ's translation *Universal Natural History and Theory of the Heavens*.

Kelvin, Lord. (William Thomson) (1824-1907) British mathematician and physicist.

Kepler, Johannes. (1571-1630) German astronomer, discovered Kepler's laws of planetary motion.

Khazini, al-, (12th century A.D.) Arab scholar, wrote treatise on mechanics.

Khwarizmi, al-. (c. 780-c. 850 A.D.) Arab mathematician, introduced Arabic numerals, wrote *Hisab al-jabr w'al muzaqalah*, a book on algebra of such popularity the names of both the book and its author are perpetuated in "algebra" and "algorithm."

Kindi, al-, (d. c. 870 A.D.) Arab philosopher and writer, one of first Arab students of the Greek philosophers.

Koyré, Alexandre. (20th century) Historian of science.

Kugler, Franz Xavier. (20th century) Archaeologist and historian. Studied Babylonian cuneiform tablets.

Kuo, Hsiang. (3rd century A.D.) With Hsiang Hsiu wrote commentary on *Chuang Tzu*, the second most important book of Taoism, put together around 300 BC.

Lagrange, Joseph-Louis. (1736-1813) French mathematician.

Lambert, Johann Heinrich. (1728-1777) German physicist, mathematician, astronomer, philosopher, devised method of measuring intensity and absorbtion of light, demonstrated irrationality of π, wrote *Cosmologische Briefe*, available as SLJ's translation *Lambert: Cosmological Letters on the Arrangement of the World-Edifice*.

Lange, Friedrich Albert. (1828-1875) German philosopher, established neo-Kantism, introduced Darwinistic sociology and philosophy into Germany, wrote *History of Materialism.*

Lao Tzu. (6th century BC) Chinese philosopher.

Laplace, Pierre-Simon de. (1749-1827) French astronomer and mathematician, worked with Lagrange, in 1773 announced discovery of the invariability of the planetary mean motions, showing that the solar system is stable.

Le Bon, Gustave. (1841-1931) French sociologist, known for his study of crowd psychology and his elitist theory of social evolution.

Leibniz, Gottfried Wilhem. (1646-1716) German philosopher and mathematician, devised calculus (his work published before Newton), developed rational metaphysics on his theory of monads.

Lemaître, Georges. (1894-1966) Belgian astronomer, priest, professor of mathematics and history of physics and mathematics at the Catholic University of Louvain. Formulated (1927) modern big-bang theory of origin of the universe.

Leonardo da Vinci. (1452-1519) Italian painter, sculptor, architect, engineer, scientist.

Levy-Bruhl, Lucien. (1857-1939) French philosopher and sociologist.

Linnaeus, Carl (Linné) (1707-1778) Swedish botanist, a father modern systematic botany, presented system of botanical nomenclature in 1735.

Lipsius, Justus. (Joest Lips) (1547-1606) Flemish Humanist and philosopher.

Littrow, Joseph J. von. (19th century) Astronomer. Director of the Vienna observatory, published 3-volume work on astronomy.

Llull, Ramon. (Raymond Lully) (c. 1235-1316) Catalan mystic and philosopher, his chief work *Ars magna* attempted to encompass all knowledge in a Neoplatonic schema.

Lorenzo dei Medici (the Magnificent). (1449-1492) Florentine statesman.

Lucretius. (c. 100 to 90-c.55 to 53 BC) Roman poet, disciple of Epicurus, wrote *De rerum natura,* treating physics, psychology, and ethics according to Epicurean doctrine.

MacMillan, William D. (20th century) Astronomer at University of Chicago, 1908-38.

Mach, Ernst. (1838-1916) Austrian physicist and philosopher, studied physics, physiology and psychology of the senses, established principles of modern scientific positivism.

Machiavelli, Niccoló. (1469-1527) Italian political philosopher, author of *Il principe,* "The Prince" (1513).

Macrobius. (fl. 400 A.D.) Latin grammarian.

Mädler, Johann H. von. (1794-1874) German astronomer, published first map of Mars with Wilhem Beer (1830) and authoritative map of Moon (1836). See SLJ's *The Paradox of Olbers' Paradox.*

Maimonides, (Moses ben Maimon) (1135-1204) Jewish philosopher. Physician to Saladin, sultan of Egypt. Wrote main works in Arabic, including *The Guide of the Perplexed.*

Mamun, al-. (786-833) Seventh Abbasid caliph, patron of philosophy and astronomy.

Manetho. (3rd century BC) Egyptian priest and historian.

Mansur, al-. (between 709 and 714-775) Second Abbasid caliph, patron of learning.

Marcus Aurelius. (121-180) Roman emperor, Stoic philosopher, opponent of Christianity, wrote *Meditations.*

Maxwell, James Clerk. (1831-1879) Scottish physicist.

Mayer, Julius Robert von. (1814-1878) German physican and physicist, studied heat, laid foundation for First Law of thermodynamics.

McVittie, G. C. (20th century) physicist, worked with Eddington on cosmology.

Meletus. (5th-4th century BC) Athenian politician, accuser with Anytus of Socrates.

Meng, Kho (Mencius). (c. 371-c.289 BC) Chinese philosopher, grandson of Confucius, considered cofounder of Confucianism.

Mersenne, Marin. (1588-1648) French mathematician and scientist, priest in order of Minims, studied primes of the form 2^p-1 where p is prime.

Meton. (fl. 432 BC) Greek astronomer, discovered 19-year Metonic cycle of solar years and synodic months.

Millikan, Robert Andrews. (1868-1953) American physicist, first to isolate electron and determine its charge, obtained precise value for Planck's constant.

Milne, Edward Arthur. (1896-1950) English astronomer.

Mo Ti (Mo-tzu) (470?-391? BC) Chinese philosopher, originally a Confucian, founder of Moism.

Moctezuma, II (Montezuma) (1466-1520) Aztec emperor.

Moleschott, Jacob. (1822-1893) Dutch physiologist, advocate of scientific materialism. (See Vogt below.)

Monod, Victor. (20th century) French scholar, wrote *Dieu dans l'univers* "in which he surveyed the influence of Platonist and Aristotelian cosmology on Christian thinking and on Newtonian and modern science." SLJ, *Bible and Science*, 126

More, Henry. (1614-1687) English philosopher and poet, leading Platonist at Cambridge, argued against Descartes and Hobbes.

More, Thomas, Saint. (1478-1535) English statesman and author, martyred under Henry VIII, known for his *Utopia*.

Nägeli, Karl. Wilhem. von. (1817-1891) Swiss botanist.

Needham, Joseph. (20th century) SLJ calls him "the leading Western historian of Chinese science and an avowed Marxist." SC 40

Nefertiti. (14th century BC) Egyptian queen.

Nemesius. (4th century A.D.) Christian philosopher and bishop.

Nernst, Walther Hermann. (1864-1941) German physicist and chemist, a founder of modern physical chemistry, Nobel laureate.

Neugebauer, Otto. (20th century) Historian of science, authority on Egyptian mathematics, author of *The Exact Sciences in Antiquity*.

Newman, John Henry. (1801-1890) English prelate, theologian, author. Anglican priest, Tutor at Oxford, converted to Roman Catholicism in 1845, ordained 1847, made cardinal by Leo XIII in 1879. See appendix for SLJ's books.

Newton, Isaac. (1642-1727) English mathematician and physicist.

Nicolas of Cusa, see Cusanus.

Nicolas of Damascus. (Damascius) (1st century BC) Greek historian.

Nietzsche, Friedrich Wilhelm. (1844-1900) German philosopher and poet. Professor of classical philology, opponent of Schopenhauer and Wagner, suffered mental breakdown (1889); known for denouncing religion, espousing doctrine of perfectibility of man through forcible self-assertion, glorification of the superman/overman (*übermensch*).

Novikov, I. D. (20th century) Astrophysicist.

Oenipodus (Oenopides or Oinopides) (5th century BC) Greek astronomer.

Oken, Lorenz. (1779-1851) German naturalist and philosopher.

Olbers, Heinrich Wilhem Matthäus. (1758-1840) German physician and astronomer, discovered 5 comets, asteroids Pallas and Vesta. See SLJ's *Olbers Studies* and *The Paradox of Olbers' Paradox*. ("Why is the night sky dark?")

Omar, Khayyam. (1048?-1131?) Persian poet, mathematician, astronomer, philosopher.

Öpik, E. J. (20th century) Astronomer, author of *The Oscillating Universe*.

Oresme, Nicole d'. (c. 1325-1382) French prelate, scholar, bishop of Lisieux, disciple of Buridan.

Origen. (185?-254?) Christian writer and teacher, one of the Greek Fathers of the Church, wrote defending Christianity against the attacks of Celsus.

Ostriker, J. P. (20th century) Astrophysicist.

Ostwald, Friedrich Wilhem. (1887-1932) German physical chemist.

Palingenius, M. (fl. 1534) Astronomer, wrote *Zodiacus vitae*, a didactic poem which gained immense popularity. See SLJ's *The Paradox of Olbers' Paradox*.

Pao, Ching-Yen. (3rd centuray) Taoist philosopher.

Pappus. (fl. 320 A.D.) Greek geometer.

Paracelsus. (Bombast von Hohenheim) (1493-1541) German alchemist and physician.

Parmenides. (b. c. 515 BC) Greek philosopher of Elea, founder of Eleatic school.

Parsons, William. (Lord Rosse) (1800-1867) Irish astronomer.

Pascal, Blaise. (1623-1662) French scientist and philosopher.

Pericles. (c. 495-c. 429 BC) Athenian statesman.

Perrin, Jean-Baptiste. (1870-1942) French physicist and chemist, Nobel laureate.

Petrarch. (1304-1374) Italian poet.

Petrus Lombardus. (Peter Lombard) (c. 1095-1160) Italian theologian, his 4-volume *Sentences* was the official textbook for medieval theological schools.

Philo (Judaeus, or of Alexandria) (c. 13 BC – between 45 and 50 A.D.) Jewish philosopher of Alexandria.

Philolaus. (5th century BC) Greek Pythagorean philosopher, may have anticipated Copernicus.

Philoponus, John. (6th century A.D.) Greek Christian theologian.

Pico della Mirandola G. (1463-1494) Italian Humanist, a leading scholar of the Renaissance.

Pius XII. (Eugenio Pacelli) (1876-1958) Pope (1939-1958).

Plato. (c. 428-348/7 BC) Greek philosopher, disciple of Socrates, teacher of Aristotle.

Pliny (the Elder) (23-79 A.D.) Roman scholar, died while trying to observe the eruption of Vesuvius which buried Pompeii. Author of *Historia naturalis* (Natural History).

Plotinus. (205-270 A.D.) Roman philosopher, chief exponent of Neoplatonism, friend of Porphyry who wrote his biography.

Plutarch. (c. 46-after 119 A.D.) Greek biographer.

Porphyry. (c.234-c.305 A.D.) Greek scholar and Neoplatonic philosopher, studied under Plotinus, vigorous defender of paganism and opponent of Christianity.

Poseidonius. (c. 135-c.51 BC) Greek Stoic philosopher.

Proclus. (410?-485 A.D.) Greek Neoplatonic philosopher, vigorous defender of paganism and opponent of Christianity.

Ptolemy. (2nd century A.D.) Astronomer, mathematician, geographer of Alexandria. Wrote *Megalê Syntaxis tês astronomias* (known as *Almagest* from its title in Arabic translation): a purely geometrical formalism on the motion of planets, presenting the "Ptolemaic System" in which all celestial bodies revolve around the Earth. He also wrote a work on astrology called *Tetrabiblos*, another called *Planetary Hypotheses*, *Analemma* and *Planisphaerium* on geometry, *Optica* on optical phenomena and *Harmonica* on music.

Pythagoras. (c. 580-c. 500 BC) Greek philosopher and mathematician.

Rankine, William Jon Macquorn. (1820-1872) Scottish civil engineer and physicist.

Ray, John. (1627-1705) English naturalist, called "father of English natural history."

Raymundus Lullus. See Llull.

Razi, ar-. (Rhazes) (865-925) Persian physician and philosopher, considered greatest physician of Islamic world, "best remembered as the author of *A Treatise on the Small-Pox and Measles*, which has been reprinted more than forty times during the last four hundred years." SC 194

Rey, Abel. (early 20th century) Director of the *Institut pour Science et Technologie* at the Sorbonne. "As a philosopher of science Rey showed sharp awareness of the ultimate origins of certain intellectual choices and attitudes." SC 343. He was "one of those rare scholars who in spite of ideological differences was willing to recognize intellectual and scholarly excellence... [he] did much between 1935 and 1939 to rally support in French academic and administrative circles to secure the publication of [Duhem's] *Système du monde*." SLJ, "Science and Censorship: Hélène Duhem and the Publication of the *Système du monde*" in *The Absolute Beneath the Relative and Other Essays*, 182.

Ricci, Matteo. (1552-1610) Italian Jesuit priest, missionary to China.

Riemann, Georg Friedrich Bernhard. (1826-1866) German mathematician, originated a general non-Euclidean geometry.

Rosse, Lord. See Parsons, William.

Russell, Bertrand. (1872-1970) English mathematician and philosopher.

Rutherford, Ernest. (1871-1937) British physicist, Nobel laureate.

Sahagún, Bernardino de, (1499-1590) Spanish Franciscan missionary and historian, went to Mexico in 1529, wrote *Historia general de las cosas de Nueva España*.

Sarton, George. *1884-1956) American scholar, historian of science, founder (1912) of *Isis*, the first professional journal for the history of science. Wrote 5-volume *Introduction to the History of Science* (1927-1947). He is "a perfect example of the fact that myopia about the stillbirths of science in ancient cultures easily becomes a myopia about the later, live birth of science, and that the myopia is clearly conditioned by one's attitude toward natural theology." SLJ *The Road of Science and the Ways to God*, 13.

Schall von Bell, Johann Adam. (1591-1666) German astronomer and Jesuit missionary to China, became head of imperial astronomical bureau.

Schelling, Friedrich William Joseph von. (1775-1854) German philosopher, leadiung figure of German Idealism, clashed with Fichte and Hegel.

Seneca (the Younger) (4? BC-65 A.D.) Roman statesman and philosopher.

Shadhili, ash-. 1196/7-1258) Moroccan theologian.

Shao, Yung. (1011-1077) Chinese philosopher.

Siger of Brabant. (c. 1240-between 1281 and 1284) French philosopher, leading representative of radical Aristotelianism, disputed against Aquinas and Bonaventure.

Simplicius. (fl. 530 A.D.) Greek Neoplatonic philosopher.

Sitter, Willem de. (1872-1934) Dutch astronomer.

Socrates. (c. 470-399 BC) Greek philosopher.

Sorokin, Pitirim Alexandrovich. (1889-1968) American sociologist.

Sosigenes of Alexandria. (1st century BC) Greek astronomer and mathematician, commissioned by Julius Caesar to reform the calendar.

Spencer, Herbert. (1820-1903) English philosopher, advocate of scientific monism.

Spengler, Oswald. (1880-1936) German writer, authored *The Decline of the West* (1918-22).

Spinoza, Baruch. (1632-1677) Dutch philosopher.

Stallo, John B. (19-20th centuries) "A Cincinnati lawyer doing philosophy of science for avocation." Wrote *Concepts and Theories of Modern Physics* (1881) which "upheld both the infinity and the finitude of the universe." SLJ, *God and the Cosmologists*, 204 and note 9, where SLJ references Easton's *Hegel's First American Followers: The Ohio Hegelians: John B. Stallo, Peter Kaufmann, Moncure Conway, and August Willich, with Key Writings* (Athens: University of Ohio Press, 1966).

Stevin, Simon. (1548-1620) Dutch mathematician and physicist.

Stewart, Balfour. (1828-1887) Scottish physicist and meteorologist, authored *The Unseen Universe* (1875) with Peter G. Tait.

Straton (also Strato) (d. c. 270 BC) Greek Peripatetic philosopher, succeded Theophrastus as head of Peripatetics.

Struve, Frriedrich-Georg Wilhem. (1793-1864) Astronomer, born in Germany moved to Russia to avoid conscription by Napoleonic armies, surveyed some 122,000 stars, one of first to measure stellar parallax(1838).

Tabit, ibn-Korra. (836-931) Arab geometer, translated works of Euclid, Apollonius, Archimedes, and Ptolemy.

Tacitus. (c. 56-c 120 A.D.) Roman orator, politician, historian.

Tait, Peter Guthrie. (1831-1901) Scottish physicist and mathematician.

Tansillo, Luigi. (1510-1568) Italian poet.

Tartaglia, Niccolò. (1499-1557) Italian mathematician, credited with discovery of solution of the cubic equation later published by Cardano as his own.

Tatian. (c. 120-173) Syrian Christian writer, broke with Rome and established school and religious community of Encratites.

Telesius (Telesio), Bernardino. (1509-1588) Italian philosopher, called "first of moderns" by Francis Bacon.

Tempier, Étienne. (1200s) Bishop of Paris, issued famous condemnation of 219 propositions March 7, 1277. SC 229

Theodore of Mopsuestia. (c. 350-428/9) Greek theologian.

Theodoric of Freiberg. (d. 1311)

Theon. (4th century A.D.) Greek mathematician.

Theophilos. (?) "...the Syrian Theophilos... served as astrologer under the first Sasanid caliphs." SC 198.

Theophrastus. (c.372-c. 287 BC) Greek philosopher and scientist, disciple of Aristotle and his successor as head of Peripatetic school.

Thierry of Chartres. (c. 1100-c.1156) French educator, theologian, Scholastic philosopher.

Thomson, William. (see Kelvin)

Thomson, George Paget. (1892-1975) English physicist, Nobel laureate.

Thorndike, Lynn. (20th century) Historian of science, author of the 10-volume "storehouse of information," *History of Magic and Experimental Science*.

Tolman, Richard Chace. (1881-1948) American physicist, determined mass of the electron and demonstrated it carried charge in electrical current.

Tung, Chung-Shu. (c. 179-c. 104 BC) Chinese scholar, established Confusianism as state cult and basis of official political philosophy.

Turner, J. E. (20th century) Professor at the University of Liverpool. Wrote to the Editor of *Nature* (126 [27 December 1930]: 995) in which he deplored the use by the Nobel-laureate physicist, G. P. Thomson, of the word "determined" in the two very different senses of "caused" and "ascertained". SC 365n17

Tut-ankh-amen. (c. 1370-1352 BC) King of Egypt during18th dynasty.

Tycho, see Brahe

Tyndall, John. (1820-1893) Irish physicist and popularizer of science, monist, wrote *Heat a Mode of Motion* (1863).

Ussher, James. (1581-1656) Irish prelate and scholar, archbishop of Armagh, propounded a chronology in which creation occurred in 4004 BC.

Varahamihira. (505-587) Indian philosopher, astronomer, mathematician.

Verbiest, Ferdinand. (1623-1688) Flemish astronomer, Jesuit missionary to China, succeeded Adam Schall von Bell as head of imperial astronomical bureau, instrumental in determining boundary between China and Russia.

Vieta, Franciscus (François Viète) (1540-1603) French mathematician and lawyer, introduced systematic (essentially modern) algebraic notation (1591), solved equations of degree 2, 3, 4, cracked cypher used by Philip II of Spain.

Virgil. (70-19 BC) Greatest of Roman poets, wrote *Aeneid, Eclogues, Georgics*.

Vogt, C. (mid 19th century) Scientific materialist. "About a hundred and fifty years ago Moleschott and Vogt speculated about intelligent life based on phosphorus, but they stopped when it was found that the brains of geese were very rich in phosphorus." SLJ "From World Views to Science and Back" in *Numbers Decide and Other Essays*, 202. The "endlessly repeated motto" of Vogt and his colleagues, "*Ohne Phosphor kein Gedanke* (without phosphorus no thought) is remembered today only as a pregnant expression of the perennial shallowness of reductionism. SLJ, *Brain, Mind and Computers*, 34.

Wang-Chhung. (fl. A.D. 80) Chinese astronomer.

Wang, Yang-Ming. (1472-1529) Chnese philosopher.

Weizsäcker, C. F. von. (20th century) Theoretical physicist, wrote *The History ogf Nature* (1949) and *The Relevance of Science: Creation and Cosmogony* (1964). SLJ: "In spite of his professed concern, expressed in the subtitle, for the notion of creation, Weizsäcker failed to do justice to the role played by that notion in the history of science." SC 343n45 Elsewhere SLJ cites him: "Gaps in knowledge have a habit of closing – and God is no stopgap." *TROP* 436. "There is no honest retreat from rational thought into naive belief. It is an old saying that the first sip from the cup of knowledge cuts off from God, but in the bottom of the cup God waits for those who seek Him." *TROP* 456.

Whitehead, Alfred North. (1861-1947) English mathematician and philsopher.

Whitrow, G. J. (20th century) Physicist, author of *The Natural Philosophy of Time*, *The Structure and Evolution of the Universe: An Introduction to Cosmology*.

Whittaker, Edmund Taylor. (1873-1956) English mathematician.

William of Alnwick. (fl. 1310s) Regent-master of the Oxford Franciscan House in the 1310s, wrote summary of Grosseteste's theory of scientific measurement. SC 222

William of Auvergne. (after 1180-1249) French philosopher and theologian.

Wright, Thomas. (fl. 1750) Astronomer, "the first to perceive in the luminous band of the Milky Way a non-uniform pattern of the distribution of stars." *TROP*

203, originator of the "grindstone theory" of the Milky Way, *TROP* 350 Wrote *An Original Theory or New Hypothesis of the Universe*.

Wundt, Wilhelm. (1832-1920) German physiologist and psychologist, "a most philosophically minded pioneer of scientific psychology" who also wrote a lengthy article, "On the Cosmological Problem." SLJ, *The Paradox of Olbers' Paradox*, 166.

Xenophon. (c. 431-c. 352 BC) Greek historian, disciple of Socrates, author of *Anabasis*.

Yu-Lan, Fung (fl. 1922) Chinese scholar.

Zeldovich, Ya. B. (20th century) Astrophysicist.

Zeno of Citium. (c. 335-c. 263 BC) Greek philosopher, founded Stoic school of philosophy.

Zöllner, Johann Karl Friedrich. (1834-1882) German astrophysicist.

Zoroaster. (c. 628-c. 551 BC) Persian religious leader, founder of Zoroastrianism (called Parsiism in India). Nietzsche's *Thus Spoke Zarathustra* is about him.

Zuñiga, Diego de. (Didacus de Stunica) (fl. 1576) Spanish theologian.

Zwicky, Fritz. (1898-1974) Swiss astronomer and physicist.

* * *

...even physicists put their trousers on one leg at a time...

SLJ, "Cosmic Rays and Water Spiders" in
The Limits of a Limitless Science, 230

V: A Bibliography for *Science and Creation*

Adam, Charles and Tannery, Paul. (eds.) *OEvres de Descartes*. [by Descartes] (nouvelle présentation; Paris: J. Vrin, 1967).

Aiken, H. D. (ed.) *Dialogues concerning Natural Religion*. [by David Hume] (New York: Hafner Publishing Co., 1948).

Aiyer, V. G. *The Chronology of Ancient India* (Madras: G. A. Natesan, 1901).

al-Farabi. *Philosophische Abhandlungen* (Leiden, E. J. Brill, 1890).

Albertus Magnus, St. *Opera omnia*, edited by S. C. A. Borgnet (Paris: L. Vives, 1895).

Alfvén, H. *Worlds-Antiworlds: Antimatter in Cosmology* (San Francisco: W. H. Freeman, 1966).

Ames, R. *Citizen Thomas More and his Utopia* (Princeton, N.J.: Princeton University Press, 1949).

Anderson, F. H. *The Philosophy of Francis Bacon*. (Chicago: University of Chicago Press, 1948).

Andreas-Salome, Lou. *Friedrich Nietzsche in seinen Werken* (Dresden: Carl Reiszner, n.d.; reprint of the first edition of 1894).

Apostle, H. G. (tr.) *Aristotle's Metaphysics*, translated with commentaries and glossary by H. G. Apostle (Bloomington: Indiana University Press, 1966).

Aquilecchia, G. *La Cena de le Ceneri*. [by Giordano Bruno] ([Turin]: Giulio Einaudi, 1955).

Aquinas, St. Thomas. *The "Summa Theologica" of St. Thomas Aquinas: Third Part (Supplement) QQ LXXXVI-XCIC and Appendices*, literally translated by Fathers of the English Dominican Province (New York: Benziger Brothers, 1922).

Aristotle. *Meteorologica*, with an English translation by H. D. P. Lee (Loeb Classical Library; Cambridge, Mass.: Harvard University Press, 1952).

—. Problems I, Books I-XXI, with an English translation by W. S. Hett (rev. ed.; London: W. Heinemann, 1953).

Arnold, Sir Thomas and Guillaume, Alfred. (eds.) *The Legacy of Islam*. (London: Oxford University Press, 1931).

Atkinson, Charles Francis. (tr.) *The Decline of the West*. (New York: Alfred A. Knopf, 1947).

Atkinson, E. (tr.) *Popular Lectures on Scientific Subjects*. [by Helmholtz] (New York: D. Appleton, 1873).

Averroës. *Aristotelis opera cum Averrois commentariis* (1562; reprinted Frankfurt-am-Main: Minerva G.m.b.H., 1962).

Babbitt, F. C. (tr.) *Plutarch's Moralia* (London: W. Heinemann, 1936).

Bachelard, G. *L'air et les songes: essai sur l'imagination du mouvement* (Paris: J. Corti, 1943).

Bacon, Francis. *The New Organon and Related Writings*, edited by Fulton H. Anderson (New York: Liberal Arts Press, 1960).

Bacon, Roger. See Bridges.

Bailey, Cyril. (tr.) *Epicurus: The Extant Remains*, with short critical apparatus, translation and notes by Cyril Bailey (Oxford: Clarendon Press, 1926).

Barach Carl S. and Wrobel, Johann. (eds.) *Bernardi Silvestris De mundi universitate libri duo sive megacosmus et microcosmus*. (Innsbruck: Wagner, 1876).

Barraclough, June. (tr.) *Sketch for a Historical Picture of the Progress of the Human Mind* [by Condorcet] (New York: The Noonday Press, 1955).

Baudin, Louis. *A Socialist Empire: The Incas of Peru*, translated from the French by Katherine Woods, edited by Arthur Goddard (Princeton, N.J.: Van Nostrand, 1961).

[BBC] *Rival Theories of Cosmology* (London: Oxford University Press, 1960). [text of a Symposium broadcast by the BBC in 1959]

Benedetti. *De coelo et elementis liber*. Joanne Benedicto Tiernaviense auctore. Ad Franciscum Vrbinatum Ducem Sereniss. (Ferrara: excudebat Victorius Baldinus, 1591, 48ff in 12°). [Included here, but SLJ implies his authorship is uncertain.]

—. *Io, Baptistae Benedicti... Diversorum speculationum mathematicarum et physicarum liber* (Turin: Haer. Nic. Bevilacquae, 1585).

Bergstrasser, G. *Hunain ibn Ishaq über die syrischen und arabischen Galen-Übersetzungen* (Leipzig: F. A. Brockhaus, 1925).

Bernard, H. *Matteo Ricci's Scientific Contribution to China*, translated from the French by E. C. Werner (Peiking: H. Vetch, 1935).

Bettray, J. *Die Akkommodationsmethode des P. Matteo Ricci S.J. in China* (Rome: Gregorian University, 1955).

Bevan, Edwyn R. and Singer, Charles. (eds.) *The Legacy of Israel*, a collection of essays edited by Edwyn R. Bevan and Charles Singer (Oxford: Clarendon Press 1928).

Bhattacharyya, Haridas (ed.), *The Cultural Heritage of India*, Vol. III. *The Philosophies* (2d rev. ed.; Calcutta: The Ramakrishna Mission, 1953).

Blanqui, Louis Auguste. *L'éternité par les astres*. (Paris: Librairie Germer Baillière, 1872).

Bliemetzrieder, F. *Adelhard von Bath* (Munich: Max Huber, 1935).

Boas, M. *The Scientific Renaissance 1450-1630* (New York: Harper & Brothers, 1962).

Bodin. *Universae naturae theatrum*. (Frankfurt: apud heredes A. Wecheli, C. Marnium, 1597).

—. Also see Chauviré.

Boehm, Walter. (ed.) *Johannes Philoponus: Grammatikos von Alexandrien* (Munich: Verlag Ferdinand Schöningh, 1967).

Bolman, Jr., Frederick de Wolfe. (tr.) *The Ages of the World*. [by Schelling] (New York: Columbia University Press, 1942).

Boltzmann. *Lectures on Gas Theory*. Translated by S. G. Brush (Berkeley: University of California Press, 1964).

—. *Populäre Schriften*. (Leipzig: J. A. Barth, 1905).

Boman, Thorlief. *Hebrew Thought Compared with Greek*, translated from the German by J. L. Moreau (London: SCM Press, 1960).

Bondi, H. *Cosmology* (Cambridge: Cambridge University Press, 1952).

Borel, E. *Space and Time* (London: Blackie and Son, 1926).

Borgnet, S. C. A. (ed.) *Opera omnia*. [by St. Albertus Magnus] (Paris: L. Vives, 1895).

Bossuet. *Discours sur l'histoire universelle*. (Paris: Emler Frères, Libraires, 1829).

Bowditch, Charles P. *The Numeration, Calendar Systems and Astronomical Knowledge of the Mayas* (Cambridge: University Press, 1910).

Boyle, Robert. *The Works of the Honourable Robert Boyle*. (new ed.; London 1772).

Breasted, James H. *Development of Religion and Thought in Ancient Egypt* (New York: Charles Scribner's Sons, 1912).

—. *The Edwin Smith Surgical Papyrus* (Chicago: University of Chicago Press, 1930).

Brennand, W. *Hindu Astronomy*. (London: Chas. Straker & Sons, Ltd., 1896).

Bridges, John H. (ed.) *The 'Opus Majus' of Roger Bacon*, edited with an introduction and analytical tables by John H. Bridges. (Oxford: Clarendon Press, 1897).

[British Association] *British Association for the Advancement of Science: Report of the Centenary Meeting: London, 1931, September 23-30.* (London: Office of the British Association, 1932).

Brundage, Burr C. *Empire of the Inca* (Norman: University of Oklahoma Press, 1963).

Bruno, Giordano. *Jordani Bruni Nolani Opera latine conscripta* (Naples-Florence: Morano-LeMonnier, 1879-91).

Also see Aquilecchia, Greenburg, Imerti, Singer, Williams.

Brunschvig R. and von Grunebaum, G. E. (eds.), *Classicisme et déclin culturel dans l'histoire de l'Islam: Actes du Symposium International d'Histoire de la Civilisation Musulmane (Bordeaux 25-29 Juin 1956)* (Paris: Éditions Besson-Chantemerle, 1957).

Brush, S. G. *Lectures on Gas Theory.* [by Boltzmann] (Berkeley: University of California Press, 1964).

Budge, Sir E. A. Wallis. *From Fetish to God in Ancient Egypt* (London: Oxford University Press, 1934).

Burckhardt, J. *Die Kultur der Renaissance in Italien* (Leipzig: Seemann, 1860).

Bury, J. B. *The Idea of Progress: An Inquiry into Its Origin and Growth* (London: Macmillan, 1920).

Butler, A. J. (tr.) *The Paradise of Dante Alighieri*, edited with translation and notes by A. J. Butler (London: Macmillan, 1891).

Butterfield H. *The Origins of Modern Science* (London: Bell, 1949).

Butterworth, G. W. (tr.) *Clement of Alexandria* with an English translation by G. W. Butterworth (London: W. Heinemann, 1919).

—. (tr.) *Origen on First Principles*, translated into English, together with an introduction and notes by G. W. Butterworth (London: Society for Promoting Christian Knowledge, 1936).

Carus, P. *The Gospel of Buddha according to Old Records.* (6th ed.; Chicago: The Open Court Publishing Co., 1898).

Caso, A. *La religión de los Aztecas* (Mexico City: Enciclopedia Illustrada Mexicana, 1936).

Cassirer, E. *The Individual and the Cosmos in Renaissance Philosophy*, translated with an Introduction by Mario Domandi (New York: Barnes & Noble Inc., 1963).

Caster, M. (tr.) *Les Stromates*, introduction by C. Mondésert, translation and notes by M. Caster (Paris: Éditions du Cerf, 1951).

[Centre National...] *Leonard de Vinci et l'expérience scientifique au XVIe siècle, Paris, 4-7 juillet 1952* (Paris: Centre National de la Recherche Scientifique, 1953).

Chace, Arnold Buffum. *The Rhind Mathematical Papyrus*, Vol. I, Free Translation and Commentary by Arnold Buffum Chace (Oberlin, Ohio: Mathematical Association of America, 1927).

Chadwick, H. (tr.) *Origen: Contra Celsum*, translated with an introduction and notes by H. Chadwick (Cambridge: The University Press, 1965). [also cited as 1953]

Chan, Wing-Tsit. *A Source Book in Chinese Philosophy*, translated and compiled by Wing-Tsit Chan (Princeton: Princeton University Press, 1963).

Chauviré, R. (tr.) *Colloque de Jean Bodin des secrets cachez des choses sublimes entre sept sçavans qui sont de différens sentimens* [*Colloquium heptaplomeres* by Bodin] (Paris: L. Tenin, 1914).

Chevalier, J. (ed.) *OEuvres complètes*, [by Pascal] (Paris: Bibliothèque de la Pléiade, Éditions Gallimard, 1954).

Clagett, M. (ed.) *Nicole Oresme and the Medieval Geometry of Qualities and Motions* (Madison: University of Wisconsin Press, 1968).

—. *The Science of Mechanics in the Middle Ages* (Madison: University of Wisconsin Press, 1959).

Clark, R. T. Rundle. *Myth and Symbol in Ancient Egypt* (London: Thames & Hudson, 1959).

Clark, W. E. *The Aryabhatiya of Aryabhata: An Ancient Indian Work on Mathematics and Astronomy* (Chicago: University of Chicago Press, 1930).

Clarke, John. *Physical Science in the Time of Nero, Being a Translation of the Quaestiones naturales of Seneca*. (London: Macmillan, 1910).

Cochrane, Charles N. *Christianity and Classical Culture: A Study of Thought and Action from Augustus to Augustine* (rev. ed.; Oxford University Press, 1944).

Condorcet. See Barraclough.

Coopland, G. W. (tr.) *Nicole Oresme and the Astrologers: A Study of his Livre de divinacions* (Liverpool: University Press, 1952).

Couderc, P. *L'astrologie* (Paris: Presses Universitaires Françaises, 1951).

Cousin, M. V. *Fragments philosophiques*. (5th ed.; Paris: Didier, 1865-66).

Crombie, A. C. *From Augustine to Galileo: The History of Science A.D. 400-1650* (London: Falcon Press, 1952).

—. *Medieval and Early Modern Science* (Garden City, N.Y.: Doubleday, 1959).

—. *Robert Grosseteste and the Origins of Experimental Science 1100-1700* (Oxford: Clarendon Press, 1953).

Crump, C. G. and Jacob, E. F. (eds.) *The Legacy of the Middle Ages*. (Oxford: Clarendon Press, 1926).

Cusanus. See Nicolas de Cusa.

Darwin, F. *The Life and Letters of Charles Darwin* (London: Murray, 1888).

Datta, B. and Singh, A. N. *History of Hindu Mathematics: A Source Book* (new ed.; Bombay: Asia Publishing House, 1962).

Dauvillier, A. *Les hypothèses cosmogoniques: théorie des cycles cosmiques et des planètes jumelles* (Paris: Masson & Cie, 1963).

Davies, P. *The Runaway Universe* (New York: Harper & Row, 1978).

Davies, P. C. W. *The Physics of Time Asymmetry* (Berkeley: University of California Press, 1974).

Dawson, R. (ed.) *The Legacy of China*. (Oxford: Clarendon Press, 1964).

de Gortari, Eli. *La ciencia en la historia de México*. (Mexico: Fondo de la Cultura Económica, 1963).

de Groot, J. J. M. *Religion in China: Universism, a Key to the Study of Taoism and Confucianism* (New York: G. P. Putnam's Sons, 1912).

—. *Sectarianism and Religious Persecution in China* (Amsterdam: J. Müller, 1903-04; reprinted in 1940).

de Sahagún, Friar Bernardino. *Historia general de las cosas de Nueva España* (Editorial Nueva España S.A.: Mexico, 1946).

De Sitter. *Kosmos* (Cambridge, Mass.: Harvard University Press, 1932).

del Castillo, Bernal Díaz. *Historia verdadera de la conquista de Nueva España* (Ediciones Mexicanas S.A.: Mexico, 1950).

D'Elia, Pasquale M. *Galileo in Cina: Relazioni attraverso il Collegio Romano tra Galileo e i gesuiti scienzati missionari in Cina (1610-1640)* (Rome: Gregorian University, 1947).

Derenbourg H. *et al.*, *Morgenländische Forschungen: Festschrift Herrn Professor Dr. H. L. Fleischer zu seinem fünfzigjährigen Doctorjubiläum am 4. März 1874* (Leipzig: F. A. Brockhaus, 1875).

Descartes, René. See Adam.

Diacceto. *Opera omnia.* (Basel: per Henricum Petri et Petrum Pernam, 1563).

Diego de Zuñiga. [Didacus de Stunica] *Didaci a Stunica Salmanticensis Eremitae Augustiniani in Job commentaria...* (Toledo: per Ioannem Rodericum, 1584).

Diels, H. *Die Fragmente der Vorsokratiker griechisch und deutsch*, edited by W. Kranz (Dublin/Zurich: Weidmann, 1968).

—. *Simplicii* in *Aristotelis Physicorum libros quattuor posteriores commentaria*, ed. by H. Diels (Berlin: G. Reimer, 1895).

Dieterici, F. *Die Naturanschauung und Naturphilosophie der Araber im zehnten Jahrhundert: Aus den Schriften der lautern Brüder* (Berlin: Verlag der Nicolai'schen Sort.-Buchhandlung, 1861).

Dieterici, F. H. *Die sogennante Theologie des Aristoteles* (Leipzig: J. C. Hinrichs, 1883).

Dikshit, Sankar Balakrishan. *History of Astronomy during the Vedic and Vedanga Periods.* (Calcutta: Government of India Press, 1969).

Dingle. H. *Modern Astrophysics* (New York: The Macmillan Co., 1927).

Dingler, H. *Geschichte der Naturphilosophie* (Berlin: Junker und Dünnhaupt Verlag, 1932).

Drake, Stillman. *Discoveries and Opinions of Galileo.* (Garden City, N.Y.: Doubleday, 1957).

—. (tr.) *Dialogue concerning the Two Chief World Systems – Ptolemaic and Copernican.* [by Galileo] (Berkeley: University of California Press, 1962).

— and Drabkin, I. E. (trs.) *Mechanics in Sixteenth-Century Italy: Selections from Tartaglia, Benedetti, Guido Ubaldo & Galileo*, translated and annotated by Stillman Drake and I. E. Drabkin (Madison: University of Wisconsin Press, 1969).

Draper, John William. *History of the Intellectual Development of Europe* (New York: Harper and Brothers, 1876).

Draper, W. H. (tr.) *Petrarch's Secret; or, The Soul's Conflict with Passion. Three Dialogues between Himself and S. Augustine*, translated from the Latin by W. H. Draper (London: Chatto & Windus, 1911).

Dreyer, I. L. E. (ed.) *Tychonis Brahe Danis Opera omnia*, [by Tycho Brahe] (Copenhagen: Libraria Gyldendaliana, 1916).

Dubs, Homer H. *The Works of Hsün Tzu* (London: Probsthain, 1928).

Duhem, Pierre. *Études sur Léonard de Vinci, ceux qu'il a lus et ceux qui l'ont lu*, 3 vols. (Paris: Hermann, 1906-13).

—. *Le système du monde: histoire des doctrines cosmologiques de Platon à Copernic*, 10 vols. (Paris: Hermann, 1913). [first five volumes 1913-15, last five 1954-59]

Dühring. *Cursus der Philosophie als streng wissenschaftlicher Weltanschauung und Lebensgestaltung* (Leipzig: Erich Koschny, 1875).

Dutt, Clemens. (tr.) *Dialectics of Nature.* [by Engels] Preface and notes by J. B. S. Haldane (New York: International Publishers, 1940; fourth printing, 1960).

Dutt, Manmatha Nath. (ed.) *The Mahabharata*, a prose English translation (Calcutta: H. C. Dass, Elysium Press, 1896).

Dyce, A. (ed.) *The Works of Richard Bentley.* (London: Francis Macpherson, 1838).

Eddington. *The Expanding Universe* (Cambridge: Cambridge University Press, 1932).

—. *The Nature of the Physical World* (Cambridge, Cambridge University Press, 1928).

—. *New Pathways in Science* (Cambridge: Cambridge University Press, 1934).

Edelstein, Ludwig. *The Idea of Progress in Classical Antiquity* (Baltimore, Md.: The Johns Hopkins Press, 1967).

Edwards, I. E. S. *The Pyramids of Egypt* (London: Max Parrish, 1961).

[Eerdmans Publishing] *A Select Library of Nicene and Post-Nicene Fathers of the Christian Church*. Second Series, Volume VI, *St. Jerome: Letters and Select Works* (Grand Rapids, Mich.: Wm. B. Eerdmans Publishing Company, n.d.). [But see Schaff, below]

Einstein, Albert. *Out of my Later Years* (New York: Philosophical Library, 1950).

Eliade, Mircea. *The Myth of the Eternal Return*, translated from the French by W. R. Trask (New York: Pantheon Books, 1954).

—. *Man and Time: Papers from the Eranos Yearbooks* (New York: Pantheon Books 1957).

[Encyclopedia Britannica] *Great Books of the Western World*, Vol. 16 (Chicago: Encyclopedia Britannica, 1952).

Eurich, N. *Science in Utopia: A Mighty Design* (Cambridge, Mass.: Harvard University Press, 1967).

Fakhry, Majid. *Islamic Occasionalism and Its Critique by Averroës and Aquinas* (London: George Allen & Unwin, 1958).

Farrington, B. *Greek Science: Its Meaning for Us* (Baltimore: Penguin Books, 1961).

Fichte, Johann Gottlieb. *The Popular Works of Johann Gottlieb Fichte*, translated by William Smith (4th ed.; London: Trübner & Co., 1889).

Ficino, Marsilio. *Opera omnia* (1561), reprint edition by Bottega Erasmo (Torino, 1959).

Filliozat, J. *La doctrine classique de la médecine indienne* (Paris: CNRS and Geuthner, 1949).

Forke, A. *The World-Conception of the Chinese: Their Astronomical, Cosmological and Physico-Philosophical Speculations* (London: Arthur Probsthain, 1925).

Forster, E. S. (tr.) *Aristotle, On Sophistical Refutations; On Coming-to-be and Passing-away* (Cambridge, Mass.: Harvard University Press, 1955).

Frankfort, H. *Ancient Egyptian Religion: An Interpretation* (New York: Columbia University Press, 1948).

Frankfort, H. and H.A., *et al*. *The Intellectual Adventure of Ancient Man: An Essay on Speculative Thought in the Ancient Near East*. (Chicago: University of Chicago Press, 1946).

Freeman, Kathleen. *Ancilla to the Pre-Socratic Philosophers* (Cambridge, Mass.: Harvard University Press, 1966).

Friedlander, M. (tr.) *Guide for the Perplexed*. [by Maimonides] (2d rev. ed., 1904; New York: Dover, 1956).

Fuhrman, Horst. *Schellings Philosophie der Weltalter: Schellings Philosophie in den Jahren 1806-1821. Zum Problem des Schellingschen Theismus* (Düsseldorf: Verlag L. Schwann, 1954).

Fung, Yu-Lan, *A History of Chinese Philosophy*: Vol. I, *The Period of the Philosophers*, translated by Derk Bodde (Peiping: Henri Vetch, 1937).

—. *A History of Chinese Philosophy*, Vol. II, *The Period of Classical Learning*, translated by D. Bodde (Princeton: Princeton University Press, 1953).

Gamow, G. *The Creation of the Universe* (New York: The Viking Press, 1956).

Garin, E. (ed.) *Disputationes adversus astrologiam divinatricem* [by Giovanni Pico della Mirandola] (Florence: Vallecchi, 1946).

Garratt, G. T. (ed.), *The Legacy of India* (Oxford: Clarendon Press, 1937).

Gerson, John. *Joannis Gersonii Opera omnia* (Antwerp: Sumptibus Societatis, 1706).

Gibson, R. W. *St. Thomas More: A Preliminary Bibliography of his Works and of Moreana to the Year 1750* (New Haven, Conn.: Yale University Press, 1961).

Gillispie, C. C. *The Edge of Objectivity: An Essay in the History of Scientific Ideas* (Princeton, N.J.: Princeton University Press, 1960).

Gilson, E. *History of Christian Philosophy in the Middle Ages* (New York: Random House, 1955).

—.*René Descartes' Discours de la méthode: Texte et commentaire.* (Paris: J. Vrin, 1925).

Glanville, S. R. K. (ed.) *The Legacy of Egypt.* (Oxford: Clarendon Press 1942).

Glockner, H. (compiler) *Hegel-Lexicon.* (Stuttgart: Fr. Frommanns Verlag, 1938).

Godley, A. D. (tr.) *Herodotus* with an English translation by A. D. Godley (London: William Heinemann, 1926).

Granet, M. *La pensée chinoise* (Paris: La Renaissance du Livre, 1934).

Granger, F. (tr.) *On Architecture* [by Vitruvius] Text and English translation by F. Granger (Cambridge, Mass.: Harvard University Press, 1962).

Grant, Edward. (ed.) *De proportionibus proportionum and Ad pauca respicientes,* [by Nicole Oresme] edited with introductions, English translations, and critical notes by Edward Grant (Madison: University of Wisconsin Press, 1966).

Greenburg, S. *The Infinite in Giordano Bruno with a Translation of his Dialogue "Concerning the Cause, Principle, and One"* [*De la causa, principio et uno*] (New York: King's Crown Press, 1950).

Greenhill, William A. *A Treatise on the Small-Pox and Measles.* (London: Printed for the Sydenham Society, 1848).

Griffith, R. T. H. (tr.) *The Hymns of the Atharua-Veda,* translated with a popular commentary by R.T.H.Griffith (2d ed.; Benares, India: E. J. Lazarus, 1917).

—. *The Hymns of the Rgveda,* translated with a popular commentary by R. T. H. Griffith (Varanasi-1, India: The Chwokhamba Sanskrit Series Office, 1963).

Grosseteste, Robert. *Opera omnia* (Paris: apud L. Billaine, 1674).

Gulick, Charles Burton. (tr.) *Athenaeus, The Deipnosophists,* with an English translation by Charles Burton Gulick (London: W. Heinemann, 1955).

Guyau, M. *Esquisse d'une morale sans obligation, ni sanction* (4th ed.; Paris: Felix Alcan 1896).

—. *Vers d'un philosophe.* (Paris: Librairie Germer Baillière, 1881).

Haines, C. R. (tr.) *The Communings with Himself of Marcus Aurelius Emperor of Rome together with His Speeches and Sayings,* revised text and a translation into English by C. R. Haines (London W. Heinemann, 1916).

Haldane, E. S. and Ross, G. R. T. *The Philosophical Works of Descartes.* (rev. ed.; Cambridge: Cambridge University Press, 1931).

Hamilton, E. and Cairns, H. (eds.) *The Collected Dialogues of Plato,* edited by E. Hamilton and H. Cairns (New York: Pantheon Books, 1963).

Hamilton, Sir William. (ed.) *The Collected Works of Dugald Stewart.* (Edinburgh: Thomas Constable, 1854).

Hartmann, L. T. (ed.) *Encyclopedic Dictionary of the Bible* (A Translation and Adaptation of A. van den Born's *Bijbels Woordenboek,* Second Revised Edition 1954-57), edited by L. T. Hartmann (New York: McGraw-Hill Book Company, 1963).

Hastie, W. *Kant's Cosmogony* (Glasgow: James Maclehose and Sons, 1900).

Hastings, J. (ed.) *Encyclopaedia of Religion and Ethics*. (New York: Charles Scribner's Sons, 1908).

Hawking, S. W. and Israel, W.(eds.), *General Relativity: An Einstein Centenary Survey* (New York: Cambridge University Press, 1979).

Heath, Sir Thomas. *Aristarchus of Samos the Ancient Copernicus* (Oxford: Clarendon Press, 1913).

Heiberg. I. L. (ed.) *In Aristotelis de Caelo commentaria* [by Simplicius] (Berlin: G. Reimer, 1894).

Heidel, Alexander. *The Babylonian Genesis: The Story of Creation* (Chicago: University of Chicago Press, 1942).

Heine, Heinrich. *Letzte Gedichte und Gedenken von H. Heine*. (Hamburg, 1869).

—. *Heinrich Heines Sämtliche Werke*, edited by E. Elster (Leipzig: Bibliographisches Institut, n.d.).

Helmholtz. See Atkinson.

Henke, Frederick G. *The Philosophy of Wang Yang-Ming*. (Chicago: Open Court, 1916).

Heron, G. (tr.) *Of Learned Ignorance*, [*De docta ignorantia* by Nicolas of Cusa] with an Introduction by D. J. B. Hawkins (London: Routledge & Kegan Paul, 1954).

Herzfeld, E. *Zoroaster and his World*. (Princeton, N.J.: Princeton University Press, 1947).

Hispalensis, Joannes. *Albumasar de magnis conjunctionibus, annorum revolutionibus ac eorum profectionibus, octo continens tractatus*. (Augsburg: E. Ratdolt, 1489).

Hitti, P. K. *History of the Arabs from the earliest Times to the Present* (1937; 8th ed.; London: Macmillan, 1963).

Hogrefe, P. *The Sir Thomas More Circle: A Program of Ideas and their Impact on Secular Drama* (Urbana: University of Illinois Press, 1959).

Hölderlin. *Hölderlin: Sämtliche Werke*. (Stuttgart: W. Kohlhammer, 1961).

Hope, Richard. (tr.) *Aristotle's Physics* (Lincoln: University of Nebraska Press, 1961).

Hoyle, Sir Fred and Wickramasinghe, Chandra. *Evolution from Space: A Theory of Cosmic Creationism*. (New York: Simon and Schuster, 1981).

Hultsch, F. (ed.) *De die natali* [by Censorinus] (Leipzig: B. G. Teubner, 1867).

Hume, David. See Aiken.

Hume, R. E. (tr.) *Thirteen Principal Upanishads*, translated from the Sanskrit by R. E. Hume (2d rev. ed.; London: Oxford University Press, 1934).

Imerti A. D. (tr.) *The Expulsion of the Triumphant Beast* [*Spaccio de la bestia trionfante* by Giordano Bruno] (New Brunswick, N.J.: Rutgers University Press, 1964).

Jaki. S. L. *Chance or Reality and Other Essays* (Lanham, Md. and London: University Press of America; Bryn Mawr, Pa.: The Intercollegiate Studies Inc., 1986).

—. *Cosmos and Creator* (Edinburgh: Scottish Academic Press; Chicago: Regnery-Gateway, 1980).

—. *Immanuel Kant. Universal Natural History and Theory of the Heavens*. (Edinburgh: Scottish Academic Press, 1981).

—. *J. H. Lambert. Cosmological Letters on the Arrangement of the World-Edifice*. (New York: Science History Publications; Edinburgh: Scottish Academic Press, 1976).

—. *The Milky Way: An Elusive Road for Science* (New York: Science History Publications, 1972).

—. *The Paradox of Olbers' Paradox* (New York: Herder & Herder, 1969).

—. *Planets and Planetarians: A History of Theories of the Origin of Planetary Systems.* (Edinburgh: Scottish Academic Press; New York: The Halstead Press of John Wiley Inc., 1978).

—. *The Relevance of Physics* (Chicago: The University of Chicago Press, 1966).

—. *The Road of Science and the Ways of to God* (Chicago: University of Chicago Press, 1978).

—. *Uneasy Genius: The Life and Work of Pierre Duhem* (Dordrecht, London, Boston: Martinus Nijhoff, 1984).

Jastrow, M. *The Religion of Babylonia and Assyria* (Boston: Ginn and Co., 1898).

Jeannin, M. (ed.) *Homélies et discours sur la Genèse* in *OEvres complètes*, edited by M. Jeannin (Bar-Le-Duc: L. Guérin, 1863-67).

Johnson, F. R. *Astronomical Thought in Renaissance England: A Study of the English Scientific Writings from 1500 to 1645* (Baltimore: The Johns Hopkins Press, 1937).

Johnson, R. S. *More's Utopia: Ideal and Illusion* (New Haven, Conn.: Yale University Press, 1969).

Jones, W. H. S. (tr.) *Hippocrates* with an English translation by W. H. S. Jones (London: Heinemann, 1923).

Jourdain, P. E. B. (tr.) *History and Root of the Principle of the Conservation of Energy.* [by Mach] (Chicago: Open Court, 1911).

Jowett, B. (tr.) *The Politics of Aristotle*, translated by B. Jowett (Oxford: Clarendon Press, 1885).

Kalbfleisch, K. (ed.) *Simplicii in Aristotelis categorias commentarium*, edited by K. Kalbfleisch (Berlin: G. Reimer, 1907).

Kamali, Sabih Ahmad. (tr.) *Tahafut al-falasifah* (Lahore: The Pakistan Philosophical Congress, 1958). [This title means "Incoherence of the Philosophers"]

Kant, Immanuel. *Cosmologische Briefe über die Einrichtung des Weltbaues* (Augsburg: Eberhart Kletts Wittib., 1761). [See Jaki for an English translation of this book with extensive notes and commentary]

Kasir, Daoud S. (tr.) *The Algebra of Omar Khayyam.* (New York: Columbia University, 1931).

Kaufmann, W. A. *Nietzsche: Philosopher, Psychologist, Antichrist.* (Princeton, N.J.: Princeton University Press, 1950).

Kautsky, Karl. *Thomas More and his Utopia* (New York: Russel & Russell, 1959).

Kaye, G. R. (tr. & ed.) *The Bakshali Manuscript: A Study in Medieval Mathematics* (Archaeological Survey of India. New Imperial Series. Vol. XLIII. Parts I & II – Calcutta: Government of India Central Publication Branch, 1927).

—. *Indian Mathematics* (Calcutta & Simla: Thacker, Spink & Co., 1915).

Kelvin. *Mathematical and Physical Papers* (Cambridge: Cambridge University Press, 1882).

—. *Popular Lectures and Addresses* (London: Macmillan, 1891).

Kepler, Johannes. *Gesammelte Werke* (München: C. H. Beck, 1938).

Kirk, G. S. (ed.) Heraclitus, *The Cosmic Fragments*, edited with an introduction and commentary by G. S. Kirk (Cambridge: The University Press, 1954).

Koestler, A. *The Sleepwalkers: A History of Man's Changing Vision of the Universe* (New York: Macmillan, 1959).

Krebs, H. A. & Shelley, J. H. (eds.), *The Creative Process in Science and Medicine: Proceedings of the C. H. Bohringer Sohn Symposium, held at Kronberg, Taunus, 10-17 May, 1974* (Amsterdam: Excerpta Medica, 1975).

Kristeller, P. O. *The Philosophy of Marsilio Ficino* translated into English by Virginia Conant (New York: Columbia University Press, 1943).

Kristeller, P. O. and Wiener, P. P. (eds). *Renaissance Essays*. (New York: Harper & Row, 1968).

Kulkarni, Chidambra. *Ancient Indian History and Culture*. (Bombay: Karnatak Publishing House, 1966).

Lake, Kirsopp. (tr.) *The Apostolic Fathers* with an English translation by Kirsopp Lake (London: William Heinemann, 1912).

Lambert, J. H. *Cosmologische Briefe über die Einrichtung des Weltbaues* (Augsburg: Eberhart Kletts Wittib., 1761). [See Jaki for an English translation of this book with extensive notes and commentary]

Lange, F. A. *The History of Materialism* (2d ed., 1873), translated by E. C. Thomas (New York: The Humanities Press, 1950).

Laplace. *Exposition du système du monde*. Fifth edition. (Paris: Bachelier, 1824).

Le Bon, Gustave. *La vie des vérités* (Paris: Flammarion, 1925).

—. *L'évolution de la matière* (Paris, Flammarion, 1908).

—. *L'évolution des forces* (Paris: Flammarion, 1912).

—. *L'homme et les sociétés* (Paris: J. Rotschild, 1881).

Le Gall, Stanislas. (tr.) *Le Philosophe Tchou Hi, sa doctrine, son influence* (2d ed; Chang-Hai [Shanghai]: Imprimerie de la Mission Catholique, 1923).

Lea, F. A. *The Tragic Philosopher: A Study of Friedrich Nietzsche* (London: Methuen, 1957).

Legge, J. (tr.) *The Chinese Classics* (3rd ed.; Hong Kong University Press, 1960).

—. *The Texts of Taoism*, translated by T. Legge, with an Introduction by D. T. Suzuki (New York: Julian Press, 1959).

Lemaître. *L'hypothèse de l'atome primitf: essai de cosmogonie* (Neuchâtel: Du Griffon, 1946).

Lenoble, R. *Mersenne ou la naissance du mécanisme*. (Paris: J. Vrin, 1943).

Leonardo. See MacCurdy and Centre.

León-Portilla, Miguel. *Aztec Thought and Culture: A Study of the Ancient Nahuatl Mind*, translated from the Spanish by Jack Emory Davis (Norman: University of Oklahoma Press, 1963).

Lerner R. and Mahdi, M. (eds.), *Medieval Political Philosophy: A Sourcebook* (New York: The Free Press of Glencoe, 1963).

Levey, M. *Chemistry and Chemical Technology in Ancient Mesopotamia* (London: Elsevier Publishing Co., 1959).

Levy, Dr. Oscar. (ed.) *The Complete Works of Friedrich Nietzsche*. (Edinburgh: T. N. Foulis, 1909-11).

Levy-Bruhl, L. *Les fonctions mentales dans les sociétés inférieures* (Paris: Félix Alcan, 1910).

Lewis, Austin. (tr.) *Landmarks of Scientific Socialism: "Anti-Dühring"* (Chicago: Charles Kerr & Co., 1907).

Lipsius. *Iusti Lipsi Opera omnia* (Vesaliae: Typis Andreae ab Hoogenhuysen, 1675).

Little, A. G. (ed.) *Roger Bacon: Essays Contributed by Various Writers on the Occasion of the Seventh Centenary of his Birth*, collected and edited by A. G. Little (Oxford: Clarendon Press, 1914).

Locke, L. Leland. *The Ancient Quipu or Peruvian Knot Record* (New York: The American Museum of Natural History, 1923).

Longair, M. S. (ed.), *Confrontation of Cosmological Theories with Observational Data* (Dordrecht: D. Reidel, 1974).

Lovejoy, A. O. and Boas, G. *Primitivism and Related Ideas in Antiquity*, with supplementary essays by W. F. Albright and P. E. Dumont (New York: Octagon Books, 1965).

Löwith, K. *Meaning of History* (Chicago: University of Chicago Press, 1949).

——. *Nietzsches Philosophie der ewigen Wiederkunft des Gleichen* (Berlin: Verlag Die Runde, 1935).

Lubbock, C. A. *The Herschel Chronicle* (Cambridge: University Press, 1933).

Lupton, J. H. (ed.) *The Utopia of Sir Thomas More*, with introduction and notes (Oxford: Clarendon Press, 1895).

MacCurdy, E. (tr.) *The Mind of Leonardo da Vinci* (New York: Dodd, Mead & Co., 1928).

——. *The Notebooks of Leonardo de Vinci*, arranged, rendered into English and introduced by E. MacCurdy (Garden City, N.Y.: Garden City Publishing Company, 1941).

MacDonald, D. B. *The Hebrew Philosophical Genius: A Vindication* (Princeton, N.J.: Princeton University Press, 1936); (New York: Russel and Russel, 1965).

Mach, E. *Die Geschichte und die Wurzel des Satzes von der Erhaltung der Arbeit* (Prague: Calve, 1872).

——. *History and Root of the Principle of the Conservation of Energy*, translated by P. E. B. Jourdain (Chicago: Open Court, 1911).

Maier, A. *Zwei Grundprobleme der scholastischen Naturphilosophie: Das Problem der intensiven Grösse. Die Impetustheorie* (2d ed.; Rome: Edizioni di Storia e Letteratura, 1951).

Mandonnet, P. *Siger de Brabant et l'averroïsme latin au XIIIe siècle, Ire Partie, Étude critique, IIe Partie, Textes inédits* (2d rev. ed.; Louvain: Institut Supérieur de Philosophie de l'Université, 1908-11).

Manitius, C. (tr.) *Gemini Elementa astronomiae*, Greek text with German translation and notes by C. Manitius (Leipzig: B. G. Teubner, 1898).

Manuel, F. E. *A Portrait of Isaac Newton*. (Cambridge, Mass.: The Belknap Press of Harvard University Press, 1968).

Marchant, E. C. (tr.) *Xenophon, Memorabilia and Oeconomicus*, with an English translation by E. C. Marchant (London: W. Heinemann, 1923).

Markham, Sir Clement R. *The Incas of Peru*. (London: Smith, Elder and Co., 1910).

Maxwell, J. C. *The Scientific Papers of James Clerk Maxwell*, edited by W. D. Niven (Cambridge: Cambridge University Press, 1890).

——. *Theory of Heat*. Third edition. (London: Longmans, Green & Co., 1872).

Mayer, Eduard. *Aegyptische Chronologie* (Berlin: G. Reimer, 1904).

Mei, Yi-Pao. *Motse: The Neglected Rival of Confucius* (London: Arthur Probstham, 1934).

Menut, Albert D. (tr. & ed.) and Denomy, Alexander J. (ed.) *Le Livre du ciel et du monde*. [by Nicole Oresme] (Madison: University of Wisconsin Press, 1968).

Mersenne, Marin. *Quaestiones celeberrimae in Genesim*. (Paris: sumptibus Sebastiani Cramoisy, 1623).

——. *Questions rares et curieuses* (Paris: chez Pierre Billaine, MDCXXX). [Originally published in 1624 as *L'impiété des déistes, athées et libertins de ce temps*.]

Métraux, G. S. and Gouzet, F. (eds.) *The Evolution of Science* (New York: The New American Library, 1963).

Meyerhof, Max. (ed. & tr.) *The Book of the Ten Treatises on the Eye*. (Cairo: Government Press, 1928).

Michel, Paul-Henri. *La cosmologie de Giordano Bruno* (Paris: Hermann, 1962).

Michelmore, P. *Einstein: Profile of the Man* (New York: Dodd, Mead & Co., 1962).

Mieli, Aldo. *La science arabe et son rôle dans l'évolution scientifique mondiale.* (Leiden: E. J. Brill, 1966). [Originally published in 1938 and recently reprinted with a new bibliography and analytical index prepared by A. Mazahéri]

Mieneke, A. (ed.) *Eclogarum physicarum et ethicarum libri duo* [by Joannes Stobaeus] (Leipzig: B. G. Teubner, 1860).

Millar, W. J. (ed.) *Miscellaneous Scientific Papers*, [by Rankine] (London: Charles Griffin & Co., 1891).

Millikan. *Science and the New Civilization* (New York: Charles Scribner's Sons, 1930).

Milne, E. A. *Relativity, Gravitation and World-Structure.* (Oxford: Clarendon Press, 1935).

Mittasch, A. *Friedrich Nietzsche als Naturphilosoph* (Stuttgart: Alfred Kröner Verlag, 1952).

Monod, Victor. *Dieu dans l'univers.* (Paris: Librairie Fischbacher, 1933).

Montet, Pierre. *Eternal Egypt*, translated from the French by D. Weightman (New York: The New American Library, 1968).

—. *Le drame d'Avaris: Essai sur la pénétration des Sémites en Égypte* (Paris: Libraire Orientaliste Paul Geuthner, 1941).

Moody, E. A. (ed.) *Quaestiones super quattuor libris de caelo et mundo* [by John Buridan on the *Quattuor libris* of St. Albertus Magnus.] (Cambridge, Mass.: The Medieval Academy of America, 1942).

More, Henry. *A Collection of Several Philosophical Writings of Dr. Henry More.* (4th ed.; London: Joseph Downing, 1712).

More, St. Thomas. See Lupton and Surtz.

Morgan Jr., G. A. *What Nietzsche Means?* (Cambridge, Mass.: Harvard University Press, 1943).

Morley, Sylvanus G. *The Ancient Maya.* (Stanford, Calif.: Stanford University Press, 1946).

Motte, A. (tr.) Cajori, F. (rev.) *Principia or Mathematical Principles of Natural Philosophy* [by Isaac Newton] (Berkeley: University of California Press, 1960).

Muckle, J. T. (ed.) *Algazel's Metaphysics: A Medieval Translation.* (Toronto: St. Michaels' College, 1933).

Mugler, Charles. *Deux thèmes de la cosmologie grecque: devenir cyclique et pluralité des mondes* (Paris: Librairie C. Klincksieck, 1953).

Myrdal, Gunnar. *Asian Drama: An Inquiry into the Poverty of Nations* (New York: The Twentieth Century Fund, 1968).

Nallino, Maria. (ed.) *Raccolta di scritti editi e inediti.* vol. V. *Astrologia, Astronomia, Geografia* (Rome: Istituto per l'Oriente, 1944).

Nasr, Seyyed Hossein. *An Introduction to Islamic Cosmological Doctrines: Conceptions of Nature and Methods Used for Its Study by the Ikhwan al Safa, al-Biruni and Ibn Sina.* (Cambridge, Mass.: The Belknap Press of Harvard University Press, 1964).

[National Catholic Welfare Conference] *The Proofs for the Existence of God in the Light of Modern Natural Science.* (Washington, D.C.: National Catholic Welfare Conference, 1951) . [English translation of an allocution by Pope Pius XII]

Needham, J. *et al.* *Science and Civilisation in China* (Cambridge: University Press, 1954-).

Neugebauer, O. *Astronomical Cuneiform Texts. Babylonian Ephemerides of the Seleucid Period for the Motion of the Sun, the Moon, and the Planets* (London: Lund Humphries, 1955).

—. *The Exact Sciences in Antiquity* (2d ed.; Providence, R.I.: Brown University Press, 1957).

Neugebauer O. and Parker, R. A. *Egyptian Astronomical Texts*, Vol. I. *The Decans* (Providence, R.I.: Brown University Press, 1960).

—. Vol. II, *The Ramesside Star Clocks* (1964).

Newman, J. H. *The Idea of a University Defined and Illustrated* (8th ed.; London: Longmans, Green and Co., 1888).

Newton, Isaac. *Opticks* (New York: Dover, 1952).

—. See Motte.

Nicolas de Cusa. [Cusanus] *Nicolai de Cusa Opera omnia* (Leipzig: Felix Meiner, 1937).

—. Also see Heron.

Nietzsche, Friedrich. See Levy.

Niven, W. D. (ed.) *The Scientific Papers of James Clerk Maxwell*. (Cambridge: Cambridge University Press, 1890).

Nordenskiöld, Erland. *The Secret of the Peruvian Quipus*. Comparative Ethnographical Studies. Göteborg Museum. Vol. VI, Part I (Göteborg: 1925).

Öpik, E. J. *The Oscillating Universe* (New York: The New American Library, 1960).

Parker, R. A. *The Calendars of Ancient Egypt* (The Oriental Institute of the University of Chicago. Studies in Ancient Oriental Civilization, No. 26; Chicago: University of Chicago Press, 1950).

Parrot, A. *Ziggurats et Tour de Babel* (Paris: Albin Michel, 1949).

Pascal, Blaise. *OEuvres complètes*, edited by J. Chevalier (Paris: Bibliothèque de la Pléiade, Éditions Gallimard, 1954).

Peet, T. Eric. (tr.) *The Rhind Mathematical Papyrus*, Introduction, transcription, translation, and commentary by T. Eric Peet (Liverpool: University of Liverpool Press, 1923).

Péronne *et al.* (eds.) *OEvres complètes de Saint Augustin*. (Paris: Librairie de Louis Vives, 1873).

Perrier, J. (ed.) *Opuscula omnia necnon opera minora*. [by St. Thomas Aquinas] (Paris: P. Lethielleux, 1949).

Perrin, B. (tr.) *Plutarch's Lives* with an English translation by B. Perrin (London: W. Heinemann, 1955).

Piankoff, Alexandre. *The Shrines of Tut-Ankh-Amon* (New York: Pantheon Books, 1955).

Pico della Mirandola, Giovanni. *On the Dignity of Man*, translated by Charles G. Wallis (Indianapolis: The Library of Liberal Arts, 1965).

Pines, Salomon. *Beiträge zur islamischen Atomlehre* (Gräfenhainichen: A. Heine, 1936).

Prescott, William A. *History of the Conquest of Mexico* (8th ed.; New York: Harper & Brothers, 1851).

Rabe, H. (ed.) *De aeternitate mundi contra Proclum*. [by Philoponus] (Leipzig: B. G. Teubner, 1899).

Rackham, H. (tr.) *Pliny, Natural History* with an English translation by H. Rackham (Cambridge, Mass.: Harvard University Press, 1938).

Randall Jr.. J. H. *The School of Padua and the emergence of Modern Science* (Turin: Editrice Antenore, 1961).

Rankine. *Miscellaneous Scientific Papers*, edited by W. J. Millar (London: Charles Griffin & Co., 1891).

Ray, John. *Three Physico-Theological Discourses.* 3rd edition. (London: W. Innys, 1713).

Ray, Praphulla Chandra. *A History of Hindu Chemistry from the Earliest Times to the Middle of the Sixteenth Century A.D.* (London: Williams and Norgate, 1902-09).

Reichardt, G. (ed.) *De opificio mundi* [by Philoponus] (Leipzig: B. G. Teubner, 1897).

Renou, L. and Filliozat, J. *L'Inde classique. Manuel des études indiennes* (Paris: Imprimerie Nationale, 1953).

Rey, Abel. *La théorie de la physique chez les physiciens contemporains* (Paris: Alcan, 1907).

—. *L'énergétique et le mécanisme* (Paris: Alcan, 1907).

—. *Le retour éternel et la philosophie de la physique* (Paris: Ernest Flammarion, 1927).

Ricci, L. (tr.) *The Prince. [Il Principe* by Machiavelli] translated by L. Ricci, revised by E. R. P. Vincent, with an Introduction by C. Gauss (New York: The New American Library, 1952).

Robbins, F. E. (tr.) *Ptolemy, Tetrabiblos*, edited and translated into English by F. E. Robbins (Cambridge, Mass.: Harvard University Press, 1964).

Roberts, A. and Donaldson, J. (eds.) *The Ante-Nicene Fathers: Translations of the Writings of the Fathers down to A.D. 325*, edited by A. Roberts and J. Donaldson; American reprint of the Edinburgh edition, revised and annotated by A. Cleveland Coxe (New York: Charles Scribner's Sons, 1925).

Rosan, Laurence Jay. *The Philosophy of Proclus: The Final Phase of Ancient Thought* (New York: Cosmos, 1949).

Rosen, F. (ed. & tr.) *The Algebra of Mohammed ben Musa.* (London: Printed for the Oriental Translation Fund, 1831).

Rouse, W. H. D. (tr.) *Lucretius, De rerum natura* with an English translation by W. H. D. Rouse (Cambridge, Mass.: Harvard University Press, 1937).

Roux, Georges. *Ancient Iraq* (London: Allen & Unwin, 1964).

Roys, Ralph. L. (tr.) *The Book of Chilam Balam of Chumayel*, translated by Ralph L. Roys (new ed.; Norman: University of Oklahoma Press, 1967).

Russell, Bertrand. *The ABC of Relativity.* (New York: Harper and Brothers, 1925).

Sachau, C. E. *The Chronology of Ancient Nations: An English Version of the Arabic Text of the Athar-ul-Bakiya of Albiruni, or "Vestiges of the Past"* (London: W. H. Allen, 1879).

Sachau, Edward C. (ed.) *Alberuni's India: An Account of the Religion, Philosophy, Literature, Geography, Chronology, Astronomy, Customs, Laws and Astrology of India about A.D. 1030.* An English edition with notes and indices by Edward C. Sachau (London: Kegan Paul, Trench, Trübner & Co., 1910).

Saggs, H. W. F. *The Greatness that Was Babylon: A Sketch of the Ancient Civilization of the Tigris-Euphrates Valley* (London: Sidgwick & Jackson, 1962).

Sajó, G. (ed.) *Boetii de Dacia Tractatus de aeternitate mundi.* (new rev. ed.; Berlin: Walter de Gruyter, 1964).

Sale, George. (tr.) *The Koran; commonly called the Alkoran of Mohammed* with explanatory notes selected by F. M. Cooper (New York: A. L. Burt, n.d.).

Salisbury, Thomas. *Mathematical Collections and Translations in Two Parts. From the Original Copies of Galileus and Other Famous Modern Authors* by Tho: Salisbury, Esq.; (London: Printed by William Leybourn, for George Sawbridge, 1667).

Sambursky, S. *The Physical World of the Greeks*, (London: Routledge and Kegan Paul, 1956).

—. *The Physical World of Late Antiquity* (New York: Basic Books, 1962).

—. *Physics of the Stoics* (New York: The Macmillan Co., 1959).

Santayana, G. *Genteel Tradition at Bay* (New York: C. Scribner's Sons, 1931).

Sarkar, Benoy Kumar. *Hindu Achievements in Exact Sciences: A Study in the History of Scientific Development.* (New York: Longmans, Green and Co., 1918).

Sarton, G. *Introduction to the History of Science.* Vol. I, *From Homer to Omar Khayyam.* (Baltimore: The Williams and Wilkins Company, 1927).

Schaff, Philip. (ed.) *A Select Library of the Nicene and Post-Nicene Fathers of the Christian Church*, edited by Philip Schaff, Vol. II, *St. Augustine's City of God and Christian Doctrine* (Grand Rapids, Mich.: Wm. B. Eerdmans Publishing Company, 1956).

Schelling. *Sämmtliche Werke.* (Stuttgart: J. G. Cotta'scher Verlag, 1860).

—. See also Bolman.

Schnabel, P. *Berossos und die babylonisch-hellenistische Literatur* (Leipzig: B. G. Teubner, 1923).

Schrecker, P. and Schrecker, A. M. (trs.) *Monadology and Other Philosophical Essays.* [by Leibniz] (Indianapolis: Bobbs-Merrill Co., 1965).

Seal, Brajendranath. *The Positive Sciences of the Ancient Hindus.* (London: Longmans, Green and Co., 1915).

Séjourné, Laurette. *Burning Water: Thought and Religion in Ancient Mexico* (New York: The Vanguard Press, 1961).

Sellery, G. C. *The Renaissance: Its Nature and Origins* (Madison: University of Wisconsin Press, 1950).

Shamasastry, R. (tr.) *Kantilya's Arthasastra*, with an introductory note by Dr. J. F. Fleet (4th ed.; Mysore, India: Sri Raghuveer Printing Press, 1951).

Shapley, H. (ed.) *Source Book in Astronomy 1900-1950* (Cambridge, Mass.: Harvard University Press, 1960).

Singer, Charles, Holonyard, E. J. and Hall A. R. (eds.), *A History of Technology*, Vol. I, *From Early Times to Fall of Ancient Empires* (Oxford: Clarendon Press, 1954).

—. *A History of Technology*, Vol. II, *The Mediterranean Civilizations and the Middle Ages.* (Oxford: Clarendon Press, 1956).

Singer, Dorothea W. *Giordano Bruno: His Life and Thought, with Annotated Translation of His Work "On the Infinite Universe and Worlds"* [*De l'infinito universo et mondi*] (New York: Henry Schuman, 1950).

Smith, E. Baldwin. *Egyptian Architecture as Cultural Expression* (New York: D. Appleton Century Co., 1938).

Smith, William. (tr.) *The Popular Works of Johann Gottlieb Fichte.* (4th ed.; London: Trübner & Co., 1889).

Smyth, Charles Piazzi. *Life and Work at the Great Pyramid* (Edinburgh: Edmonston & Douglas, 1867).

—. *Our Inheritance in the Great Pyramid* (London: A. Strahan, 1864).

Sorokin, Pitirim A. *Social and Cultural Dynamics*, vol. II, *Fluctuation of Systems of Truth, Ethics, and Law*, (New York: American Book Company, 1937).

Soustelle, J. *La pensée cosmologique des Anciens Mexicains: Représentation du monde et de l'espace* (Paris: Hermann, 1940).

Spedding, J., Ellis, R. L., and Heath, D.D. (eds.) *Works of Francis Bacon*. (Boston: Taggard & Thompson, 1863).

Spencer, Herbert. *Education: Intellectual, Moral, and Physical* (New York: D. Appleton, 1889).

—. *First Principles* (3rd ed.; London: Williams and Norgate, 1870).

Spengler, O. *The Decline of the West*, translated by Charles Francis Atkinson (New York: Alfred A. Knopf, 1957).

Spinden, Herbert J. *Ancient Civilizations of Mexico and Central America* (New York: American Museum of Natural History, 1917).

—. *Maya Art and Civilization* (rev. ed.; Indian Hills, Col.: Falcon's Wing Press, 1957).

Spitzer, Alan B. *The Theories of Louis Auguste Blanqui* (New York: Columbia University Press, 1957).

Stahl, William Harris. (tr.) *Macrobius, Commentary on the Dream of Scipio*, translated with an Introduction and Notes by William Harris Stahl (New York: Columbia University Press, 1952).

Stevenson, Mrs. Sinclair. *The Heart of Jainism*. (London: Oxford University Press, 1915).

Steward, Julian H. (ed.), *Handbook of South American Indians*. Vol. 2, *The Andean Civilizations*. Smithsonian Institution. Bureau of American Ethnology. Bulletin 143 (Washington, D.C.: United States Government Printing Office, 1946).

Stewart, B. and Tait, P. G. *The Unseen Universe* (9th rev. ed.; London: Macmillan 1880).

Stewart, H. F. and Rand, E. K. (tr.) *Boethius, The Theological Tractates*, with an English translation by H. F. Stewart and E. K. Rand, *The Consolation of Philosophy*, with an English translation of "I. T." (1609) revised by H. F. Stewart (Cambridge, Mass.: Harvard University Press, 1962).

Stimson, D. *The Gradual Acceptance of the Copernican Theory of the Universe* (Hanover, N.H. 1917).

Surtz, Edward and Hexter, J. H. (eds.) *The Complete Works of St. Thomas More*. (New Haven, Conn.: Yale University Press, 1965).

Surtz, E. *More's Utopia* (Cambridge, Mass.: Harvard University Press, 1957).

Suter, H. *Die Mathematiker und Astronomen der Araber und ihre Werke*, in *Abhandlungen zur Geschichte der mathematischen Wissenschaften* (Leipzig: B. G. Teubner, 1900).

Taton, R. (ed.) *History of Science*, vol. I, *Ancient and Medieval Science from the Beginnings to 1450*, edited by R. Taton, translated by A. J. Pomerans (New York: Basic Books Inc., 1963). [also cited as 1957]

—. (ed.) *History of Science*, vol. II, *The Beginnings of Modern Science from 1450 to 1800*, translated by A. J. Pomerans (New York: Basic Books, 1964).

Taylor, Thomas. *The Philosophical and Mathematical Commentaries of Proclus on the First Book of Euclid's Elements* (London: Printed for the Author, 1792).

Thayer, H. S. (ed.) *Newton's Philosophy of Nature: Selections from his Writings*. (New York: Hafner, 1960).

Thompson, J. Eric S. *Maya Hieroglyphic Writing: An Introduction* (new ed.; Norman: University of Oklahoma Press, 1960).

—. *The Rise and Fall of Maya Civilization*. (Norman: University of Oklahoma Press, 1954).

Thompson, R. Campbell. *The Epic of Gilgamish* (London: Luzac & Co., 1928).

—. *The Reports of Magicians and Astrologers of Nineveh and Babylon in the British Museum*, Original texts, with translation, notes, and introduction (London: Luzac & Co., 1900).

Thomson, N. H. (tr.) *The Florentine History*. [by Machiavelli] (London: Archibald Constable, 1906).

Thorndike, L. *History of Magic and Experimental Science*, 10 vols. (New York: Columbia University Press, 1923-58).

Tolman, Richard C. *Relativity, Thermodynamics and Cosmology*. (Oxford: Clarendon Press, 1934).

Tulk, A. (tr.) *Elements of Physiophilosophy*. [by Lorenz Oken] (London: Printed for the Ray Society, 1848).

Tyndall, John. *Heat a Mode of Motion*. Fourth edition. (New York: D. Appleton, 1881).

Ussher, Archbishop. *The Annals of the World...* (London: E. Tyler, 1658). [Latin version published in 1650.]

Vaillant, George C. *Aztecs of Mexico: Origin, Rise and Fall of the Aztec Nation* (Garden City, N. Y. Doubleday, 1953).

Van den Bergh, Simon. (tr.) *Tahafut al-tahafut* (London: Luzac, 1954). [This title means "Incoherence of the Incoherence"]

van der Waerden, B. L. *Science Awakening*, translated by Arnold Dresden (New York: John Wiley & Sons, 1963).

van Grunebaum, G. E. *Islam: Essays in the Nature and Growth of a Cultural Tradition* (2d ed. London: Routledge & Kegan Paul, 1961).

Venturi, P. Tacchi. (ed.) *Opere storiche del P. Matteo Ricci S.J.*, edited by P. Tacchi Venturi (Macerate: F. Giorgetti, 1911-13).

Vitelli, H. (ed.) *Joannis Philoponi in Aristotelis physicorum libros quinque posteriores commentaria* (Berlin: G. Reimer, 1888).

—. (ed.) *De generatione et corruptione* [the commentary of Philoponus on this book of Aristotle] (Berlin: G. Reimer, 1887).

Voigt, G. *Die Wiederbelebung des klassischen Althertums, oder das erste Jahrhundert des Humanismus* (Berlin: G. Reimer, 1859).

von Arnim, J. (ed.) *Stoicorum veterum fragmenta* (Leipzig: B. G. Teubner, 1903-24).

von Braunmühl, A. *Vorlesungen über Geschichte der Trigonometrie* (Leipzig: B. G. Teuhner, 1900-03).

von Hagen, Victor W. *The Aztec and Maya Papermakers* (New York: Augustin, 1943).

—. *The Aztec: Man and Tribe* (rev. ed.; New York: The New American Library, 1961).

—. *Realm of the Incas* (rev. ed.; New York: The New American Library, 1961).

—. (ed.) de Onis, Harriet (tr.) *The Incas of Pedro de Cieza de León* (Norman: University of Oklahoma Press, 1959).

von Hanstein, Otfrid. *The World of the Incas: A Socialistic State of the Past*, translated by Anna Barwell (London: George Allen and Unwin Ltd., 1924).

von Weizsäcker, F. *The Relevance of Science: Creation and Cosmogony* (New York: Harper & Row, 1964).

Waddell, W. G. (tr.) *Manetho*, with an English translation by W. G. Waddell (Loeb Classical Library; Cambridge, Mass.: Harvard University Press, 1964).

Walker, D. P. *Spiritual and Demonic Magic from Ficino to Campanella* (London: The Warburg Institute, 1958).

Wallis, Charles G. *On the Dignity of Man.* [by Giovanni Pico della Mirandola] (Indianapolis: The Library of Liberal Arts, 1965).

Warren, H. C. *Buddhism in Translations* (Cambridge, Mass.: Harvard University Press, 1896).

Way, Sr. A. C. *The Fathers of the Church: A New Translation*, Vol. XLVI (Washington, D.C.: The Catholic University of America Press, 1963).

Wedel, Theodore O. *The Medieval Attitude toward Astrology, particularly in England* (New Haven, Conn.: Yale University Press, 1920).

Weinberg, S. *The First Three Minutes.* (London: André Deutsch, 1977, p. 154).

Wensinck, J. *The Muslim Creed: Its Genesis and Historical Development* (Cambridge: The University Press, 1932),

Westacott, E. *Roger Bacon in Life and Legend.* (New York: Philosophical Library, 1953).

Whitehead, A. *Science and the Modern World: Lowell Lectures, 1925.* (New York: The Macmillan Company, 1925).

Whitrow, G. J. *The Natural Philosophy of Time* (London: Thomas Nelson, 1961).

Whittaker, Sir Edmund T. *The Beginning and End of the World* (Oxford: Oxford University Press, 1942).

—. *Space and Spirit: Theories of the Universe and the Arguments for the Existence of God* (Hinsdale, Ill.: Henry Regnery Co., 1948).

Whittaker, Thomas. *Macrobius or Philosophy, Science and Letters in the Year 400* (Cambridge: Cambridge University Press, 1923).

Willey, B. *The Seventeenth Century Background* (London: Chatto 1934).

Williams, L. *The Heroic Enthusiasts* [*De gl'heroici furori* by Giordano Bruno] (London: George Redway, 1887).

Wilson, H. H. (tr.) *The Vishnu Purana: A System of Hindu Mythology and Tradition*, translated from the original Sanskrit and illustrated by notes by H. H. Wilson (London: John Murray, 1840).

Wright, E. Ramsay. (tr.) *The Book of Instruction in the Elements of the Art of Astrology*, by Abu'l-Rayhan Muhammad ibn Ahmad al-Biruni. Translation facing the Arabic original by R. Ramsay Wright (London: Luzac & Co., 1934).

Yates, Frances A. *Giordano Bruno and the Hermetic Tradition* (Chicago: University of Chicago Press, 1964).

Zehnder, L. *Der ewige Kreislauf des Weltalls.* (Braunschweig: F. Vieweg, 1914).

Zimmer, H. *Myths and Symbols in Indian Art and Civilization*, edited by J. Campbell (New York: Pantheon Books, 1946).

Zöllner, J. C. F. *Über die Natur der Cometen: Beiträge zur Geschichte und Theorie der Erkenntniss.* (Leipzig: Wilhelm Engelmann, 1872).

Zycha, J. (ed.) *Sancti Aureli Augustini De Genesi ad litteram libri duodecim*, edited by J. Zycha, in *Corpus Scriptorum Ecclesiasticorum Latinorum*, vol. XXVIII, Sec. III, Pars 1 (Vienna: F. Tempsky, 1894).

VI: Some Major Events in the History of Science

Note: in this chronology, *SC* = *Science and Creation*, *TROP* = *The Relevance of Physics*.

ΕΝ ΑΡΧΗ ΗΝ 'Ο ΛΟΓΟΣ
ΚΑΙ 'Ο ΛΟΓΟΣ ΗΝ ΠΡΟΣ ΤΟΝ ΘΕΟΝ
ΚΑΙ ΘΕΟΣ ΗΝ 'Ο ΛΟΓΟΣ

In the beginning was the WORD
And the WORD was with God
And the WORD was God...

B.C.
3102 India: the great Bharata battle. SC 17
2700s-2400s Babylon: Sumerian period. SC 84
2660(ca) Egypt: start of "Old Kingdom" SC 73
2371 Babylon: Sargon (through 2316) SC 84
2180 Egypt: end of "Old Kingdom" SC 73
2080 Egypt: start of "Middle Kingdom" SC 73
1900s Egypt: Probable date of Rhind mathematical papyrus. SC 77
1800s-1600s Babylon: Hammurabi dynasty. SC 84
1640 Egypt: end of "Middle Kingdom" SC 73
1579 Egypt: start of "New Kingdom" SC 75
1370 Egypt: Akhenaton's monotheism. SC 77
1075 Egypt: end of "New Kingdom," start of "Late Period" SC 75
800(ca) China: *Chou Pei Suan Ching* (Arithmetic in Nine Sections) compiled. SC 31
753 Traditional founding of Rome
740 Isaiah called as prophet in a vision: "Holy, holy, holy" (Is 6:1-13)
600(ca) India: the *Vedas*. SC 5
587 Jews taken to captivity in Babylon
551 Death of Zoroaster
538 Babylon: Persian occupation begins. SC 84
528(ca) Meditating under a banyan tree at Buddha Gaya, Siddhartha Gautama achieves enlightenment
509 Overthrow of the Roman monarchy; the Republic of Rome founded
500 Death of Pythagoras
500(ca) Lao-Tzu, principal proponent of Taoism, composes parts of *Tao Te Ching*. SC 28
483 Death of Buddha
480 Defeat of the Persian fleet by the Athenians at Salamis

479   Death of Master Kung (Confucius) SC 25

425(ca) Death of Mo Ti. SC 25

399   Death of Socrates

384   Birth of Aristotle.

350(ca) China: Shih Shen draws up catalog of 800 stars. SC 32

350(ca)-270(ca) Berossos, author of *Babyloniaka*, a history of Babylon. SC 96

347   Death of Plato

332   Egypt: end of "Late Period" SC 75

323   Death of Alexander the Great.

323   Babylon: Persian occupation ends. SC 84

322   Death of Aristotle

300(ca) Composition of the *Chuang Tzu*, "the second most important book of Taoism" SC 29

300(ca) Euclid's *Elements*, the master-text of geometry. SC 103

289   Death of Meng Kho (Mencius) SC 26

280(ca) Herophilus and Erasistratus establish medical schools at Alexandrian Museum. SC 102

270   Death of Epicurus

264-254 First Punic War

218-201 Second Punic War, Hannibal crosses Alps

212   Death of Archimedes

250(ca) Founding of the Museum and Library at Alexandria.

200s Babylon: Seleucid era. SC 86-7

200s Manetho, Egyptian historian. SC 73

232(ca) Death of King Asoka, the "great champion of Buddhism... had all his monuments inscribed with the swastika." SC 11

200(ca) Eratosthenes, custodian of the Alexandrian Museum, accurately computes circumference of the earth. SC 102

165   Last Bactrian invaders leave India. SC 5

150(ca) Hipparchus discovers precession of equinoxes. SC 102

150(ca) Composition of the Book of Wisdom.

150(ca) Aristarchus measures the sizes and distances of the moon and sun. *God and the Cosmologists* 176

149-146 Third Punic War and the destruction of Carthage

136   Tung Chung-Shu makes Confucianism the official state doctrine. SC 26-7

54   Death of Lucretius

46   Sosigenes, astronomer of the Alexandrian Museum, aids Julius Caesar in calendar reform. SC 102

44   Assassination of Julius Caesar

27   Augustus Caesar becomes emperor of Rome

+

ΚΑΙ ‘Ο ΛΟΓΟΣ ΣΑΡΞ ΕΓΕΝΕΤΟ
Et VERBUM caro factum est
"And the WORD was made flesh..."
+
The Conception, Birth, Public Life,
Passion, Death, and Resurrection of
OUR LORD JESUS CHRIST
+

A.D.

14   Death of Emperor Augustus, succeeded by Tiberius Caesar

150(ca)   Ptolemy's *Almagest* and *Tetrabiblios*.

240   Censorinus alludes to the Sothic Cycle as the "Great Year" of the Egyptians. SC 71

317   Start of Maya "Old Empire." SC 57

325   Council of Nicea; its Creed applies the term μονογενης, *unigenitus* = "only-begotten" to Jesus Christ. SC 173

350(ca)   India: *Mahabharata* composed. SC 9

350(ca)   India: Buddhaghosa compiles *Visuddhi-Magga*, "the great synthesis of Buddhist doctrine." SC 11

410(fl)   Macrobius: "one of the last non-Christian Roman writers on scientific matters" SC 126

426   St. Augustine completes his work, *The City of God*

430   Death of St. Augustine

496   Aryabhata composes *Aryabhatiya*, "that little gem of ancient Hindu astronomy... its author ... seems to have recognized the rotation of the earth on its axis." SC 15

500(ca)   India: *Puranas* composed. SC 1

510(fl.) Damascius (Nicolas of Damascus). SC 98

517   John Philoponus' commentary on Aristotle's *Physics*. SC 185

622   Mohammed flees from Mecca to Medina (the Hegira).

711   Spain invaded by Muslims from North Africa

731   Start of Maya "Great Period" of Old Empire. SC 57

732   Muslim advance stopped in France by Charles Martel

980   Birth of Avicenna

987   Maya "Old Empire" ends, "New Empire" starts. SC 57, 61

1054   Chinese astronomers record supernova in Taurus. SC 33

1061   China: oldest cast-iron pagoda. SC 32

1030(ca) Persian scholar al-Biruni tours India. *SC* 15-16, 198-200

1037   Death of Avicenna

1125(fl.) Adelard of Bath travels the Muslim world. SC 219-20

1126   Birth of Averroës

1178   Medieval monks noted an exceedingly brief eruption of huge flames from the moon's surface, reported by Gervase of

Canterbury in his *Chronicle. Bible and Science* 185, note 19

1198   Death of Averroës

1220(ca) Birth of Roger Bacon

1247   Roger Bacon enters Franciscans

1249   Death of William of Auvergne, Bishop of Paris. SC 223

1253   Death of Grosseteste, Bishop of Lincoln, scholar of philosophy and science. SC 221-2

1274   (March 7) Death of St. Thomas Aquinas

1277   (March 7) Étienne Tempier, bishop of Paris, issues list of 219 condemned propositions. SC 229

1280   Death of St. Albert the Great

1292   Death of Roger Bacon

1330(ca) Buridan, professor at the Sorbonne, enunciates impetus theory. *Numbers Decide* 133.

1358(ca) Death of Jean Buridan

1382   Death of Nicole Oresme

1400(ca) Europe recovers Greek mathematical corpus. SC 87

1452   Birth of Leonardo

1473   Birth of Copernicus

1479   Aztecs make 13-foot calendar stone. SC 50

1492   Columbus discovers the western hemisphere.

1502   White men with beards appear off Mexican shore. SC 54

1503   Moctezuma II ascends Aztec throne. SC 53

1519   Death of Leonardo

1519   Cortéz conquers Aztec empire. SC 53-4

1543   Death of Copernicus, publication of his *De Revolutionibus Orbium Coelestium*

1558   *Leyenda de Soles*, an Aztec creation story, is written. SC 51

1561   Birth of Francis Bacon

1564   Birth of Galileo

1571   Birth of Kepler

1572   (November 6) Supernova in Cassiopeia, observed by Tycho on Nov. 11; he showed it to have a "superlunary" position, and published a book on it. *TROP* 240, *The Limits of a Limitless Science* 58-9, *The Paradox of Olbers' Paradox* 26-7, *Burnham's Celestial Handbook* 503

1583   Father Matteo Ricci arrives on the Chinese mainland. SC 36

1584   Publication of Bruno's *La cena de le ceneri*. Jaki's translation, *The Ash Wednesday Supper*

1588   Birth of Mersenne

1596   (March 31) Birth of Descartes

1596   Publication of Kepler's *Prodromus dissertationum cosmographicarum continens mysterium cosmographicum* (usually called "*Mysterium cosmographicum*")

1604 (October 9) Supernova in Ophiuchus (V843 Ophiuchi) on which Kepler publishes a book (1606). *The Limits of a Limitless Science* 59, *Burnham's Celestial Handbook* 1249

1607 Dutch opticians offer their telescopes to States General of the Netherlands.

1608 Chinese translation of Euclid's *Elements* is printed. SC 37

1610 Galileo claimed before the Venetian Senate that the telescope was his invention. Two months later he had to admit that he merely improved the techniques of some Dutch opticians. *The Absolute Beneath the Relative* 127

1610 Galileo observes mountains on moon, sunspots, Jupiter's four major moons, phases of Venus, and the innumerable stars in the milky way; reported in his *Sidereus Nuncius* or *Starry Messenger*. *The Paradox of Olbers' Paradox* 35n1; *A Late Awakening* 93

1623 Birth of Pascal

1626 Death of Francis Bacon

1630 Death of Kepler

1637 Publication of Descartes' *Discourse on the Method*, a book "totally barren of science." *A Late Awakening* 65

1642 Death of Galileo

1642 Birth of Newton

1644 Publication of Descartes' *Principia philosophiae*

1645 Pascal builds a calculating machine. *Brain, Mind and Computers* 22

1648 Death of Mersenne

1650 Death of Descartes

1662 Death of Pascal

1665 Newton devises calculus

1675 Roemer measures the speed of light based on the motion of Jupiter's moons. *Bible and Science* 117n19

1682 Leibniz presents his calculating machine. *Brain, Mind and Computers* 25

1684 Leibniz publishes work on calculus

1687 Publication of Newton's *Philosophiae naturalis principia mathematica*. *The Origin of Science and the Science of its Origin* 103, *The Absolute Beneath the Relative* 200

1697 End of Maya "New Empire" SC 61

1713 Second edition of Newton's *Philosophiae naturalis principia mathematica* with General Scholium. SC 267, 287

1718 Halley discovers the proper motion of stars. *The Paradox of Olbers' Paradox* 173, *Burnham's Celestial Handbook* 1255

1724 Birth of Kant

1727 Death of Newton

1735 Linné (Linnaeus) publishes *Systema Naturae*, presenting a system of botanical nomenclature; his 1753 *Species Plantarum* is considered foundation for modern system.

1744 Birth of Lamarck

1755 Publication of Kant's *Allgemeine Naturgeschichte*. Jaki's translation, Kant's *Universal Natural History*.

1758 Birth of Olbers

1761 Publication of Lambert's *Cosmologische Briefe*. Jaki's translation, Lambert's *Cosmological Letters*.

1770 Birth of Hegel

1783 Herschel discovers Uranus. *The Road of Science* 148.[49]

1789 Lavoisier's *Elements of Chemistry* is published. *TROP* 151-2

1791 Birth of Charles Babbage

1795 Lavoisier is sent to the guillotine.

1799 Juan Yuan writes *Chhou Jen Chuan* (biographies of Chinese and Western mathematicians). SC 39

1801 (January 1) Father Giuseppe Piazzi discovers the first asteroid, Ceres. *Olbers Studies* 9

1802 (March 28) Olbers discovers the second asteroid, Pallas

1804 Harding discovers the third asteroid, Juno

1804 Death of Kant

1807 Olbers discovers the fourth asteroid, Vesta

1809 Birth of Darwin

1819 Birth of Foucault

1820 Birth of Engels

1821 Cauchy provides the "limit" (the foundation of calculus) with logical rigor. *Chance or Reality* 131

1822 Birth of Hermite; birth of Pasteur

1824 Birth of William Thomson (Lord Kelvin)

1820s Babbage develops his "difference engine"

1828 Wöhler synthesizes urea from inorganic substances (i.e. not taken from living creatures). *Numbers Decide* 154; "Ammonium cyanate ($CNONH_4$) white solid formed by reaction of sodium cyanate and ammonium sulfate solutions is transformed to urea upon being heated at 100°C. This reaction was carried out in 1828 by Wöhler and is the first record of a so-called inorganic substance being transformed outside a living organism into a so-called organic substance." *Van Nostrand Scientific Encyclopedia*, 334

1829 Death of Lamarck

1831 Death of Hegel

---

[49] But see Jaki, *Olbers Studies*, 19. According to Sidgwick, "No fewer than 19 pre-discovery observations of Uranus have been identified, from 1690 (by Flamsteed) onward." Sidgwick, *Amateur Astronomer's Handbook*, 513.

1831 Darwin's voyage on the *Beagle* (through 1836)

1832 Henderson observes stellar parallax of 0.92 seconds in α Centauri (modern value 0.75) but was "uncertain" and did not publish his results. *TROP* 248

1837 Publication of Babbage's *Ninth Bridgewater Treatise*

1837 Struve observes stellar parallax in α Lyrae. *TROP* 248

1838 Bessel observes stellar parallax in 61 Cygni. *Bible and Science* 117n19, *TROP* 248

1840 Death of Olbers

1844 Birth of Nietzsche

1845 Leverrier discovers Neptune. *The Limits of a Limitless Science* 60

1847 Helmholtz's paper, *Über die Erhaltung der Kraft*, "On the Conservation of Force," i.e. the conservation of energy.

1851 Foucault's pendulum experiment. *Bible and Science* 117n19

1854 B. Riemann's essay on non-Euclidean geometry, "On the hypotheses which lie at the bases of geometry" which "brought to a culmination Gauss's work on the geometry of curved surfaces." SC 298, *TROP* 116, *The Paradox of Olbers' Paradox*, 163-4, 194n60.

1858 Birth of Planck

1859 Publication of Darwin's *The Origin of Species*

1860s John Tyndall's *Heat a Mode of Motion* goes through 4 editions; its "most startling feature... was its author's silence about the Second Law of thermodynamics." SC 295

1861 (June 9) Birth of Pierre Duhem

1865 Maxwell proposes more general form of Ampère's law

1868 Work on the Fraunhofer lines in the solar spectrum led to the discovery of a hitherto-unknown element which was named *helium. TROP* 208

1868 Death of Foucault

1872 Zöllner's *Über die Natur der Cometen...* abandons an infinite universe for a non-Euclidean space. SC 298, n142

1872 Blanqui's *L'éternité par les astres*, "the lengthiest assertion of the topic [of eternal recurrences] written by a modern author." SC 314-5, 319

1873 Cave paintings discovered in Altamira, Spain

1873 Nietzsche's essay "Philosophy during the Tragic Age of the Greeks" SC 319

1873 Lange's *History of Materialism*, second and vastly revised edition. SC 320

1874 Tyndall addresses British Association for the Advancement of Science meeting in Belfast. SC 295

1875 Eugene Dühring, privatdozent at the University of Berlin declared himself a convert to socialism. SC 313

1876 Kelvin (William Thomson) constructs machine to analyze tides, and with his brother James constructs a machine by which a "general differential equation of the second order with variable coefficients may be rigorously, continuously, and in a single process solved by a machine." Its use could cut to one-tenth or less the work of skilled mathematicians engaged in the computation of "any one of the simple harmonic elements of a year's tides recorded in curves in the usual manner by an ordinary tide-gauge." *Brain, Mind and Computers* 42 and notes 92 and 93

1878 Total solar eclipse, but "Vulcan" (hypothesized to orbit inside the orbit of Mercury) was not spotted. *TROP* 245

1879 Birth of Einstein

1881 Nietzsche conceives his *Thus Spake Zarathustra* (on eternal recurrence). SC 319

1881 Michelson invents interferometer (used in measuring diameter of stars, also in attempt to detect "ether").

1882 Death of Darwin

1884 Newcomb puts the advance of the perihelion of Mercury at 43 seconds of arc per century as "unaccountable by any known or conceivable factor." *TROP* 245

1886 Crookes' famous presidential address of 1886 to the Chemical Section of the British Association. *TROP* 155-7

1887 Michelson-Morley experiment gives null result of motion of the earth with respect to the ether. *TROP* 82-3

1888 Nietzsche's autobiographical *Ecce Homo*. SC 319

1892 Lord Rayleigh writes to *Nature* about a minor discrepancy in the molecular weight of nitrogen depending on its origin; experiments by Ramsay led to the discovery of argon, an inert gas. *TROP* 254-5

1894 Chinese imperial sanctioning of Chu Hsi's work on cycles. SC 34

1895(ca) Newcomb said that engine-powered flight is a physical impossibility. *Numbers Decide* 154

1895 Roentgen discovers X-rays. *God and the Cosmologists* 193

1895 Death of Engels

1896 Becquerel discovers natural radioactivity. *TROP* 172

1898 The Hundred Days Reform [in China] was initiated through the influence of Kang Yu-Wei. SC 27

1900 Death of Nietzsche

1900 Due to his work on black-body radiation, and despite profound misgivings, Planck announces the "quantum" of energy. *TROP* 88-9

1901 Birth of Heisenberg

1902 Einstein's father goes bankrupt. *God and the Cosmologists* 193

1904 J. B. Stallo warned physicists that because of the breakdown of mechanistic theories it was useless to search for units smaller than molecules, that is, atoms. *TROP* 163

1905 Einstein formulates Special Theory of Relativity ($E=mc^2$), theory of Brownian motion, photon theory of light.

1907 Death of Lord Kelvin

1912 As a result of her observations of variable stars in the Small Magellanic Cloud, Miss Henrietta Leavitt of Harvard discovered a definite relation between the periods and luminosities of certain regularly pulsing stars called Cepheid variables. Worked into a useful formula by Shapley in 1917, this permits these stars to be used as a "galactic yardstick." *TROP* 213 and *Burnham's Celestial Handbook* 590-92.

1913 Bohr devises model of hydrogen atom using the quantum which explained the Fowler spectra. *TROP* 95, *God and the Cosmologists* 193

1913 Rutherford gives Marsden reluctant permission to look for large-angle scattering of alpha-particles shot at a thin gold foil. Rutherford called it "the most incredible event" when such were found. *TROP* 172

1913 Publication of volume (1) of *Le Système du Monde*, Duhem's 10-volume masterwork. Volume (2) came out in 1914, (3) in 1915, (4) in 1916, (5) in 1917.[50]

1915 Einstein formulates General Theory of Relativity

1916 (September 14) Death of Pierre Duhem

1916 E. Barnard discovers a "runaway" star in Ophiuchus with huge proper motion. *Cosmos and Creator* 129, *Burnham's Celestial Handbook* 1251

1917 Einstein publishes paper: "Cosmological Considerations on the General Theory of Relativity"

1919 (May 29) Solar eclipse in West Africa. Measurements taken of the bending of starlight around the sun verified Einstein's prediction due to General Relativity. *God and the Cosmologists* 75-6, *Road of Science* 190-1, 195n80.

1920s Vannevar Bush uses the principle embodied in Kelvin's differential analyzer to develop the first modern computer. *Brain, Mind and Computers* 49

1920 Rutherford in Bakerian Lecture predicts neutron, deuterium, tritium. *TROP* 174

---

[50] Also see the entry for 1954, and *Le Système du Monde* under Major Sources.

1922 A. Friedman shows "an oscillating type of universe" as a "possible solution of the cosmological equations of Einstein," estimating its period as "2.4 billion years." SC 336, 350

1924 (August 17) birth of S. L. Jaki

1924 With Mt. Wilson's 100-inch telescope Hubble resolves a Cepheid variable in the Andromeda nebula, thereby deriving a tentative distance of 900,000 light years, thereby proving it to be a galaxy independent of the Milky Way. *TROP* 213, also *Burnham's Celestial Handbook* 133-5 and 593-4.

1925 William D. MacMillan "devoted his lengthy address to the American Mathematical Society... to the defence of Euclidean infinity as the true structure of actual physical reality, and the only logical framework of cosmological speculations." SC 337

1927 G. Lemaître's paper "*Un univers homogène de masse constante...*" proposes an "intermediate solution" between Einstein's original, static cosmological model and W. de Sitter's interpretation of it. SC 337n10. He was "the first to connect the instability of the Einsteinian universe and the recession of the nebulae... [his] idea of an expanding universe of finite radius and finite mass became almost overnight the central point of cosmological thought." *TROP* 215

1927 Eddington's famous Gifford Lectures, *The Nature of the Physical World*. SC 340, *Lord Gifford and His Lectures* 45

1928 Gamow works out theory of alpha-tunneling. *God and the Cosmologists* 193

1928 Millikan: "With the aid of this assumption [that high energy cosmic rays kept turning into atoms] one would be able to regard the universe as in a steady state now, and also to banish forever the nihilistic doctrine of its ultimate 'heat-death'." SC 342

1930s The work of Kugler and Neugebauer advance the knowledge of Babylonian astronomy. SC 88

1930s Swiss astronomer F. Zwicky postulates extra mass "to reconcile the rotational velocity of the outer parts of spiral galaxies with Kepler's Laws." SC 361

1930 Regarding the denial of causality presumed to arise from Heisenberg's uncertainty principle: J. E. Turner, of the University of Liverpool, points out the equivocation in which "two different meanings of the word 'exact,' one operational and the other ontological, are equated." SC 365 n 17

1931 Eddington's presidential address to the Mathematical Association speaks of the irreversible expansion of the galaxies. SC 339

1931 At the Centenary Meeting of the British Association for the Advancement of Science, "The vocal prejudice among men of science in favour of a 'never-ending cycle of rebirth of matter and worlds' evidenced, indeed, a baffling oversight of the historical background of the question." SC 341

1932 Chadwick discovers the neutron. *TROP* 174

1933 Eddington lectures at Cornell on a cyclic universe. SC 340

1934 Richard C. Tolman "through an analysis of irreversible cosmic processes, found the model of an oscillating universe with increasingly longer periods to be free of contradictions." SC 362

1934 Rutherford declared that talk about the industrial utilization of nuclear energy was moonshine. *Numbers Decide* 154

1938 Commenting on a paper by F. von Weizsäcker, Walter Nernst, a Nobel-laureate, angrily contended that "the view that there might be an age of the universe was not science." SC 343

1940 The American Association of Social and Psychological Studies stated "The principal reason which turns some men to astrology and other superstitions is that they lack the necessary resources to solve the serious problems with which they are faced. Frustrated, they give in to the pleasant suggestion that there is a golden key within their reach, a simple solution, an ever present help in times of trouble." SC 354

1941 Jean Perrin, Nobel-laureate and president of the French Academy of Sciences in 1938, declared the idea of an age of the universe of some hundred billions (10^{11}) of years as "almost derisory." SC 345

1942 Sir Edmund T. Whittaker, in his Riddell Lectures "set great store by the radical difference between the Great Year of antiquity and the Christian belief in creation and on the bearing of that difference on the past and future of science." SC 346

1945(ca) ENIAC (Electronic Numerical Integrator and Calculator) is constructed, a differential analyzer using electronic tubes.

1947 Death of Planck

1948 Bondi and Gold's paper on Steady-State cosmology. SC 347

1950 Conference in Delhi of scholars on the history of science in India and Southeast Asia. SC 15

1950 Vannevar Bush, the captain of American technology during World War II, insisted that it was impossible to construct intercontinental ballistic missiles. *Numbers Decide* 154

1950 (Dec. 21) S. L. Jaki arrives in New York. *A Mind's Matter* 20

1951 Pope Pius XII addresses Pontifical Academy of Science with respect to creation and the age of the universe. SC 347

1953 H. Dingle's presidential address to the Royal Astronomical Society: "a masterpiece of scientific criticism" on the Steady-State theory. SC 348

1953 Difficulties resulting from surgery on S. L. Jaki's tonsils brings an end to his teaching. *A Mind's Matter* 21-22

1954 After heroic work on the part of Duhem's daughter Hélène, volume (6) of *Le Système du Monde* is published. Then followed (7) in 1956, (8) and (9) in 1958, and (10) in 1959.

1955 Death of Einstein

1959 Michelson-Morley experiment repeated using masers, again giving a null result. *TROP* 257

1961 Frank Drake formulates his equation to predict Earth-like planets. *Numbers Decide* 143

1961 Symposium on the History of Sciences in Ancient and Medieval India held in Calcutta. SC 16

1962 (fall) S. L. Jaki conceives the outline of his *The Relevance of Physics. A Mind's Matter*, 28

1966 S. L. Jaki publishes his first book, *The Relevance of Physics*

1967 Peebles and Wilkinson's "The Primeval Fireball" article on cosmic expansion in *Scientific American*. SC 349 and n87

1974 S. L. Jaki publishes *Science and Creation*.

1974-75,75-6 Jaki gives the Gifford Lectures at the University of Edinburgh. *The Road of Science and the Ways to God.*

1976 Death of Heisenberg

1984 Hut and White disclose that "if heavy neutrinos existed the galaxies could not have formed even up to now." SC 364

1986 S. L. Jaki publishes the revised edition of *Science and Creation* with Postscript.

1990 Pope John Paul II appoints S. L. Jaki as an honorary member of the Pontifical Academy of Sciences

2009 (April 7) Death of S. L. Jaki

+

Requiem aeternam dona eis Domine, et lux perpetua luceat eis.
Requiescant in pace.
Animae eorum et animae omnium fidelium defunctorum
per misericordiam Dei requiescant in pace. Amen.

Appendix I: The Books of S. L. Jaki

Just a brief note before we plunge into the list. Every one of Jaki's books is what most will call "scholarly"; they are rarely descend to the crass (and all too often inaccurate) level of popular treatments of science. However, that does *not* mean they are unreadable by the Common Man, but it does mean one might want to have some reference works around while one is reading since he rarely explains the material he references. One also should keep a notebook handy to record interesting citations. While Jaki's texts are rich in footnotes, this is by no means a disadvantage: it means the material presented is backed up by the actual literature. Whenever possible Jaki used the primary sources:

> There is no substitute to the perusal of primary texts, which, incidentally, hardly ever fail to reveal something that has not yet been noticed by others. SLJ, *A Mind's Matter*, 5-6

and this imparts a firm foundation for additional scholarly work, as he expects curious and enthusiastic students to follow his lead.

Notes:
1. The dates in parenthesis give the year of the book's publication; if more than one, these are later editions *or* reprints.
2. The publishers are indicated by the following codes:

    rvb   New Hope, KY: Real View Books [51]
    sap   Edinburgh: Scottish Academic Press
    isi   Bryn Mawr, PA: Intercollegiate Studies Institute
            (also University Press of America)
    cp   Front Royal, VA: Christendom Press
    ucp Chicago, IL: University of Chicago Press
    shp New York: Science History Publications
    wbe Grand Rapids, MI: Wm. B. Eerdmans

In general, check the Real View Books website,

                 http://www.RealViewBooks.com

for current availability of their titles. Most other titles are out of print.

* * *

The Absolute Beneath the Relative and Other Essays. (ici 1988) 233 pages. A collection of essays, most of which had appeared previously in various sources. See Appendix II for the list of titles.

Advent and Science (rvb 2000) 92 pages.

---

[51] Note that some books give Fraser, Royal Oak, or Pinckney, Michigan as the location. In 2017 it is located in New Hope, Kentucky.

And on This Rock: The Witness of One Land and Two Covenants.
(Notre Dame, IN: Ave Maria Press, 1978, Manassas, VA: Trinity Communications, 1987, cp 1997) 128 pages. A study of the term "rock" (Aramaic *kepha*, Greek πετρος) in the Bible, and of the place "in the neighborhood of Caesarea Philippi" where Jesus gave that name to a man named Simon. (Mt 16:13-19)

Angels, Apes and Men. (La Salle, IL: Sherwood Sugden and Company, 1983, rvb 2006) 128 pages. Originally presented as three lectures at the Institute for Christian Studies, Toronto. It takes "a close look... at the ravages of inner logic which is at work when either man's body or man's soul is ignored in modern philosophic and scientific discourse."

Apologetics as Meant by Newman (rvb 2005)

Bible and Science. (cp 1996) 225 pages.

Brain, Mind, and Computers. (New York: Herder and Herder, 1969, South Bend, IN: Gateway Editions 1978, Washington, DC: Gateway Editions, 1989) 267 pages. SLJ examines the mind-body connection and computers. Notable for SLJ's exposition of Babbage's argument about God and miracles based on his mechanical computer and its programming, presented in his *Ninth Bridgewater Treatise.*

Catholic Essays (cp 1990) 176 pages. A collection of essays, most of which had appeared previously in various sources. See Appendix II for the list of titles.

Chance or Reality and Other Essays (isi 1986) 250 pages. SLJ's first collection of essays, most of which had appeared previously in various sources. See Appendix II for the list of titles.

Chesterton: A Seer of Science. (Urbana, IL: University of Illinois Press, 1986, rvb 2001) 164 pages. A brilliant and far too short study of the work of English journalist and author G. K. Chesterton with reference to science under four heads: (1) Interpreter of Science, (2) Antagonist of Scientism, (3) Critic of Evolutionism and (4) Champion of the Universe.

The Church of England as Viewed By Newman (rvb 2004)

Cosmological Letters on the Arrangement of the World-Edifice. (shp 1976) 245 pages. SLJ's translation from the German of Lambert's *Cosmologische Briefe über die Einrichtung des Weltbaues*, a series of 18 long letters about the cosmos, originally published in 1761. SLJ provides a lengthy introduction and copious notes. Lambert presents the idea of a hierarchy of stellar systems orbiting a central massive non-luminous "dark regent"; his cosmology was tuned to teleology and so demonstrates the risks of hypothesizing using the mind's eyes rather than data obtained by observation.

Cosmos and Creator (sap 1980, South Bend, IN: Gateway Editions, 1981) 168 pages. As SLJ states in his preface, this book was written at the urging of his "esteemed friend, the Reverend Dr. Thomas F. Torrance, for many years Professor of Christian Dogmatics at the University of Edinburgh, and winner of the Templeton Prize for 1978. He felt that the major points made in my other, at times lengthy, books about creation, both as an article of Christian faith and as a foundation of natural science, should be made available in a concise form for the wider public."

Cosmos in Transition: Essays in the History of Cosmology (Tucson, AZ: Pachart Publishing House 1990) 248 pages. A collection of essays, most of which had appeared previously in various sources. See Appendix II for the list of titles.

Culture and Science (Windsor, Canada: University of Windsor Press, 1975) 52 pages. The two essays ("A Hundred Years of Two Cultures" and "Knowledge in an Age of Science") in this hard-to-find booklet are reprinted in *Chance or Reality*.

The Ethical Foundations of Bioethics (rvb 2007) 136 pages

Genesis 1 through the Ages. (London: Thomas More Press, 1992, rvb 1998) 315 pages. A study of the various interpretations of the Six Days of Creation.

The Gist of Catholicism and Other Essays (rvb 2001) 255 pages. A collection of essays, most of which had appeared previously in various sources. See Appendix II for the list of titles.

God and the Cosmologists. (sap 1989, rvb 1998) 286 pages.

God and the Sun at Fatima (rvb 1999) 386 pages. A study of the evidence regarding the "miracle of the sun" witnessed by thousands of believers and unbelievers at Fatima, Portugal on October 13, 1917, including a possible explanation of what happened (an explanation which is emphatically *not* a debunking), and a discussion of the nature of miracles.

Impassible Divide, or the Separation Between Science and Religion (rvb 2008) 108 pages.

Is There a Universe? (New York: Wethersfield Institute 1993) 138 pages.

Justification as Argued by Newman (rvb 2007) 286 pages.

The Keys of the Kingdom: A Tool's Witness to Truth. (Chicago, IL: The Franciscan Herald Press, 1986, rvb 2001) 226 pages. A study of "key" as tool and term, with particular reference to the commissioning of St. Peter in Mt 16:19.

A Late Awakening and Other Essays (rvb 2006) 256 pages. A collection of essays, most of which had appeared previously in various sources. See Appendix II for the list of titles.

Lectures in the Vatican Gardens. (rvb 2011) 196 pages. A collection of papers given at meetings of the Pontifical Academy of Sciences, most of which appear in SLJ's other essay collections. See Appendix II for the list of titles.

Les tendances nouvelles de l'ecclésiologie. (Rome: Herder and Herder, 1957) 274 pages. SLJ's doctoral dissertation for S.T.D., Pontificio Ateneo S. Anselmo, Roma, 1950. Reprinted in 1963.

The Limits of a Limitless Science and Other Essays (isi 2000) 247 pages. A collection of essays, most of which had appeared previously in various sources. See Appendix II for the list of titles.

Lord Gifford and His Lectures: A Centenary Retrospect. (sap 1986) 138 pages.

Means to Message: A Treatise on Truth (wbe 1999) 233 pages.

The Milky Way: An Elusive Road for Science. (shp 1972, shp1975) 352 pages. One of SLJ's case studies in the history of astronomy, it examines the history of theories about the "milky way" (the dim glowing band which crosses the night sky), the theory of galaxies and congeries of stars, and its relation to cosmology.

A Mind's Matter: An Intellectual Autobiography (wbe 2002) 309 pages. SLJ also released booklets, *Five Years Later* (2006) and *Three More Years* (2011), which are extensions of this work.

Miracles and Physics. (cp 1989) 114 pages.

The Mirage of Conflict between Science and Religion. (rvb 2011) 83 pages

Neo-Arianism as Foreseen by Newman (rvb 2006) 267 pages

Newman's Challenge (wbe 2000) 321 pages.

Newman to Converts: An Existential Ecclesiology (rvb 2001) 531 pages.

Numbers Decide and Other Essays (rvb 2003) 267 pages. A collection of essays, most of which had appeared previously in various sources. See Appendix II for the list of titles.

Olbers Studies: With Three Unpublished Manuscripts by Olbers. (Tucson, AZ: Pachart Publishing House 1991) 96 pages.

The Only Chaos and Other Essays. (isi 1990) 278 pages. A collection of essays, most of which had appeared previously in various sources. See Appendix II for the list of titles.

The Origin of Science and the Science of its Origin. (sap 1978) 160 pages. The enlarged text of the Fremantle Lectures SLJ gave in the spring of 1977 at Balliol College, Oxford, England, which (as SLJ says in the foreword) "aim at showing the crucial role played in the origin of science by a widely shared belief in the first article of Christian creed, an article placing the origin of all in the creative act of God, the Father Almighty, Maker of heaven and earth."

The Paradox of Olbers' Paradox: A Case History of Scientific Thought. (New York: Herder and Herder, 1969, rvb 2000) 325 pages. One of SLJ's case studies in the history of astronomy, it examines the history of the question "Why is the night sky dark?" and its relation to cosmology.

Patterns or Principles and Other Essays (isi 1995) A collection of essays, most of which had appeared previously in various sources. See Appendix II for the list of titles.

The Physicist As Artist: The Landscapes of Pierre Duhem. (sap 1988) 188 pages, quarto. A collection of the works of art of Pierre Duhem, with a lengthy introduction and commentary.

Planets and Planetarians: A History of Theories of the Origin of Planetary Systems. (sap 1978) 266 pages. One of SLJ's case studies in the history of astronomy, it examines the history of theories about the origin and motion of the planets (Mercury, Venus, Mars, Jupiter, and Saturn) as well as the sun and moon.

Praying the Psalms (wbe 2000) 248 pages.

The Purpose of It All. (sap 1990) 297 pages. The text of SLJ's eight lectures given in 1989 for the Farmington Institute for Christian Studies, at Corpus Christi College, Oxford.

Questions on Science and Religion (rvb 2004) 201 pages. A study of various questions touching these two fields.

The Relevance of Physics. (ucp 1966, sap 1992) 604 pages. This is SLJ's first book, a history and commentary of physics. Its four parts examine
- (1) the study of the world as
  - (a) an organism,
  - (b) a mechanism, and
  - (c) a pattern of numbers;
- (2) the central themes of physics:
  - (a) the layers of matter,
  - (b) the frontiers of the cosmos, and
  - (c) the edge of precision;
- (3) its contact with other disciplines, in particular:
  - (a) biology,
  - (b) metaphysics,
  - (c) ethics, and
  - (d) theology; and finally
- (4) explores the question "Physics: Master or Servant?" treating
  - (a) its fate in scientism and
  - (b) its place in human culture.

Among many other notable things, it contains his first presentation of the effect of Gödel's incompleteness theorem on physics.

Reluctant Heroine: The Life and Work of Hélène Duhem (sap 1992) 335 pages. A biography of the daughter of Pierre Duhem. Her heroic efforts finally accomplished the long-suppressed publication of the last five volumes of her father's masterwork, *Le Système du Monde*, on the history of science.

The Road of Science and the Ways to God: The Gifford Lectures 1975 and 1976. (ucp 1978, 1980) 475 pages. Text of the 20 lectures SLJ gave in Edinburgh in 1975 and 1976, the aim of which, as he wrote in the book's introduction, "is to demonstrate what is intimated in their title, namely, the existence of a single intellectual avenue forming both the road of science and the ways to God. Science found its only viable birth within a cultural matrix permeated by a firm conviction about the mind's ability to find in the realm of things and persons a pointer to their Creator. All great creative advances of science have been made in terms of an epistemology germane to that conviction, and whenever that epistemology was resisted with vigorous consistency, the pursuit of science invariably appears to have been deprived of its solid foundation."

The Savior of Science. (Washington, DC: Regnery Gateway 1988, sap 1990, wbe 2000) 268 pages.

Science and Creation: From Eternal Cycles to an Oscillating Universe. (sap 1974, 1986, Lanham, MD: University Press of America 1990, rvb 2016) 367 pages. Where SLJ's *Relevance* examines science in a topical manner, this book examines it in a more chronological manner. The first six chapters show the "stillbirths" of Science in ancient India, China, meso-America, Egypt, Babylon, and Greece due to the entrenched philosophy of the "Great Year" (the idea that *all* things repeat in unending cycles). Then follows a chapter full of surprises: an amazing study of Science *vis-à-vis* the ancient Hebrews. The eighth chapter examines Science with respect to early Christianity; it provides a most important quote from St. Augustine on the proper relation between faith and science as it relates to statements of strictly physical matters in the Bible. The ninth chapter considers Science as related to the rise of Islam. The tenth is the most surprising of all, because it is here one learns of the work of Buridan and Oresme discovered by Pierre Duhem, specifically the concept of impetus which anticipated Newton's First Law of Motion by some 300 years. The remaining chapters examine the history and philosophy of Science since the Middle Ages, considering its astounding growth and its dalliance in "murky backwaters.

Scientist and Catholic: Pierre Duhem (cp 1991) 204 pages. Further information about the great French physicist and historian of science, with special attention to his Catholicism.

Sigrid Undset's Quest For Truth (rvb 2007) 296 pages

Theology of Priestly Celibacy (cp 1997) 223 pages.

Uncodified Conspiracy and Other Essays. (rvb 2014) 303 pages. A collection of essays. See Appendix II for the list of titles.

Uneasy Genius: The Life and Work of Pierre Duhem (Dordrecht: Martinus Nijhoff, 1984) 472 pages. SLJ's masterful biography of the great French physicist and historian of science.

Universe and Creed. (Milwaukee, WI: Marquette University Press, 1992) 86 pages. Text of the 1992 Père Marquette Lecture in Theology, given at Marquette University.

Booklets and Small Books

These works are shorter presentations of topics covered in detail in other publications, or meditational studies of various Catholic prayers or devotional practices. They are paper-bound and 32 pages long unless otherwise noted. All are published by Real View Books.

Apostles' Creed: a Commentary (2008) 100 pages.

Archipelago Church (2006) 77 pages.

The Brain-Mind Unity: the Strangest Difference (2004)

Christ and Science (2000) See SLJ's *The Savior of Science*.

Confidence in God? (2003) 76 pages.

The Creator's Sabbath Rest (1999) See SLJ's *Genesis One Through the Ages*.

Darwin's Designs (2006) 16 pages.

The Drama of Guadalupe (2009)

Death? (2004) 75 pages.

The Drama of Quantities (2005) 76 pages.

Eastern Orthodoxy's Witness to Papal Primacy (2004)

The Eight Beatitudes: a Commentary (2009) 82 pages.

Evolution For Believers (2003)

Fifty Years of Learning (2007)

Fourteen Stations (2001) Meditations on the Stations of the Cross.

Galileo Lessons (2001)

The Garden of Eden: Why, Where, When, How Long? (2009)

Giordano Bruno: A Martyr of Science? (2000) See also SLJ's translation of Bruno's *The Ash Wednesday Supper* and the essay "Giordano Bruno's Place in Science" in *Numbers Decide*.

Hail Mary: a Commentary (2008) 84 pages.

Intelligent Design? (2005) 12 pages.

Jesus, Islam, Science (2001)

The Litany of the Holy Name (2007) 141 pages. A meditation and study of the litany on the Holy Name of Jesus.

The Litany of Loreto (2005) 224 pages. A meditation and study of the litany to the Blessed Virgin Mary, the mother of Jesus.

The Litany of the Sacred Heart (2007) 152 pages. A meditation and study on this prayer in which the love of Christ for us is presented under the symbol of his most Sacred Heart. It contains some amazing information about the history of the devotion, in particular about what Pope Leo XIII called the "most important action" of his papacy, the consecration of the world to the Sacred Heart of Jesus.

The Litany of the Precious Blood (2010) 116 pages.

The Litany of St. Joseph (2002) 116 pages. A meditation and study of the litany to St. Joseph, the spouse of Mary, the mother of Jesus.

Mary's Magnificat (2007) 46 pages. Study and meditation on the *Magnificat* canticle (Luke 1:46-55).

Maybe Alone in the Universe, after All (2000) See SLJ's *Planets and Planetarians*)

One True Fold: Newman and his Converts (1998)

Original Sin? (2003) 77 pages.

Ours a Dearest Father (2008) 81 pages.

The Parable of the Good Samaritan (2009)

The Perennial Novelty of Jesus (2008) 89 pages.

Sigrid Undset: Through Moral Crises to Catholicism (Reply to a Parish Priest) (2008)

The Sun's Miracle or of Something Else? (2000) See SLJ's *God and the Sun at Fatima.*

To Rebuild or Not To Try? (the Temple of Jerusalem) (1999) Insights into the question with regard to a strange event occurring during the reign of the Roman emperor Julian.

Resurrection? (2004) 78 pages

Science and Religion: A Primer (2004)

Themes of Psalms (2005) 92 pages.

Thy Kingdom Come? (2004) 76 pages

Twenty Mysteries (2003) 103 pages. On the mysteries of the Holy Rosary, including the Luminous Mysteries proposed by St. John Paul II.

The Virgin Birth and the Birth of Science. (1990). See SLJ's *The Origin of Science and the Science of Its Origin*.

Why Believe in Jesus? (2002) 79 pages.

Why Believe in the Church? (2002) 74 pages.

Why the Mass? (2003) 76 pages.

Why the Question: Is There a God? (2001) 65 pages

Why the Question: Is There a Soul? (2002) 68 pages.

Zechariah's Canticle and Ours (2008) xx pages. Study and meditation on the *Benedictus* canticle (Luke 1:68-79).

Appendix II: The Essay Collections

Father Jaki wrote a number of journal articles on various subjects, sometimes in support of (or in development of) arguments and topics more fully presented elsewhere, and sometimes on matters not mentioned in his other writing. Their original location in scholarly journals would make such articles difficult to obtain, but from an early date Jaki began publishing collections of them in book form. For convenience, here is the list of the chapter titles from these collections.

Chance or Reality and Other Essays (1986)

1. Chance or Reality: Interaction in Nature Versus Measurement in Physics
2. From Subjective Scientists to Objective Science
3. Maritain and Science
4. Chesterton's Landmark Year: The Blatchford-Chesterton Debate of 1903-1904
5. Goethe and the Physicists
6. A Hundred Years of Two Cultures
7. Knowledge in an Age of Science
8. The Role of Faith in Physics
9. Theological Aspects of Creative Science
10. The University and the Universe
11. The Greeks of Old and the Novelty of Science
12. Christian Culture and Duhem's Work
13. On Whose Side Is History?

The Absolute Beneath the Relative and Other Essays. (1988)

1. The Absolute Beneath the Relative: Reflections on Einstein's Theories
2. The Impasse of Planck's Epistemology
3. The Metaphysics of Discovery and the Rediscovery of Metaphysics
4. God and Man's Science: A View of Creation
5. Brain, Mind, and Computers
6. The Role of Physics in Psychology: The Prospects in Retrospect
7. Order in Nature and Society: Open or Specific?
8. Scientific Ethics and Ethical Science
9. The Physics of Impetus and the Impetus of the Koran
10. The Last Century of Science: Progress, Problems, and Prospects
11. Science and Censorship: Hélène Duhem and the Publication of the *Système du Monde*
12. Monkeys and Machine-guns: Evolution, Darwinism, and Christianity
13. The Demythologization of Science
14. Science and Hope

The Only Chaos and Other Essays (1990)

1. The Only Chaos
2. The Cosmic Myth of Chance
3. The Modernity of the Middle Ages
4. The Transformation of Cosmology in the Renaissance: Facts, Myths and Mythmaking
5. The History of Science and the Idea of an Oscillating Universe
6. Extra-Terrestrials and Scientific Progress
7. Science: Revolutionary or Conservative?
8. The Three Faces of Technology: Idol, Nemesis, Marvel
9. Normalcy As Terror: The Naturalization of AIDS
10. Evicting the Creator
11. Physics or Physicalism. A Cultural Dilemma
12. Science and Antiscience
13. Teaching Transcendence in Physics
14. Physics and the Ultimate
15. The Hymn of the Universe
16. The Universe in the Bible and in Modern Science
17. Address on Receiving the Templeton Prize

Catholic Essays (1990)

1. Science for Catholics
2. The Case for Galileo's Rehabilitation
3. The Creator's Coming
4. A Most Holy Night
5. Christ, Catholics and Abortion
6. Man of One Wife or Celibacy
7. G. K. C. as R. C.
8. The Business of Christianity and the Christianity of Business
9. The Intelligent Christian's Guide to Scientific Cosmology
10. Commencement

Cosmos in Transition: Essays in the History of Cosmology (1990)

1. The Milky Way Before Galileo
2. The Milky Way from Galileo to Wright
3. Lambert and the Watershed of Cosmology
4. The Wronging of Wright
5. The Five Forms of Laplace's Cosmogony
6. The Early History of the Titius-Bode Law
7. Soldner and the Bending of Light
8. The Gravitational Paradox of an Infinite Universe

Patterns or Principles and Other Essays (1995)

1. Patterns or Principles: The Pseudoscientific Roots of Law's Debacle
2. Ecology or Ecologism?
3. Socrates or the Baby and the Bathwater
4. Medieval Creativity in Science and Technology
5. Telltale Remarks and a Tale Untold

6.   Determinism and Reality
7.   History as Science and Science in History
8.   Science: Western or What?
9.   Gilson and Science
10. The Nonsense and Sense of Science
11. The Mind: Its Physics or Physiognomy?
12. The Last Word in Physics

The Limits of a Limitless Science and Other Essays (2000)
1.   The Limits of a Limitless Science
2.   Extraterrestrials, or Better Be Moonstruck?
3.   Computers: Lovable but Unloving
4.   The Biblical Basis of Western Science
5.   The Inspiration and Counter-inspiration of Astronomical Phenomena
6.   Words: Blocks, Amoebas, or Patches of Fog?
7.   Beyond Science
8.   The Reality of the Universe
9.   A Telltale Meteor
10. Cosmology: An Empirical Science?
11. To Awaken from a Dream, Finally!
12. Science and Religion in Identity Crisis
13. Science, Culture, and Cult
14. The Paradox of Change
15. Cosmic Rays and Water Spiders

The Gist of Catholicism and Other Essays (2001)
1.   The Gist of Catholicism
2.   The Catholic Intellectual
3.   Faith, Reason and Science
4.   The Immaculate Conception and a Conscience Immaculate
5.   Liberalism and Theology
6.   Undeceivably Infallible
7.   Peter's Chair: A Professorial Chair?
8.   Authoritatively no-authority to ordain women
9.   The True Origin of Man
10. The Purpose of Healing
11. Life's Defense: Natural and Supernatural
12. Consistent Bioethics and Christian Consistency
13. The Ethical Foundations of Bioethics
14. The Dilution of Essence
15. The Future of Bioethics and the Soul's Future
16. The Catholic Church and Astronomy
17. Two Miracles and a Nobel Prize
18. Creation: Once and for All
19. Beyond the Tools of Production

Numbers Decide and Other Essays (2003)

1. Numbers Decide or Planck's Constant and Some Constants of Philosophy
2. The Power and Poverty of Science
3. Non-Darwinian Darwinism
4. Pluralism in Education and Education in Pluralism
5. The science of education and education in science
6. Myopia about Islam, with an Eye on Chesterbelloc
7. Islam, Science, and Christianity as Seen by a Muslim Physicist
8. The Origin of the Earth-Moon System and the Rise of Scientific Intelligence
9. Cloning and Arguing
10. Cosmology in Science and Theology: Some Perennial Differences
11. The Relevance of Materials Science
12. Quantities and Everything Else
13. From World Views to Science and Back
14. Giordano Bruno's Place in Science
15. A Thousand Years from Now

A Late Awakening and Other Essays (2006)

1. A Late Awakening to Gödel in Physics
2. Myopia with Lynx Eyes about a Text of Aristotle
3. Pierre Duhem: Uneasy Genius
4. Christ and the History of Science
5. What God Has Separated... Reflections on Science and Religion
6. Christ, Creation, and Science
7. Christ, Extraterrestrials, and the Devil
8. Relativity and Religion
9. Purpose Redux
10. The Metamorphoses of Human Dignity
11. The Parasitical Society and Its Parasite Families
12. A Dire Need and Vain Hopes: Bioethics at the Third Millennium
13. Jewish Psychiatrist Turns Catholic
14. Chesterton a Seer of Science
15. Heretics and Dogmatists: or the Gist of Chesterton's *Heretics*
16. A Non-Thomist Thomism
17. Thomas and the Universe

Uncodified Conspiracy and Other Essays (2014)

1. Uncodified Conspiracy
2. Dickens, Darwin, and Chesterton
3. Darwin's Designs
4. The Blessings and Banes of Quantities
5. On a Discovery of Gödel's Theorem
6. Science as Prediction and the Unpredictability of Science
7. Relativity and Religion
8. The Reality Beneath: the World View of Rutherford

9.   Knowledge, Personal and Impersonal: Reflections on Polanyi's Thought
10. The Demarcation Line Between Science and Religion
11. From a Chain of Instant *Now*'s to an Eternal NOW
12. Christianity: From a Corner Into Many Others and Yet Not Cornered
13. Hail Mary: a Legal Dilemma
14. What God Has Separated... Reflections on Science and Religion (same as *A Late Awakening* #5)
15. Pragmatism Then and Now: From Tacit Amorality to Public Immorality
16. Priestly Celibacy
17. Newman: an Anti-Liberal or Much More
18. The Mind and Its *Now*
19. The Christian Spark for Exact Science
20. Inspiration and Counter-Inspiration of Astronomical Phenomena (same as *Limits* #5)
21. The Relevance of Materials Science (same as *Numbers Decide* #11)
22. Fifty Years of Learning

Lectures in the Vatican Gardens (2011)
1.   Ecology or Ecologism (same as *Patterns or Principles* #2)
2.   Simplicity Before Complexity or Second General Commentary
3.   Science, Culture, and Cult (same as *Limits* #13)
4.   The Origin of the Earth-Moon System and the Rise of Scientific Intelligence (same as *Numbers Decide* #8)
5.   The Christological Origins of Newton's First Law
6.   The Science of Education and Education in Science (same as *Numbers Decide* #5)
7.   From World Views to Science and Back (same as *Numbers Decide* #13)
8.   On a Discovery of Gödel's Incompleteness Theorem (same as *Uncodified Conspiracy* #5)
9.   Science as Prediction and the Unpredictability of Science (same as *Uncodified Conspiracy* #6)
10. Evolution as Science and Ideology
11. The Demarcation Line Between Science and Religion (same as *Uncodified Conspiracy* #10)

* * *

Appendix III: Bibliography for the Scholium

(For the works of S. L. Jaki see Appendix I)

Burnham, Robert, Jr. *Burnham's Celestial Handbook*. (New York: Dover Publications, Inc., 1978).

Cary, M. *et al*. *The Oxford Classical Dictionary*. (London: Oxford at the Clarendon Press, 1949, 1957).

Chesterton, G. K. His collected works (CW) are published by Ignatius Press in San Francisco.

—. *Chaucer*. (In CW 18)

—. *Heretics*. (In CW 1)

—. *The Man Who Was Thursday*. (In CW 6)

—. *Orthodoxy*. (In CW 1)

—. *St. Thomas Aquinas* (In CW 2)

—. *The Innocence of Father Brown*. (In CW 12)

—. *The Thing. Why I Am a Catholic*. (In CW 3)

—. *The Well and the Shallows*. (In CW 3)

Curtius, E. R. *European Literature and the Latin Middle Ages*, tr. from the German by W. R. Trask (London: Routledge and Kegan Paul, 1953).

Fowler H. W. and Fowler, F. G. *The Concise Oxford Dictionary of Current English*. 5th edition. (Oxford: at the Clarendon Press, 1964).

Glasstone, Samuel. *Sourcebook on Atomic Energy*. (Princeton, NJ: D. Van Nostrand Company, 1950).

Grun, Bernard. *The Timetables of History*. New Third Revised Edition. (New York: Simon & Schuster, 1991).

Harrow, Benjamin. *Eminent Chemists of Our Time*. Second Edition. (New York: D. Van Nostrand Company, Inc. 1927).

Hellemans, Alexander and Bunch, Bryan. *The Timetables of Science*. (New York: Simon and Schuster, 1988).

Lewis, Charlton T. and Short, Charles. *A Latin Dictionary*. (Oxford University Press, 1996).

Liddell, Henry George and Scott, Robert. *A Greek Lexicon*. (Oxford: at the Clarendon Press, 1953).

Liguori Publications. *Catechism of the Catholic Church*. (Liguori, MO: Liguori Publications, 1994).

Marchant, J. R. V. and Charles, J. F. *Cassell's Latin-English and English-Latin Dictionary*. (Toronto: Cassell and Co., 1910).

Merriam-Webster, Inc. *Webster's New Biographical Dictionary*. (Springfield, MA: Merriam-Webster Inc, Publishers, 1988).

—. *Webster's New Collegiate Dictionary*. (Springfield, MA: G. & C. Merriam Co., Publishers, 1961).

Newman, John Henry. *The Idea of a University*. (New York: Doubleday Image, 1959).

Runes, Dagobert. D., *et al*. *Dictionary of Philosophy*. (Totowa, New Jersey: Littlefield, Adams & Co., 1976).

Sidgwick, J. B. *Amateur Astronomer's Handbook*. (New York: Dover Publications, Inc., 1971).

(Sixtus V.; De Quelen, ed.)

'Η Παλαια Διαθηκη κατα τους 'Εβδομηκοντα. *Vetus Testamentum Graecum juxta Septuaginta interpretes*. 2 vols. (Paris: Ambrosio Firmin Didot, 1855). [The Greek Septuagint edition of the Old Testament, with parallel Latin]

Van Nostrand's Scientific Encyclopedia. (New York: D. Van Nostrand Co., 1938).

Weast, Robert C., ed. *CRC Handbook of Chemistry and Physics*. 62nd Edition. (Boca Raton, FL: CRC Press, Inc., 1981).

For more information and links to other useful and interesting sites, visit:

http://DeBellisStellarum.blogspot.com
http://theduhemsociety.blogspot.com
http://www.sljaki.com

For the works of S. L. Jaki, visit the publisher, REAL VIEW BOOKS:

http://www.RealViewBooks.com

* * *

S. L. Jaki and the author.

Peter J. Floriani holds the Ph.D. in computer science and has over 30 years of experience in diverse fields such as numerically controlled machine tool software, ad insertion and spot distribution for cable television, compilers, device drivers, and other system software. His doctoral work presented algorithms for finding prokaryotic rRNA "signatures" for use in *in-situ* hybridization experiments. He is the author of a number of books including the multi-part adventure saga *De Bellis Stellarum*, three collections of short stories, and a mystery novel. His non-fiction includes a study of Subsidiarity resulting from his work in cable television, a study of the epistemological classification scheme known as the Tree of Virtues, another on the implementation of the Tree in an academic setting, and works on the relations between science and the Faith; also a series of monographs, *Case Studies in Computer Science*, on technical matters.

Printed in Great Britain
by Amazon

22867646R00089